The Bridges Before Us

The Fix It or Get Out Series

Christine Ardigo

Published by the author as a member of the
Alexandria Publishing Group

The Bridges Before Us

Copyright © 2016 by Christine Ardigo

No part of this book may be reproduced or transmitted in any form or by any means, electronic or mechanical, including photocopying, recording, or by any information storage and retrieval system without the written permission of the author, except for the use of brief quotations in a book review. This book is a work of fiction. Names, characters, places, and incidents either are products of the author's imagination or are used fictitiously. Any resemblance to actual persons, living or dead, events of locales is entirely coincidental.

The Wiggles 'Fruit Salad'
Written by Murray Cook, Jeff Fatt, Anthony Field, Greg Page
(Wiggly Tunes Pty Ltd)
Used by Permission

First Edition, February 2016

Cover Design by JC Clarke at The Graphics Shed
Interior Book Design by Rik Hall
Author's photo by Limpuiu Photography

Acknowledgements

I would like to thank my critique partners, Sahara Foley, Rebecca Warner and Sheila Kell.

Sahara Foley is the author of eight mythical and suspenseful stories. Her advice and keen eye to details has helped steer this novel to near perfection.

Rebecca Warner is the author of three magnificent novels where smart, feminine, and powerful women take center stage. Rebecca's remarkable insights pushed my book to new heights and transformed it in so many ways.

Sheila Kell is the author of the smokin' hot H.I.S. Series. She has provided so much support throughout the writing, editing, and publication of this book, I call her my book-wifey. I could not have finished this book without her. I can't thank her enough for all her encouragement and sense of humor when I needed it the most.

*Dedicated to my quirky daughters, Ashley and Autumn.
Don't change so people will like you.*
Be yourself and the right people will find you.

Chapter 1

Samantha Hart exited her car and enjoyed the sound her black combat boots made as they crunched their way through the grimy snow left over from last week's Nor'easter. Her breath fogged the air while her eyes followed the wandering trails of footprints in the parking lot. A stray, red mitten livened up the enormous mound they had plowed against a lone lamppost.

She zipped her fleece-lined, flannel coat up, and pulled her black ski cap down, while Guster, the alternative rock band she loved, played in her head - bongos and symbols energized her on an otherwise dreary day. After kicking the snow out of the deep treads in her boot's soles, she hopped onto the sidewalk that lead into the Plainview Public Library and hurried into the overly lit building.

High school students studied at workstations with private barriers, while senior citizens flipped through newspapers in cozy chairs. One of the librarians stuffed stickers and funny bookmarks into the transparent cube on the checkout desk. Only the whir of the copy machine or a quiet flip of a page whispered behind her as she made her way down the spiral staircase towards the small auditorium.

Once downstairs, she hung her coat in the hallway that led to the meeting room. The familiar musty smell from the burgundy carpeting greeted her. She quickly lapped up a few mouthfuls from the water fountain, and skipped into the welcoming children's area. Posters of famous children's books lined the lavender painted walls.

Bob, a retired furniture maker in his seventies, set up the stage with a microphone, several books, and of course, his hand puppet, Ralph. Bob had volunteered at the library for almost two years now, always with Ralph in tow. The puppet, with its long, tousled hair, looked like a hippy. Its disheveled clothes (the yellow shirt she could swear had a coffee stain on it) and big nose (that was once white, now appeared tan) resembled Bob quite a bit. She'd never tell him that, though. Widowed for over three years, Bob was generous and caring, but his puppet needed a serious bath.

"Samantha!" Bob beamed. He raised his arms in the air, *The Little House* in one hand and *The Snowy Day* in the other. Both books her all-time favorites. "How are you? Keeping warm?"

"Trying to. It melted a little this afternoon, but it's supposed to drop in the lower thirties tonight." She rubbed her arms up and down.

"Nothing like those surprise snow storms in March. Just when your heart's set on spring, Mother Nature wallops you with one last storm."

"That's Long Island for you. Hope it melts before Easter next week."

"Supposed to warm up real good by weeks end." Bob picked up Ralph and stroked his matted hair. "Ralph's getting cabin fever."

Did Bob have any friends? "Why don't you invite Ms. Nelson in reference out to dinner? She's kinda cute." Why was she playing matchmaker when her own love life needed help?

"That old crab? She needs to get laid, alright, but not by me!"

Samantha laughed, then pretended to look through various music sheets even though she knew all the songs by heart. Bob was way too open with her.

"I need a younger woman. One that can keep up with me! Know anyone like that?" His minty breath hit her. *Was he talking about her?*

Before she could answer, the Dawson triplets scurried in and hopped onto three folding chairs in the front row. Bob glided Ralph onto his hand and ran over. "Hey guys! How are we today?" The boys squealed, then ran a lap around the room unable to contain their excitement.

Every Sunday, Samantha and Bob entertained the neighborhood kids with two stories and a handful of songs. Even though her mother said she sounded like a foghorn warning ships of her position, she loved the buzz of performing on stage, and the children loved hearing their favorite tunes while stomping around like wild animals. At times, she felt like shouting: "The circus animals are loose!"

When the room filled with chatty kids, all ten and younger, Bob grabbed Ralph and began reading *The Snowy Day*. Samantha pulled out a chair next to him and made various facial expressions that corresponded with the book's mood. It got her juices flowing and pumped her up for her performance. For the final song of the night, she let everyone climb on stage and dance beside her. *Wanna see raw energy come to life?* There was nothing like the thrill of twenty energetic children swarming you, then running out of breath from dancing and giggling uncontrollably.

Bob, or actually smelly Ralph, finished reading *The Monster at the End of This Book*, and Samantha leaped onto the twelve-inch-high platform and flipped on the stage lights. Several children, knowing the routine, left their chairs and wandered closer to the stage.

"Ready everyone?" Her bubbly voice excited the crowd further.

"Ready!" the children shouted - their eyes wide and gleaming.

Samantha cued Bob, who grabbed his acoustic guitar and gave her the thumbs up. *What songs would he play tonight?* Always one to surprise her, Bob kept her on her toes. His song choices were the only unpredictable thing in her life right now. Would it kill to have a little spontaneity? Toss in a few adventures? Experience some reckless abandon?

"Okay, here we go." With almost four-dozen eyes on her, Samantha, empowered from all the adrenaline, grasped the microphone and swayed her hips. As soon as Bob strummed the first few chords, the children bounced and flung their arms in the air.

"John Jacob Jingleheimer Schmidt..." She tapped her foot, keeping Bob up to speed. At times, he seemed to daydream. Portly and grayed, he probably pretended to be Elvis Presley in his youth.

A little girl in the front swayed her incredibly long, blonde locks back and forth, unaware she was smacking every kid in the face with them. She bobbed and thrashed as if in a trance. Or, high on some acid trip. The little boy next to her gave her a big shove, but she didn't seem to notice.

Samantha chuckled in between lyrics and tried to compose herself. "...I know a weenie man...someday I'll change his life. I'll be his weenie wife..." At this point, she'd date a weenie man. Samantha scanned the room for any hot dads. Older brothers would be fine, too. Her sex life a distant memory, dates were nonexistent. When was the last time she had sex?

Glenn, her Ex-boyfriend. No. Had it really been three years? At twenty-four, she should be hooking up with a new guy every week. At least every month. She hated thinking about it.

"...Boom, boom, ain't it great to be crazy?" Samantha removed the microphone, leaped back and forth, and thrust her fist into the sky, acting her best 'crazy'. She wiggled her butt, puffed her cheeks, and jumped up and down like a pogo stick. The children copied Samantha's wacky movements and their parent's laughter filled the room. Her energy never wavered on stage, as if her audience's enthusiasm flowed directly into her veins.

She glanced over at Bob and crossed her eyes. He squinted his, then touched his nose with his tongue. *His wife had probably loved that trick.* Then, he deliberately changed the song mid note to trip her up, but Samantha caught it and switched lyrics immediately. Why was he picking such weird songs tonight? Was the long winter getting to him also?

"...People come and step on me, that's why I'm so cracked you see. I'm a nut, I'm a nut..." She grasped her right foot, lifted it in the air, and hopped on her other foot. Before losing her balance – which happened once – she lowered her leg, then waved her free hand near her ears and wiggled her fingers. The children burst into fits of laughter, then tossed their best silly faces back. Unable to compose herself any longer, Samantha curled over, clutched her stomach, and tried desperately to sing the final verse through her own cackles and howls.

"Okay, kids." Bob stood with his guitar. "Last song. You know what that means!"

The kids charged the stage, whooping loudly, and surrounded Samantha. A few hugged her legs and others gave her a high-five. One tiny tot kissed her hand. Her smile grew and she chuckled right along with them. The little girl with the incredibly long, blonde locks reached up and touched Samantha's belly. "I want to sing on stage like you one day."

Samantha patted her on the head and cupped her chin. "You can. You will." She loved singing for the children, and wished she could hug and kiss every one of them. This was the highlight of her week, and the intoxicating feeling kept the grin on her face while working her regular job at the hospital.

Bob strummed the guitar strings and Samantha's face tightened. She glared at him and opened her mouth to protest, but kept quiet when he smirked and winked back. She missed the first set of lyrics and the youngest of the children, tapped her on the butt.

"Sing. Sing," the five-year-old hollered.

Samantha took a breath, perked up her posture, then reluctantly positioned the mic under her mouth. "Ohhh, I stuck my head in the little skunk's hole..."

Bob broke into hysterics. He tried to keep up, but his fingers gave in to the laughter. She continued to sing, hoping the faster she sang, the quicker the gross song would be over. Who wrote these songs and what drugs were they on?

The hour ended with applause and cheers. The joy in their eyes meant the world to Samantha. It made her feel valuable, like she was doing *something* right in her life.

The youngest children scurried out with their parents. A few older ones remained - their parents yet to return. Bob didn't mind entertaining them while they waited, but some parents abused the hour and returned fifteen, twenty, minutes after their performance had ended.

A whimper from behind turned Samantha's head. Emily, a ten-year-old wearing one of her usual pretty dresses, stood with her head down eyeing her pink sparkly boots, as three girls surrounded her. Emily had come every Sunday since school started and was one of the kindest children here. Why was she upset?

The tallest of the girls wore a scowl on her face. Her finger poked the sweet girl in the shoulder. Samantha carried a stack of books to the milk crate and eavesdropped.

"Who dressed you? Angelina Ballerina?"

The two other girls laughed at her insult. Emily tried to leave, but the bully stepped in her path. Samantha cringed, remembering her own horrible childhood. She dropped the books into the crate and marched in their direction. Emily's tears fell now, but she tried desperately to hide them.

"Cinderella is crying. Aww...."

"Excuse me." Samantha stepped between them. "What's your name?" She glared at the tall girl.

"Lisa." She crossed her arms and looked at the ceiling.

"We don't tolerate bullying. I'm sure your parents taught you that."

The girl rolled her eyes. Samantha put her palm on Emily's shoulder, then squatted down beside her. "Emily, Bob has a goodie-bag full of stickers. Why don't you ask Ralph to pick out a few for you?"

Emily darted toward the stage, thankful for the rescue, and Samantha gave Bob a knowing look. She turned her attention back to the bully. The two other girl's mothers entered the auditorium as Samantha started to speak. The girls grabbed their winter coats and took off - the look of guilt clearly plastered on their faces.

"Where's your mother?" Samantha stepped in Lisa's view.

"Getting her nails done."

Ugh. "Do you want to be here, Lisa?" Samantha kneeled on the burgundy rug attempting to connect with the girl.

"Nope. It's babyish." Lisa refused to look at her.

"Then why do you come?"

"None of your business."

Samantha clenched her fist. "Why were you picking on Emily? She's such a nice girl. If you took the time to get to know her, you'd really like her. She's a lot of fun and—"

"She dresses like a dork."

Samantha glanced at Lisa's clothes. Her hair chaotically pulled into a loose ponytail. Jeans. Sneakers. New York Giants sweatshirt. *At least she had taste.*

"You can't judge someone by the way they look. She really is a nice—"

"Blah. Blah. Blah." Lisa pretended to yawn.

Samantha stood, trying to compose herself. "Please, go sit over there until your mother arrives."

Lisa *hmphed* and then plopped into the folding chair so hard, it almost tipped over. Samantha stormed back to the stage to help Bob.

"What was that all about?" Bob scratched his head.

"*Lisa*, was picking on Emily. I told *Lisa* how I don't tolerate bullying." Visions of Randi, her bully from the seventh grade, returned. The girl had tormented her all year. Shoved mean notes in her locker. Snuck on her bus and terrorized her. Every day Samantha sat alone at lunch and hid.

After Emily left, Bob and Samantha placed the microphone, along with the milk crate full of books and songs, in the small closet. Samantha shut the lights over the stage while Bob set his guitar back in its case.

A well-dressed woman strutted in, purple clutch hanging from the crook in her elbow. Her long, highlighted hair corkscrewed at the ends and draped over her tight, red sweater that let everyone know she had a boob job. Her knee-high boots with the stiletto heels pounded the rug as if she'd arrived late for a Jimmy Choo sale. How she made it in here safely through the snow and ice was a mystery. Despite the cold temps, her coat was nowhere to be found – obviously due to her still wet nails. Oh. And, seventeen minutes late.

"I'll grab our coats. Be right back." Bob hurried down the corridor.

Samantha waited for Lisa and her mother to leave, but the evil queen whipped her head up and charged over to her.

"Excuse me. Did you tell my daughter she's no longer allowed to attend a public children's event?"

Samantha's chest tightened. Time appeared to stall. "What? No! I was just explaining how—"

"I'll have you know, my husband pays your salary."

"I don't get paid. I volunteer." Her shaky voice, obvious.

"Huh! Then you have no right abusing your authority."

"Abusing? Your daughter was picking on another child. I'm responsible for making sure all the children are safe and—"

"It's bad enough you yell at an innocent little girl and tell her she can no longer attend a group that she *loves*, but lying? Is this how you intend to get ahead in life?"

"What? I didn't lie. She was making fun of—"

"Let's go, Lisa." She seized her daughter's hand, then frowned at Samantha. "I plan on taking this up with the manager."

Lisa looked back and stuck her tongue out.

Samantha collapsed against the wall behind her. Bob passed Lisa and her mother on their way out and met Samantha by the stage. "What's wrong, my darling?"

Her entire body trembled from the encounter. She thrust her hands into her jean pockets and took a few deep breaths. With her pulse still racing, she relayed her confrontation with the mother from hell.

Bob handed Samantha her coat. "Don't let that witch get ya down, hun. You're a good person."

"I don't get it. I give back to my community, stick up for a girl that's getting bullied, and I get reamed out by one of the mothers?"

"Karma. That little snot-nosed brat has to live with that beast. And, vice versa." Bob placed his hand on her shoulder. But, it wasn't Bob. It was Ralph. Ralph disappeared under her brown hair and his nose tickled her ear. It lightened the mood.

"You think you're funny with that puppet of yours, eh?"

"It's all part of the entertainment, Samantha." Bob wrapped his arm around her shoulders - Ralph still perched on his hand. "I play the guitar, you sing. I have my puppet, you wear your silly clothes."

She flinched. "Silly?"

"Yeah. What do you guys call it? Punk rock? No. No. I'm dating myself. Goth? Always dressed in black. Dark makeup. I love your getups. I mean, look at this great T-shirt you have on." He pointed to her chest. "Where do you buy these things?"

Ice crystals tore through her. Her eyes bulged, then traveled to her black T-shirt. Zombie fruits and vegetables were chasing a poor defenseless tomato right off the edge of her shirt. She thought it was fitting since she worked as a Registered Dietitian at St. Elizabeth's Hospital.

She turned away. Were her clothes scaring people away? "Do…" she hesitated. "Are the kids scared of me?"

Bob chuckled, then swatted her away. "What? No way! You know kids. They love all that weird, stuff."

Weird? She looked weird? A lump formed in her throat. Her fingernails, painted in her favorite Black Licorice color, dove through each armhole in her jacket. She glanced at her black jeans and the stud-embellished ankle straps on her combat boots. *This wasn't a costume.*

The two exited the library. Frost speckled the windowpanes and thickened along the edges. The clean, cold scent of a winter's night pricked her nose. Bob led Samantha by the elbow to her car, pointing out slippery spots. A crusty cushion of ice beneath her shoes caused her to skid. He held on tighter.

Samantha waited for Bob to leave the parking lot safely, then leaned her seat back. She retracted the sunroof's interior panel and took in the astounding display of stars set against the black, velvety background. Was she some constellation lost in all that darkness?

No one took her seriously. Not even Bob. Did Ralph think she was a weirdo, too?

She did not just ask that.

The way Lisa's mother spoke to her - did she see Samantha as some joke? Some stupid kid she could tell off? The pride she had gained from giving back to the community, shriveled. Her lack of confidence resurfaced. Samantha had always volunteered her time. Helped anyone that needed it. Put herself last. She *was* a good person. Then why did that woman speak to her that way?

She glanced at her outfit. The studs on her army boots reflected the light from the lamppost. Suddenly, her zombie shirt looked childish. Samantha sprung her seat back to its upright position. She gripped the steering wheel and her black nail polish, something she always loved, shot a blow through her. Her fingers wrapped around the wheel to hide the glaring disaster. No wonder no one took her seriously. Was she scaring guys off, too?

Were her work clothes any better? Layers of black clothes. Chunky boots under dress pants. Her clothes had become some sort of shield. Something to hide under, bury her fears and protect her self-esteem. She turned the ignition one notch and pressed play on her CD player. The car filled again with her favorite Guster song.

She thought about what Bob had said about Lisa's mom and shook her head. Screw that witch. Samantha refused to let her ruin her night. She needed to put this behind her. She had a big surprise for the children in her Pediatrics Unit this week. Despite the snow, Easter was on its way.

Chapter 2

Samantha bounced down the corridor leading to the Pediatrics Unit she had covered at St. Elizabeth's Hospital for the past two years. Despite the range of illnesses and surgeries behind these doors, working in this unit lifted her spirits. She couldn't do enough for the children, and holidays here were always her favorite time. Although she also covered a medical/surgical floor, this unit gave her life purpose. The small amount of joy she brought made her feel like she wasn't a complete disappointment, as she apparently was to a few people. Namely, her mother. And, let's not forget her Ex, Glenn.

She neared the double doors that volunteers from the high school had decorated with a brightly painted mural of a curious, lively monkey hanging from a tree in the jungle. His foot, caught on a vine, allowed him to dangle and plan what mischief he'd get into next. Various shades of greens and yellows made the perfect backdrop for the wily, brown monkey to cause trouble.

"Samantha!" Before she could push the door open, her co-worker, Cara McCormick, strutted towards her. Her short, red skirt and white, button-down blouse clung to her, accentuating every curve, oozing a sensual appeal. Her long, black hair bounced like she was in one of those shampoo commercials. Her ankle-strapped heels resounded over the hustle and bustle in the hallway, drowning out conversations and beeping Pulse-Ox machines.

Before walking the mere ten-yards, a doctor waved hello to Cara, and a phlebotomist stopped to chat. Like a magnet, Cara attracted anything within fifty feet of her. Samantha waited, her shopping bag full of goodies weighed down her hand. Deep-red marks imprinted in her fingers.

"Nice…um, ears, Samantha. What's shaking?" Cara pointed to her head.

"Just a little Easter Bunny visit to my kids." She adjusted the bunny ears with her free hand.

Cara looked into the shopping bag. "Wow. Lotta stuff. You went all out this year." She glanced at Samantha's fingers. "Pink nail polish? What gives?"

She averted her gaze and rubbed the back of her neck hiding her nails. "I just thought it looked cheery."

"Since when? You love your black."

The incessant ringing of a nearby phone worsened her uneasiness. "Trying something new."

"Love it! Maybe we can get you in some dresses and heels next." Cara winked.

Samantha eyed her gorgeous co-worker's outfit. You'd think she worked as a model and not a dietitian. She'd never master Cara's techniques - it came naturally to her. Cara continued to ramble on how she'd love to make her over like some Barbie doll, while Samantha's fingers turned blue. She switched hands and glanced at her watch.

"You have a cute figure, Sammy. Why not show it off?" Cara grabbed both sides of Samantha's waist, judging her size. "Samantha Hart! You have a skinny waist! What the f—"

Samantha stepped back and knocked into an empty stretcher tearing down the hallway with the reckless transporter scurrying behind it. "Ooh. Sorry."

"My bad! Running behind!" He tore down the hall, but not before Samantha noticed his cute ass.

"Wow. Who's that?" Samantha adjusted her posture.

"Frankie? New transporter. Started two weeks ago. He's twenty-three, lives in North Bell—"

It figured she knew him. Was there anyone she didn't know? "Look, Cara. I gotta run. I haven't started my work yet. I'll catch up with ya later."

"Sure, toots. Save some candy for me, okay? Oh, and don't forget. We have that meeting with boss lady in an hour."

"Totally forgot. Thanks." Samantha turned to leave and almost knocked into a group of family members whispering to a resident. She glanced around looking for Dr. Chambers, a third year resident she had her eye on all year. She hadn't really noticed him two years ago. Quiet, exhausted and shy, first year residents only had time to listen to orders barked at them. Last year, a bit more confident, Dr. Chambers stood out from the rest. Sure, he was handsome and striking, not to mention hot, but his confidence and boldness made employees turn heads when he spoke.

All this time she'd been too nervous to approach him. He probably didn't even know she existed. She had asked Cara about him – always up on the latest gossip - and Cara thought he had dated some flirty nurse from the E.R. in the fall, but couldn't confirm.

Samantha detoured around the family members, her thick boot catching on the freshly waxed floors, and stumbled. She toppled three more steps, caught herself and then scowled at her thick footwear. Tingling swept up the back of her neck and suddenly her ears felt impossibly hot. *Must she always embarrass herself?*

She pushed the doors open and her boots clobbered the linoleum like Frankenstein lumbering across a graveyard. Cara's dainty heels echoed in her head and reminded her of the smooth, fluid moves she made as she glided toward her.

The glossy, polished flooring in the Pediatrics Unit instantly put anyone in a good mood. Infused with color, the tiles arranged themselves in patterns, forming various shapes and numbers like a giant hopscotch drawing. Quirky zoo animals painted in abstract forms greeted you and lined the walls leading toward each patient room. Everything from baby powder to apple juice filled her nose. The ongoing sound of a video game from the playroom, along with both laughter and sobbing, entered her ears.

Samantha stopped at the nurse's station and held up the shopping bag. The secretary and two nurses surrounded her.

"Oh! They'll be so excited."

"I love your Bunny ears."

"What a wonderful surprise for them!"

They peeked into the bag. "Samantha! How much money did you spend?"

She squirmed, her knees pulling together. "Don't worry about it. I don't have expenses like you guys. I still live at home and I have an old car. Plus, I love spending it on them."

"I wish I still lived at home." The unit secretary gazed at the ceiling. "No bills. Home cooking. No dragging your clothes to the laundromat."

"Trust me. It's no picnic living with my mom. I'd trade places with you any day."

"What's so bad about her?" A nurse's aide joined in on the conversation.

"Over protective, controlling, selfish…"

"From what you've told me, she sounds almost narcissistic."

Samantha placed the bag on the counter. "I'm here to have fun. Let's not talk about the *grumbler*. I've got goodies to hand out and smiles to create."

Samantha checked the patient's diet orders noting which children were allowed to eat, otherwise, she had brought Easter pencils, along with tiny activity books filled with spring-themed puzzles. She handed the nurses a bag full of plastic Easter eggs filled with stickers, and headed for her first room.

The bug room.

Samantha hated the bug room. Each room had a theme. One was painted like a sky, complete with stars and planets. Another like the ocean – various fish and a giant, grinning octopus with big eyelashes covered that rooms' walls. Others had flowers, a colorful hot air balloon, or a treehouse with long, twisting branches.

But, the bug room was cursed. Or, at least she thought so. Not because the bugs were scary or anything. The various insects couldn't be cuter. But, whenever something went wrong, it happened in there. A few months ago, a father picked up his discharged son, but they later discovered the parents were in the middle of a custody battle and the father could only see his son with supervision. Last year, a seven-year-old boy died from an asthma attack. On Monday, somehow a nine-year-old girl ran out of the unit despite the door alarm, and hid for over an hour under a chair in an unused workstation. The bug room.

Samantha entered the room with her usual cheery countenance. She bucked her teeth like a bunny and hopped in. "Easter Bunny's here to melt away the rest of the snow and welcome in the spring!" The boy in the first bed tossed off his covers with his good arm – the other in a cast – and squealed. "How's it going Zach?"

"Good. Good!" He scooted to the end of the bed and rested his hand on Samantha's wrist. His bright, blue eyes mirrored hers. Large and wide, his expression reminded her of a photograph taken of her at his age. Eyes eager to please.

"I have an activity book for you and goodie bag full of jelly beans. If your mom says it's okay."

The boy peeked at his mom, who fanned out her palm and let him accept the goodies. "Yay! Thank you, Easter Bunny."

Some Easter Bunny. She looked more like the grim reaper with ears. "You're very welcome. Enjoy." Samantha approached the next bed, and the giant fly with huge teeth painted near the window, grinned at her. "Good morning, Richard."

"It's Richie." The boy frowned, but the hand on his stomach let her know it was from pain, not her screwing up his name. Sweat-soaked hair stuck to his forehead.

"Sorry. I'm Samantha. How are you feeling?"

"Bad." He crooked his chin into his chest.

"I'm sure you'll be feeling better in a few days. I have some surprises for you."

Richie perked up. The laugh track on the television cartoon coincided perfectly with his facial expression.

"I know you can't eat yet. You're going for a procedure today?" Samantha shot a glance at his mother.

"It's just a test, actually." His mother, sitting on the bed, answered for him. "But, I can save whatever you have for later."

Samantha hesitated. Her voice tense, "I'm not really allowed to give him anything to eat, but I can come back later. I have activity books, pencils—"

"That's not fair!" Richie screamed. The half-baked spider on the wall behind him appeared to be laughing. *Dumb bug room.*

"What if you leave the candy with me, and I can give it to him after the test?" His mother's eyebrows raised.

"Sometimes the test," her words cautious, "might...allow him to eat."

Richie started to cry. The spider snickered. His mother stood and took Samantha's arm. "I promise I won't give it to him. I'll save it for when he can eat again. I'll keep it in my bag."

Unable to resist, she handed the goodie-bag over. Richie immediately stopped crying, the corners of his mouth rose. All in a day's work. This was why she did this.

She exited the room, made her way into the other nine rooms, and then left the remainder of treats with the nursing staff, making sure to grab one for Cara. The whisper of slippered feet scampered behind her. Toby, a girl from the flower room, took her IV stand for a walk and met Samantha at the double doors. "Thank you again," she said, holding her pencil with the little, yellow chicks in the air.

Samantha squatted down. "No problem." Zach tiptoed out of his room and spied on her. She let her eyes roll to their corners. "Can I sign your cast, Zach?"

"Sure!" He nodded several times like Samantha was some famous celebrity. She took the purple sharpie from her lab coat and signed: *The Easter Bunny*. Zach's eyes lit up.

"Be good. Do well in school both of you." She bucked her teeth one last time, bent her hands under her chin, and hopped toward the double doors. Not even two feet out the door, her beeper vibrated in her lab coat.

Roselyn Hardstroud. Her boss. They were patiently awaiting her arrival.

****

The department's food service director leaned back in her chair and shoved a pen behind her ear. She took in a long, sustained, concentrated breath, but never appeared to release it. Samantha waited for her face to turn blue. Cara rhythmically kicked the bottom of the desk's leg and kept her eyes on the rug.

Roselyn dressed impeccably – perfectly tailored, expensive suits. Her office, not frilly or feminine, but business-like and professional. No pictures on her desk. No knickknacks or personal items. She looked at least fifteen years older than Samantha did. Her heavy makeup made her appear older, or perhaps hid a weathered appearance. She had a constant drained look on her face.

Karen and Melissa, both diet clerks, sat on the opposite side of the room. Heather, the other dietitian, had off, as well as several other diet clerks that were working this weekend. Roselyn had a habit of conducting meetings when half her staff was off, leaving them confused and misinformed. Organization and communication was not one of her strong points.

"As you all know…" she began. (Which was funny, since they never knew what was going on.) "The Nutrition Department is not a money making department. We feed patients. What little we make in the cafeteria pays for the food and salaries of our employees."

And, the point being? Samantha nodded a few times, but her thoughts were on her clothes. Even the diet clerks dressed more fashionably than she did. *Hmm.* The mall stayed open until nine…

Roselyn whipped her pen up and down. "The laying off of your Clinical Manager was a much needed step in reducing costs in our department."

Seriously? Not even a spec of remorse for ruining a person's life? She was merely an unnecessary expense? Let's not discuss the fact that Roselyn divided the Clinical Manager's responsibilities among the three dietitians. With no extra pay.

Samantha took in slow, deep breaths. Why did it smell like wine in here? She turned her attention toward Cara and her ensemble - from her dangling earrings, to her three-inch heels. Cara never seemed to need help with anything. How she paid her way through college, rented an apartment, furnished it, and bought a brand new car, amazed her. She really had it all. Looks. Independence. Financial stability. Men. Lots of men.

She felt Melissa's gaze on her, and glanced over. Melissa crossed her eyes and pretended to hang herself. Samantha's body froze. *Was she crazy?*

"Melissa, is there a problem?" Roselyn did not look amused.

Melissa even dressed nice. Her hot pink skirt, with a fitted, long-sleeved cotton top came across professional, yet sexy. The bold silver-and-black necklace pulled it all together. Melissa's sensual appeal and witty sense of humor, always had others flocking around to hear her insane stories.

The sales associates at the mall would be able to help her pick out a new wardrobe, right? It had been so long since she wore anything feminine.

Roselyn coughed. Samantha jerked her head back in her direction. Was she trying to get her attention? *Thump!* For added emphasis, Roselyn's fist pounded her desktop. "We need to find a way to bring more money into this department, otherwise more jobs will be lost!"

Cara leaned forward until her elbows rested on her knees. "Don't *you* have any ideas?"

Roselyn's nostrils flared. She stared at Cara for a good minute. Cara loved pushing her buttons, but it made Samantha anxious. You didn't want to mess with someone like Roselyn. Samantha kept her mouth shut during most of the meetings.

Although Cara was out of line – not to mention cheeky, brazen and, well…you get the idea, she was one-hundred percent right. Roselyn had a habit of stealing everyone's ideas.

Karen, in her stylish blue and green form-fitting dress, cleared her throat. "Other hospitals have an out-patient dietitian. Shouldn't we?"

"The amount of money it would cost to pay a part-time dietitian would exceed any monies brought in. Next!" Roselyn rolled her eyes and turned her attention to Melissa. *Nothing.* Then Cara, who pretended to fix her shoe.

Samantha leaned forward, hesitant. "What about the cafeteria? The food's…not that good. If we had healthier items, a few vegetarian choices, a salad bar that actually had fruits and vegetables in it, ones that weren't drowned in mayonnaise or oils, maybe that would generate some significant profits, and then—"

Roselyn's chin shot into the air. Her mouth fell open. She stared at the ceiling as if it had opened up, then clenched her eyes and shook her head. *Had she said something wrong?* Samantha turned slightly toward Cara who yawned and picked at her nails.

"Samantha. I'm sorry. Aren't you a Registered Dietitian?"

Confused, she nodded her head.

"Then act like one. Your job is with patients. Not food. Leave that to Apollo. That's why he's the Cafeteria manager."

And, obviously Apollo didn't have a strong understanding or any clear vision for the cafeteria. Instead of inspiring his staff with bold, new ideas, he was... well, who knows what the hell he was doing all day.

Roselyn seized her yellow note pad and held it up. "Empty. You see this? Not one single idea from the four of you."

Huh? She gave her a fantastic idea. Everyone on the floors complained about the food. Healthier, more appealing food would bring in more customers, thus bringing in more sales. This woman was impossible.

Samantha went back to admiring her co-workers outfits. If she hit the mall right after work, she had a good three hours to shop. Better than spending another Friday night at home. She had to deal with her family all weekend anyway. Too bad she wasn't working Easter weekend.

It was bad enough her brother was home from college for the weekend. His lazy-ass would lie around whining how hard it was being a college junior, living in a dorm with a bunch of rowdy, partying guys. But, her mother would bemoan about all the cooking she did, even though Samantha would do most of the work.

Hmm. Maybe Heather wouldn't mind switching with her. She had two kids. Wouldn't she rather be home watching them open their Easter baskets? Wasn't that what Easter was about, anyway? New beginnings. A total departure from our past.

"Samantha, are you listening?" Roselyn sighed heavily. Her pinched expression let everyone know she reached her boiling point.

Crap. Had she suggested some great, new money making scheme? Not wanting to annoy her further, Samantha grinned. "Of course I am."

"Good. I want your suggestions on my desk by the end of the day."

Uh, oh.

Cara stood, letting Roselyn know she was done. Samantha joined her before she unleased any more firestorms. They quickly exited, tore down the hallway, and decided to grab lunch early.

They entered the barren cafeteria. The clattering of dishes emanating from the dish room next door drowned out the muffled chatter and chairs scraping across the floor. Bright fluorescent lights emphasized the awkward table and chair arrangements that had been in place since she started working here almost two years ago. A long forgotten menu board hung over the self-serve dining trays -

cobwebs had been the only thing on the menu for months.

"You doing anything this weekend, Sammy?" Cara scanned the room.

"Not much. Family stuff, of course." Her fingers slipped under a hard, fiberglass tray. An elderly man struggled with his own tray while trying to push a walker. Samantha removed the blue rectangle for him and placed it on the counter. He smiled and tipped his pretend hat.

"Eryn and I are meeting up for happy hour tonight. Wanna come? You haven't hung out with us in a while."

Eryn, also a dietitian, only worked with Samantha and Cara at St. Elizabeth's Hospital for three months. She had covered Heather's maternity leave. In the mere twelve weeks, they formed a strong bond and happy hours began shortly after. Despite Heather returning to work, something they hoped wouldn't happen, they promised to meet every month. This year, their get-togethers became more haphazard, and the crappy weather kept Samantha away altogether.

Despite Cara and Samantha working together every day, it was obvious Cara had more in common with Eryn. Clubs were never Samantha's thing, but to the other two, it was their second home.

"Actually, I think I'm hitting the mall tonight. And, all day tomorrow. My Wicked Witch of the West look has to go."

"Really? No way!" Cara slowed her pace, then eyed Samantha from top to bottom. "Why *do* you dress like that?"

Samantha had dressed this way for so long, she failed to see herself anymore. "I didn't have any friends in middle school. Got picked on a lot." *Her protection. Her security blanket.* "I was such a nerd. Everyone wore ripped jeans, flannel shirts and cool sneakers, or those brown, suede Thom McAn Exersole shoes."

"I had those!"

"Exactly. See my point?" The strong odor of burnt grease pushed Samantha down the cold, metal counter and past the unattractive desserts. One of the servers slopped a pile of barbequed ribs on the elderly man's plate. The only other choice was fried chicken wings. *Gross.* "My mother wouldn't let me out of the house. I had no friends. I couldn't wear makeup. Had to wear dresses and skirts through seventh grade—"

"At least your mom cared."

"Cared? She constantly criticizes me. I'm never good enough in her eyes."

"Then move out. I've been telling you for years."

"I can't. Not now." Samantha wandered to the salad bar and grimaced at the mayonnaise-covered items through the scratched-up sneeze guard covering the food selections. With no other choices, she plopped a blob of tuna fish in her plate and snatched a banana. She turned and searched for a seat.

Cara met Samantha at the booth and dusted the crumbs off her seat. With her shoulders back, chin up, and boobs out, her dazzling, white teeth bit into her hearty turkey sandwich. "How'd you go from nerd to grunge?" Her words garbled.

Samantha wiped the cold mayonnaise blob from the corner of her mouth. "When I started high school, I met this girl Autumn. She taught me to lie to my mom. Brought in makeup and clothes for me to put on in the school bathroom. Even took me into this creepy store where they sold drug paraphernalia. I remember using my babysitting money to buy a black Led Zeppelin T-shirt. It had a giant airship on it, you know, a blimp, and I was so stupid, I thought it was a submarine all those years, Ha ha! But, I can't tell you what it felt like to walk down the school halls wearing that shirt. This one druggie guy, Timmy Houseman, actually high-fived me when we passed in the corridor."

"No way! He high-fived you? Holy shit!" Cara's sarcastic tone turned heads. "Sorry." She lowered her voice. "So, basically you want your Led Zeppelin T-shirt back?"

"I just want guys to notice me again." After a long, hard inspection of herself in the mirror last night, Samantha was ready to change. She couldn't spend another summer single. A tingling spread between her legs. Had it really been three years since she had sex?

"So, what're you thinking? A splash of femininity? A dash of sophistication? Lighter makeup. Some heels. Show some leg—"

Samantha scooped up some tuna and let the lump squish between her teeth. "I don't know where to start. Hopefully, one of the sales associates that attack you as soon as you walk into a store will ask if I need any help and I'll say, Yes! Please!"

"How 'bout ditching the tuna for lunch every day, too? Unless you want to be known as tuna breath."

Samantha pushed her plate away. "If the hot food didn't suck so badly, I wouldn't eat it."

Cara rambled on about the mall and her favorite shops, while Samantha poked her nail into the tip of her banana. She peeled the three skins down imagining herself being stripped from her shell. Her safety blanket. Her mask. Revealing the new 'feminine her' underneath. Naked and exposed, the banana looked sexy, and sultry. It was time.

Chapter 3

Samantha's heart pounded. Dr. Chambers stood in the hallway on Samantha's unit outside a patient's room. He flipped through a clipboard, then ran his fingers through his hair - dark brown with blonde highlights and spiked like one of the Backstreet Boys. What resident had time to style their hair in the morning and put gel in it?

Samantha pushed herself up from the high-back chair and removed her lab coat. She wobbled in her high heels. Hours of practice walking in them yesterday during their Easter celebration had better pay off. At least she wasn't five-foot-one anymore. They raised her self-esteem up a notch, as well.

Her new, aqua dress hugged her curves. Tight, yet still professional, but with the thirty dollar push up bra from Victoria Secrets she suddenly had cleavage. The soft pinks dusted across her face, and the shiny pink lip-gloss reminded her that her mask was gone.

Compliments from Cara and the diet clerks gave her the confidence she needed to approach Dr. Chambers, finally. Today she'd ask him to join her for lunch. Every second she waited would result in another lost chance. Without giving it another thought, she hurried down the corridor.

The unit secretary glanced up from her computer and did a double take. "Samantha! You look amazing."

"Thank you." She turned her head to hide her burning cheeks and continued forward.

"Is that you Samantha?" The case manager squinted. "Oh my, God. What a difference. I'd never recognize you."

"Time for a change." Her stomach hardened. Maybe this wasn't such a great idea. Maybe she should wait another week? *No. She could do it. Smile.* "Good morning, Dr. Chambers." Samantha sighed so forcefully, it sounded like she just outran a wild pack of zombies.

His eyes slid to their corners, then back to the clipboard. She had expected him to say something. Anything. But, the harsh silence clobbered her like cracking open someone's ribs.

She grinned. "I was wondering how—"

Ahhh! A confused patient's hollering escalated until it soared past them, destroying her confidence further. *Ahhh!*

No. Not now. "I was wondering how everything's going?" she yelled over the howling.

"With what?" His sarcastic tone choked off her rehearsed dialogue. He dumped the clipboard back in its wall holder.

"Just wondering if you're having a great day. I know it can...get busy, you know, with being a resident and all."

"What? Sweetie, I'm a third year. The word of the day is delegate." He let out a thunderous roar that drowned out the confused patient's wailing, and echoed in the hallway. "That's what the first and second years are for." He tugged on a pair of latex gloves and snapped the wrist piece in her face.

A painful lump formed in her throat carrying a sour taste with it. What. An. Ass. This is the man she drooled over all year? The one she dreamed about every night? She shook her head.

Bleh! A patient gagging and throwing up rumbled through the halls. *Yup. Got that right. Sickening.*

She returned to her lab coat. Her beeper bounced in the pocket. *What now?* After clicking on the number, Samantha tossed it back in her pocket. Roselyn.

Roselyn ignored the fact that Samantha sat in front of her for a good three minutes. Rustling papers in her drawer, intercoming her secretary, picking something out of her tooth. What was that smell? Tequila? She pulled her hem down. Was the dress too short? Had someone reported her? Roselyn calling you into her office was never a good thing. If just once she called you in to compliment you, or tell you what a great job you were doing, maybe Samantha wouldn't be so edgy.

"Samantha. I'm going to cut right to the chase. Did you, or did you not hand out candy to children in Pediatrics on Friday?"

If someone could hyperventilate that quickly, it would be her. With her heart beating rapidly, her palms in full clammy-mode, she kicked off her heels and rubbed her toes together in awkward bursts.

"Yes." What could she say? Guilty as charged. Every possible scenario flew through her mind. Did a child choke? Was someone allergic to jelly beans? Did one of them stick a religious cross tattoo on their leg and the surgeon operated on the wrong body part?

"Well, because of you, a child that had a procedure scheduled that morning, ate the candy and the test had to be postponed."

Samantha cringed. Her big toe dug between two other toes.

"Was it the bug room?

"What?" Her bloodshot eyes went cold. Dead. Flat. Her eyebrows collapsed so profoundly, she thought her face was melting. "You delayed care and you're wondering if there were bugs in the room?"

"There's a room with insects."

"Don't try switching the blame to the housekeeping department. You had—"

"No. The rooms all have themes. There's a room with bugs painted on the walls. Was it the bug room?"

"Who cares!"

Although half-naked, her body grew impossibly hot and desperately needed some fanning. She wanted her shield back. Every ounce of confidence she built, completely shattered with each word spewed from Roselyn's mouth.

After a hefty reprimand, and Samantha having to sign a verbal warning that she would no longer hand anything out to the children in the Pediatrics Unit, she retreated down the hall to her office, infuriated and defeated.

****

Cara shook her head. "Unbelievable. Roselyn's an idiot. And, well, Dr. Chambers is a conceited ass."

"I was just saying hello to him. I don't get it."

"Stay away from the third years. They go from humble, exhausted, pee-ons, to these monstrous, inflated heads of arrogance. And, no one can get Dr. Chambers. He's untouchable."

"Untouchable? No. It's me. New makeup and clothes aren't going to change what's inside." They exited their office and the smells of bleach from housekeeping mixed with the aroma of Swedish meatballs from the kitchen entered her nose.

"What you have inside is golden. You're compassionate, loving and always helping others."

Samantha's face flushed with warmth. "Thank you, but between my mother and Glenn, I feel like a complete failure. When I'm around children, I feel safe. I hope I'm someone they can look up to. Like a big sister. A mentor. And, they don't judge me. They look up to me. They make me feel good about myself."

"Screw Glenn."

"No. I can't. Something made him break up with me. Everyone we hung out with vanished from my life, too. As if it were planned. They all must've known. The joke was on me."

"Then you don't need them. Glenn sounded like a jerk anyway. I think you let people walk all over you. You need to stand up for yourself more. Just because someone says something, doesn't mean they're right."

"Guess I'm afraid to put myself out there. Afraid of making a fool of myself. Getting hurt. Maybe I shouldn't be hitting on doctors. Maybe I should take Bob up on his offer. Or, Ralph. Or, maybe one of the ninety-year-old volunteers."

Cara laughed. "Yeah. Okay. You do that. I think people that go after residents are desperate anyway. They're all like, "marry me, so I can quit my job and not have to work ever again." Right?"

"Gee, thanks."

"Oh, God! So sorry. I did not mean you."

"I know. It's fine."

The two of them ambled outside onto the busy Queens street towards their cars. A *woosh* of traffic flew past them, car exhaust followed close behind. Cara reached into her coat pocket, keys dangled in her hand.

Samantha skipped down the street in her heels and swung her pocketbook around like Little Red Riding Hood. "Look how good I can walk in my heels now. La la la." She twirled around twice, then danced a few steps, ending with a hip shake.

A truck flew by and sank into a pothole. The impact sprayed thick, brown water all over Samantha, from her perfectly, straightened hair to her panty-hosed legs. Cara jumped away and raised her hands. She stared at Samantha, her jaw dropped. Samantha, speechless, could only shake.

"This…is…not…happening." She chucked her bag onto the sidewalk and screamed.

Her beautiful aqua dress was ruined. The filthy liquid dripped from her bangs, onto her cheeks. The stench of sewage coated her. Something planted itself square on her nose. She swiped it off and a glass-breaking screech flew from her mouth. "What the fuck was that! I think it was an insect, creature thingy!"

Cara, still silent, gaped, then snapped her jaw shut.

"Say something, dammit."

Cara handed Samantha a McDonald's napkin from her jacket. "Did you just curse?"

"Hell yeah, I did."

Cara smirked. "What would your mother say?"

****

Samantha yanked on the shower curtain - metal rings skid along the pole - then turned the knob until the water burned her skin. How'd she drive home in this filth? Her favorite dress. The light and airy makeup that finally showed off her features, covered up once again by black crud.

She switched on her shower radio, pressed play on the '80s Greatest Hits CD, and increased the volume as loud as it would go. After changing the settings on the showerhead, water pelted her grimy skin. Steam filled the bathroom quickly and once she poured half a bottle of coconut-frosting scented shampoo on her head, she started to sing.

The lyrics flowed as if she had written them herself. Word after word left her mouth and drifted off with the steam. As her nails scrubbed her scalp, she swayed side to side. Her voice intensified until she imagined herself on stage singing in front of a crowd.

Samantha grabbed the bottle of conditioner and pretended it was a microphone. The shower curtain fluttered, then pulsated. She shouted every verse. When the chorus began, she returned the bottle to the shelf and flung her arms high in the air. Jumping on the rubber shower mat, she extended the final note and howled into the condensation-streaked mirror in the shower.

Bam! Bam! Bam!

The pounding on the door startled her and she gripped the soap dish to prevent herself from falling.

"What the hell did I tell you about that horrible screaming in the shower? Get out now. I've had enough. I can't even rest."

"I wasn't screaming, mom. I was singing." Samantha rotated the knob until the water trickled to four last drops.

"Ha! You call that singing. You sound like a wounded walrus."

Samantha dried herself, threw sweats on, and twisted the towel around her drenched hair. She slapped the light switch off, the whir of the overhead fan silenced. Why couldn't there be a switch for her mother? She charged into her bedroom and closed the door, then made her way toward the dresser for her hair dryer and flat iron.

The dresser was lined with picture frames her mother had bought, along with photographs pre-selected and placed inside. All four photographs were of her mother. One of her mother at her brother's high school graduation. Her brother wasn't even in the picture. One sitting at her office desk that everyone decorated with cards, gifts and balloons for her fiftieth birthday. A hint to Samantha that she obviously didn't do enough for her. One of her in the backyard. Alone. She wasn't sure who took that picture. Had she placed the camera on a table and set the timer?

The final one, shockingly, was of her mother and her at the beach. Another zinger, though. Samantha was only fourteen in the picture. The last time, her mother insinuated, that they had hung out together. Not true of course, but she arranged the four photographs to remind Samantha daily of the lack of love and support.

Samantha looked at her door. Left an inch ajar, she stepped to the right, away from the opening. She sprang toward her desk, raised her arms, and practiced the dance move she saw on a show last night. She squatted down, kicked out her right leg, then her left. She leaped onto the bed in one fluid motion, bounced several times, then jumped off with a mighty *Thump!* She was a ninja!

With her adrenaline pumping out good vibes, she opened the drawer for her hair supplies. Before she could turn on the hair dryer, her door creaked. She tilted her head, then spun towards the left. Her mother's arm inched away from the door that was now open two feet.

"Stop opening my door!"

Her mother's dramatic facial expressions paired with her theatrical performance would've won her a Tony award on Broadway. Both hands raced to her cheeks. She fell back into the wall as if she might faint. "Excuse me?"

"Don't touch my door. It's my room and I want privacy."

Her mother stood there with a perfectly hair-sprayed coif. Gold hoop earrings dangled, matching the gold necklace and bracelets. Her red sweater draped flawlessly over her body, on top of her winter-white pants and matching white, cuffed boots. "You know the rules. No one closes their door."

Samantha chucked the wet towel on the rug. "I'm twenty-four—"

"Don't put wet towels on my carpet."

Samantha gritted her teeth. "What could possibly be going on in here that you need my door open?"

"I heard pounding on the floor. What were you doing?" Her mother examined the room for the apparent gang of men she kept hidden behind the furniture, then scurried over to the towel and plucked it off the floor. "Keep the door open. And, why are you taking another shower? Are you going out again?"

"Again? I haven't been out since that Halloween party."

"And thank God. What were you thinking wearing that ridiculous Viking costume? You should've heard the neighbors!"

"The neighbors didn't see me. It was dark and I had a coat on."

"You were wearing a gold helmet with giant, white horns shooting out of your head. Are you insane?"

Oh, please. Here we go. Even having fun on Halloween was an issue.

"You've been nothing but an embarrassment to me. This is just another act of betrayal. What would my family say?" Her hands secured themselves to her hips. "Your brother would never embarrass me like that. He always helps me when he's home on break."

"Helps? He stays out 'til 3 a.m. every night and then sleeps all day."

"Michael works very hard in college. He needs his rest. Besides, he washed my dishes Saturday morning."

"What the h…" She bit her lip so hard she thought it would bleed. "He's twenty, not seven."

"You bought a flat iron?" Her tiny white boots sashayed over to the desk. "Are you trying to burn down the house?"

"Yes. Yes, I was. I decided the best way to burn down the house was to buy a flat iron and leave it plugged in on the desk with the hope it would eventually, in a few days, burn my desk, catch fire, and eat away at my rug. You got me. You're too smart for me."

"Damn right I am." She grinned, pleased at herself, but then a minute later, her bottom lip quivered. "Don't you care about anyone but yourself? After all I've done for you!" Her eyelids grew heavy. Just as she looked like she was about to cry… "Why are you treating me so badly? Are you even listening to me?"

Samantha ignored her delusions.

"I've had it! We'll continue this conversation when you've calmed down and aren't so hysterical."

Samantha's face contorted. *What?*

Her mother stomped out, entered her own room, and *Slam!*

Good. Some peace. With her hair still dripping onto her shoulders, she threw a hooded sweatshirt on, snatched her pocketbook, and headed out of her room.

"Where do you think you're going?" Her mother stood in the hallway. Apparently, her door slamming shut was a farce.

"Out."

"Now? On a Monday? Where?"

Before she had time to answer, the phone in the kitchen rang. Samantha snatched it off the wall. *Ms. Christensen from the library.* Her sweet voice immediately calmed her.

"Hello, Ms. Christensen. How was your Easter?"

"Wonderful. Beautiful."

"I missed seeing the children yesterday. It's my favorite part of my week."

Silence ensued. Was she whispering to someone behind her? "Um, yes. I...Samantha, I need to tell you something."

Oh no. Did something happen to Bob? Heart attack? Car accident? "What's wrong? Please, tell me. Is it Bob?"

"There's no easy way to tell you this. The library has to let you go. An incident was reported last week from one of the parents and I have to—"

"Lisa."

"Um, yes. Her mother reported some serious accusations."

"No. Lisa's lying. Bob was there. Ask him."

"We did. He said, although he was in the room, he wasn't able to hear what you and the child were saying. He also said, when Lisa's mother spoke to you, he had left the room. We can only go by what the mother and daughter said, and, they were quite upset. Hysterical, I should say."

"But, they're lying. You know me. I'd never—"

"Samantha. I'm very sorry. I appreciate you volunteering your time, but it's only a volunteer position. It's not that big of a deal."

It was to her. Her chest ached. The kitchen swirled. She couldn't even volunteer correctly. Her muscles tensed as if ambushed by rage. Disbelief turned to disgust. Anger boiled through her veins. Dr. Chambers laughter hit her hard in the chest.

Samantha ran out of the house and down the driveway. The distinct sound of the front door pulling away from its frame, followed.

"You can't just pick up and leave! What's wrong with you lately? Where are you going?" Her mother stepped onto the front porch, a frigid aura surrounded her.

Samantha careened out of the driveway and away from her home. She entered Jericho Turnpike and maneuvered along the congested road, blasting the stereo. Despite the chilly evening, she rolled her window down, and the wind rushed in, whipping her hair onto her face. She thrust her head out, and sang so loud and dramatic, you'd think she was an escaped psych patient. Drivers stopped to look. A few honked their horns or danced along, but most tossed dirty looks. *Jerks.*

She gripped the steering wheel lighter. Her mother's words cut through her again. The daily insults and attacks, followed by the deliberate guilt trip for never being good enough, caused her eyes to lose their focus as they grew with tears. How much more could she do for that woman? Was she that much of a failure?

Twenty minutes and five songs later, her ears frostbitten and her throat dry, she pulled into a small shopping center. Rob Roy's Deli called to her. Her car smashed into one of the many potholes created from the never-ending blizzards and she rolled the window back up. She flipped the hood on her black sweatshirt over her head, instantly finding security in the armor.

She slammed the door closed, kicked her car's tire, and screamed. She refused to shed another tear. Rage tore through her instead. Tired of being nice and people taking advantage of her. Tired of always doing the right thing and being the good girl while other's walked all over her. She was done.

After exiting the deli with a big fat tuna fish hero, she yanked her car door open. The sandwich rolled onto the seat, the paper unraveled, and tuna fish scurried out from the suffocating and confining bread. She wanted to escape, too. Maybe hanging out with Cara and Eryn would do her some good. Try 'sinful and scandalous' for a while. Nice was getting her nowhere.

Chapter 4

Two Months Later

A fruity cosmopolitan slid down Samantha's throat, while she swiveled back and forth on a stool in The Liquid Ambassador Bar, waiting for Cara to return from the bathroom. According to Cara, if she wanted to catch a sophisticated guy, she had to drink a sophisticated drink. Beers had been off limits since they started hanging out again, as were bar snacks, going to dingy pubs, and dancing with old men. No wonder she failed to meet anyone these past two months.

The icy liquid quenched her thirst and made its way through her veins. With any luck, it'd go straight to her head. A good buzz was more than needed. She had yet to do anything exciting. Tonight, in the new bar, with its packed capacity, her chances of meeting someone increased, as the refreshing atmosphere lifted her spirits.

The tiny dance floor already had ten to twelve people hopping around on it. The band, The Bitter Orphans, positioned themselves on the small stage. The lead singer leaped off and made his way through the crowd, singing to various hot girls and welcoming the ones that had no problem running their fingers through his hair or down his chest. They cheered and roared, then surrounded him, grinding their crotches into his thighs and butt. He was a God to them.

Like a scene in a movie, where all the noise and commotion suddenly pauses, Cara strutted back to the bar - all eyes on her. Her strawberry-colored nails fluffed her long black hair and then clutched onto her short, red mini-dress tugging it back down around her hips. It could've easily fit a ten-year-old. The flashing laser lights from the dance floor reflected off her wire choker collar. An array of gold chains hung from it and wedged themselves in her notable cleavage. In the packed bar, with a typical Friday night happy-hour crowd, Cara looked six-feet tall towering over the already half-drunk patrons, clearly from her five-inch stilettos.

Cara charged through the crowd toward her. "Holy crap, it's

packed." Cara plopped onto the bar's leather stool. "Looks like Cara's getting lucky tonight!"

Samantha chuckled. "When haven't you?" Samantha locked her heels on the bar's brass foot rail. The whir of a blender shifted her view to the hot bartender. His soft, brown curls bounced as he rolled up his shirtsleeves to pour the colorful concoction. Samantha adjusted her gold-sequined, V-neck, spaghetti-strap tank top – the lowest cut shirt she had ever worn. She paired it with a black mini-skirt. No stockings needed on this warm June night.

Cara slapped Samantha on the knee. "Hey, did you meet the new kitchen manager yet? Cooper, I think his name is."

"Cooper? No. The diet clerks were talking about him this morning, though. You?"

"Unfortunately. He's big and fat and mean."

"Mean?"

"Yeah. I went in the kitchen to talk to Bruce and he introduced me to the new storeroom guy. In fact, I invited both of them tonight in case the bar was a flop.

"But, Eryn's meeting us. I thought it would just be the three of us—" Her voice disappeared under the roar of excitement from the Mets game on T.V.

"We did invite her. But, hey, the more the merrier, right? Anyway, Cooper hushed me, then shooed me out of the kitchen like I was some preschooler. Told me I wasn't allowed in there! Then he followed me to make sure that I—"

As if on cue, a feisty redhead burst through the entrance and immediately removed her short, black jacket. Curls of fire dipped over her shoulders and down her back. Eryn grabbed her jacket's collar, flipped it over her shoulder and cut through the crowd like a runway super model. Her short, dark-blue dress clung to every inch of her curvy body. She wore black pumps as well, but they were only a *measly* three-inches high. She searched the room for her former co-workers.

Eryn located Samantha at the bar and tore over, throwing her arms around her and crushing Samantha with the mountains that exploded from beneath the blue stretch fabric. Flowery perfume invaded her nostrils and fused to her skin. Samantha peered down and couldn't help notice Eryn's toned, tight butt. Neither could the guys behind them.

"So glad it's finally Friday!" Eryn hugged Cara next. "How you guys doing?"

"Good. How's the nursing home?" Cara finished off her martini.

"*Uck.* Sucks. I sent my resume to a bunch of hospitals last week. Gotta get the hell out of there. Hey, did you guys do anything Memorial Day weekend?"

Cara licked the salt off the rim of her glass. "I did. Didn't get home 'til 5 a.m." She tossed Eryn a wink.

"What about you, Samantha? Move out of your house yet? Any boyfriends?" Eryn tilted her head.

"Not yet." Samantha locked her ankles together and avoided Eryn's contemptuous smile. The last few weeks, she'd given Samantha little digs. Was she mad that she was hanging out with them again?

"You gotta get out there more. And the emphasis is on *get out*." Eryn slipped her tiny jacket over the stool's backrest.

"Working on it." Samantha peeked to her right. The *glug glug* of a beer poured into a tall glass caught her attention. She could almost taste the hops and barley bubbling up in the foam. She licked her lips, but the sugary remnants from her Cosmo prevailed. *Bleh.*

She turned her attention back to Cara and Eryn who lit up the bar as usual. Dynamic, gorgeous, fun, and lively. Who didn't notice them? Men flocked to them, showered them with drinks, and they always ended up with a phone number or two. Their smiles radiated across the room. Their laughter drew a crowd. And, forget the dance floor - hot men surrounded them in no time. The two of them held their beverages high and clinked glasses as continuous laughter drained from their lungs. Cara closed her eyes and shimmied to the music, while Eryn twirled her hips like a belly dancer.

"So, Eryn," Cara eyed a man at least six-foot-five and smiled. "Any new guys in your life?"

"Just broke up with one actually. Hoping tonight I'll find someone to replace him."

"I don't think you'll have a problem. This place is on fire!" Cara threw her arm around Eryn and gave her a tight squeeze.

Eryn went through guys faster than Samantha's mother tossed insults. Her gushing sex appeal and all around gorgeousness reeled the men in, but her vibrant personality kept them around. In the short three months they had worked together, Eryn managed to date at least five different men. Some at the same time. One usually overlapping the other. Eryn claimed she broke up with them, but after a few drunken revelations, Samantha sensed they had dumped her.

The band began their rendition of "Pour Some Sugar on Me," and the dance floor flooded with screaming girls. This place *was* on fire! Cara leaned in closer to Eryn and pointed to the tall guy and his cute friend. They giggled and then launched into their own private conversation. Samantha felt like a third wheel. She scooted off the bar stool, noticed her entire boob almost popped out from beneath the loosely-draped V-neck, then wandered away from the hordes of patrons laughing and shouting over one another, wanting to be closer to the powerful energy on the dance floor.

The deafening conversations softened as she neared the dance floor. Samantha stayed at the perimeter and smiled at the enthusiasm of the crowd. The lead singer drifted down the two stairs and zigzagged through the crowd. Shrieking ensued, as the bass player took center stage for his mini solo. When the lyrics began again, the singer held the microphone up to various women, letting them sing the chorus.

Samantha's heart thundered. Would he hold it under her mouth? It'd been so long since she sang in front of an audience. And, that was to small children. She always dreamed of singing to a large crowd, but her mother's insults strangled her courage.

The lead singer approached and she froze. He closed in, held the mic up to a girl with a nose ring, then turned and faced Samantha dead on. *Here we go.* Her mouth opened wide, "Pour some..." But, the singer coasted back toward the stage and sang the last chorus himself. He leaped over the two steps and landed flat on the platform. Warmth shot through Samantha's body and she huffed a long breath, unsure if it was from relief or disappointment.

Samantha lifted her foot and used the heel to scratch the itch that was brewing on her calf. Cheers erupted to her left. A girl with black and white striped hair, slipped and crashed to the floor. Her spread legs revealed a black lace thong beneath her pink, satin mini-skirt.

"Quite a sight." The deep voice floated past her ear. A guy with a beer in hand, stood less than four inches behind her.

"If you hang around long enough, there's always plenty of sights." She clinked her delicate glass with his beer bottle. *That's it. Be cool.* "I'm Samantha."

"I'm Lou. Lucky night for me."

Her heart twitched. Unable to compete with his steely gaze, Samantha took a sip of her Cosmo, avoiding his striking eyes. Although not terribly tall, his broad shoulders made up for it. He could probably lift her effortlessly in his strong arms and carry her across his bedroom.

"So, I'm new to the area. Is this the hot spot?" His picture-perfect, white teeth sparkled with a smile so large it immediately sucked her in.

She couldn't pull her eyes away this time. Not exactly her fantasy guy, but his interest in her was more than flattering. After the rejection from Dr. Chambers, her confidence still wavered. She tapped her foot nervously, trying to compose herself. "Seems to be. My co-worker Cara found it a few weeks ago and—"

"Cara?" His eyebrows narrowed.

Oh, great. Finally, a handsome guy was interested in her - a man she could see herself dating, a man she had chemistry with - and it was probably one of Cara's old toss-aways. "Yes. Cara McCormick. She works at St. Elizabeth's Hospital. You know her?" *Please say no.*

"Not really. Just started working there in the storeroom. Met her today. She invited me and this guy Bruce I work with to come."

"Bruce?" Samantha snickered. "You work with Bruce in the kitchen?"

"Yeah. You know him?"

She held out her hand. "I'm one of the dietitians there."

"No kidding. How come I haven't seen your pretty face around?"

"Hmm. You're slick, aren't you?"

The band took a break and the overhead sound system turned on. Christina Aguilera's "What a Girl Wants" chimed in, and a group of girls next to her sang along with such intensity, Lou pulled her away and back towards the bar. A server weaved through the patrons with her tray held high to avoid a collision.

"You're a dietitian? Do all dietitians dress like you two?"

Samantha became aware of her top inching dangerously close to her nipple. "What do you mean?"

"You ladies are hot." Lou placed his hand around her waist, not wasting any time, and swayed to the music.

"Thank you." Although more comfortable in her new clothes, tonight Samantha pushed her limits. But, maybe it was working. Maybe this is what she needed to do.

She casually glanced over at her co-workers. Eryn's legs were wrapped around some guy's hips. She put one hand on his shoulder, then dragged her long fingernail down his cheek, under his chin, and across his lips. In less than a wink, Eryn and the guy were kissing.

Cara entertained the tall guy. With her shoulders pulled way back, her boobs floated under his chin. He focused on them and his finger reached into her cleavage and swept out the long strands of gold beads hiding in there. Cara shook her head back and forth, glass held high, and her hips gyrating like she was having sex.

This was what she had to do? Dressing the part was one thing, but—

"Need a shot?" Lou motioned to the bar.

She shifted back to reality, "Um, well..." She jiggled her full glass. *Just go with it.* "Sure. Why not. Let's have some fun."

They strolled to the bar and leaned their elbows on the counter. Upside-down shot glasses, half-empty wine goblets, and crumpled napkins littered the top. The mirrored wall behind the bar reflected a blue neon sign, but she caught their reflection in it as well. *This was happening.* Butterflies soared in her stomach, and her heart leaped with excitement. Lou was interested in her. And, what a good looking catch he was. Sweet. Friendly. Welcoming. Maybe Dr. Chambers *was* out of her league.

"How do you like the hospital so far?" Samantha asked.

"Not bad. Bruce's cool. He's teaching me a thing or too."

"I'm sure he is."

"You know it, darling." He nudged her in the shoulder.

Something hard slammed Samantha behind her knee causing her leg to buckle. She recovered, twisted her upper body around from the scare, and met Bruce's ogling gaze. His eyes followed a route up the back of her leg, and when they reached her tank top, they widened. Samantha peeked down and gasped. Turning rapidly had knocked her boob out from the plunging neckline. Her hardened nipple thrust out for all to see. She yanked it closed, but not before Lou caught sight of it, too. *How embarrassing!*

"Didn't know where you went." Bruce kept his eyes on Samantha's chest, but directed his question toward Lou.

"Found myself something sweet to look at." Lou clasped his palm around Samantha's elbow, claiming her.

Bruce's expression changed. Was he intrigued or pissed off? Bruce had to be over six-feet tall. His dark, Puerto Rican skin and thread-like mustache, matched his scrawny body. He fit in perfectly with the rest of the players here. His thick gold chain reflected the fluorescent light above. His relentless gaze on her, unnerving. He bit down on his lower lip and looked like some horny beaver.

"Hey, Sam. You have a pencil?" Bruce wiggled his eyebrows.

"No. I didn't bring my—"

"Cause I wanna erase your past and write our future." He licked his top lip, gliding over the bottom of the mustache.

Lou pushed him away. "I was about to order some shots. Want one?" Lou took out his wallet.

"I'll get them." Bruce tried to drive himself between the two of them. "You bought the beers." Lou shoved back, sending Bruce to the other side of her.

The bartender approached, looking exhausted and irritated. "What'll you guys have?"

Bruce threw a crumpled ten-dollar bill on the bar. "Shots. Two buttery nipples and a blow job."

The bartender, unamused, shook his head in disgust. "You shitting me? I'm in no mood, buddy."

Lou leaned in. "Three shots of tequila. Ignore him."

"I will. And for the rest of the night." The bartender stormed off and threw his rag into one of the sinks.

Bruce snorted, then gulped his beer, finishing it off.

Samantha turned her back to Bruce and smiled. Two guys fighting over her. She should be flattered. "Where'd you work before, Lou?"

"Supermarket near my house. My mom's friend, Angie, told her there was an opening in the hospital for the storeroom position."

"Oh! Angie's so sweet. What a doll. Glad she hooked you up." Angie, one of the tray-line supervisors in the kitchen, had worked there for almost two years and managed to warm the hearts of everyone in the department. Always smiling and laughing, Angie could cheer anyone up. Her tall, thin frame, and dark-brown, pixie-haircut made her appear much younger than the forty-year-old she was.

"It seems easy enough. Lotta food though. Man." Lou slanted in, leaving only inches between them. His fingers gently caressed her bare shoulder, causing her heart to hammer in her chest.

Samantha attempted to talk to Lou for the next half hour, but Bruce continued to interject. Couldn't he take a hint? Couldn't he find his own girl? She never liked him. Although married, not once had he resisted the urge to hit on anything that walked past him. She overheard him many times flirting with the nurse's aides and secretaries, exchanging phone numbers, and touching them, while he passed out patient trays. He made her want to vomit.

Bruce continuously dug his paws into the bowl of peanuts in front of her. His breath smelled of nuts and stale beer. When she thought she couldn't stand the annoyance any longer, Cara located them. "Hey guys!" Cara raised her empty glass in the air and shook her boobs like two maracas.

"Now the party's starting!" Bruce placed his hand on her lower back and grinded her thigh as if she was some teenage boy's bed.

Gross! Samantha threw her bag over her shoulder. "I need to use the bathroom." *Use it to puke.*

After Samantha's mouth sparkled with her pink lip-gloss again, she adjusted her ridiculous top one more time, and exited the heavily perfumed bathroom into the swollen crowd with its packed booths and amplifying music. Before she could take two steps, a hand grabbed hold and pulled her behind the wall. White teeth sparkled at her.

"Sorry to scare you." Lou ran his fingers through his hair. "I figured we could use some alone time without Bruce drooling on your shoulder."

Samantha's lips stretched into a grin. "Thank you. It was a little annoying." *Incredibly annoying.*

"Wanna get out of here?" His smile created chaos in her mind.

Samantha became breathless. Her stomach stiffened. *Say yes. Just say yes, dammit.* "Well, I'm here with Cara and Eryn, and it wouldn't be cool." Who was she kidding? They always blew her off. Fear gripped her, though. She barely knew Lou.

What happened to being a badass? Didn't she want more spontaneity in her life?

She tracked the outline of his neck, over his wide shoulders, and down his arms. What he'd probably do to her. Her imagination ran wild with visions of him naked on his bed, towering over her.

How many dates had she had over the past three years? None. Unless you count that loser she made out with at the Halloween party. *Lame.* So was his kiss. Wonder what Lou kissed like.

"You're right. My fault. Wouldn't be the right thing to do—"

That was all he had to say. She was tired of being the good girl. Where had that gotten her? Samantha eased in for a kiss. And…instantly melted. Strong. Powerful. Juicy and *Wow!* Something about him was intense. She hadn't felt this way in years.

Suddenly, Samantha wished she had said yes. Wished he'd lift her up in those big strong arms and carry her to his place. Lustful urges coursed through her body. Wicked and sinful thoughts spilled over, but she knew she wasn't ready. Why'd she say no! What was she so afraid of? Being hurt again? She needed to put herself out there. Take chances. What's the worst that could happen, right?

She'd have to dig deeper next time and find more courage. Tonight, a kiss would have to do.

Chapter 5

Samantha couldn't wipe Lou from her mind. Why hadn't she left with him that night? She'd been kicking herself all week. She finally had her chance to do something wild and spontaneous, then blew it. Talking to Lou every day this week at the hospital, only heightened the chemistry between them. Next time things would be different. No holding back.

Cara and Eryn's personal magnetism and charisma came naturally. Samantha's actions felt artificial. She had to dress a certain way. Act a certain way. Speak a certain way. She didn't feel like herself anymore, but was that a good thing? According to Cara, she'd been going about it the wrong way.

Maybe her mother was right about her being an embarrassment. Maybe Glenn dumped her because she didn't fit in with his friends. They did all dress flawlessly. Name brand clothes and bags. Samantha glanced at her new stilettos. Had Glenn dumped her for the way she looked? The way she acted? What had she done that was so horrible that he said he couldn't *do* this anymore?

Whatever it was, whatever she'd been doing wrong, she was definitely doing something right now. Of all the women in the bar that night, Lou approached her.

Samantha strutted into the hospital's kitchen in her highest heels, and traipsed across the battered kitchen flooring with the excuse of needing a can of Glucerna for one of her patients. Onion skin fragments and dried spills dotted the tiles, but she kept her head high and grinned. Her short, burgundy skirt and tight, gray top clung to every twist and turn on her body.

The lunch line had ended a few minutes prior, and the staff cleared away trays full of cellophaned bread slices and brown-spotted bananas. Others returned perishable foods to the refrigerators while the rest wiped down their stations. The lingering odor of garlic remained. With the hustle and bustle of the routine distracting everyone, Samantha snuck into the storeroom.

The silence from within let her know it was vacant. *Damn*. Where could Lou be? Lunch break? She fiddled around for a can of

Glucerna, grabbed a second one, changed it to chocolate, then pretended the can was stuck. Five minutes later, feeling like a moron, she turned to leave.

A rustling of papers brought her to a stop. Was Lou in the storage area behind her? She tiptoed to the back, peeked around the corner, and recoiled. A man in an extra-large lab coat was crouched over a box of green beans, tugging at the cover to tear it open. The scent of intoxicating cologne, something that always drove her crazy and left her powerless, replaced the garlic stench. She couldn't move. Cooper Timmons.

Big and fat and mean. Samantha had yet to meet the new kitchen manager, and now was not the time. The last thing she needed was to get in trouble again. She swiftly turned and bee-lined for the exit. Angie, the tray line supervisor, with her larger-than-life grin, waved her arm wildly as if she was a drowning victim, holding on to a tree branch for dear life.

Samantha waved back - less enthusiastically - then scrambled by as fast as possible in her four-inch heels. The door leading toward the hallway was less than ten yards away. With the gnawing grind of a can opener behind her, she high-tailed it, looked over her shoulder one last time, and crashed right into a hard, warm being.

"Well, well. Another lucky day for me." Lou bit his lip and clutched her hips. The electric energy shot fireworks through her body.

"You are a very lucky person, aren't you?" She practiced her seductive voice all weekend.

"And what do I owe this visit?"

"Actually, I was just getting a can of Glucerna for a patient. But...it's definitely nice to bump into you."

"It is. Especially the bumping part." He glanced at her chest, which looked abnormally large in her extra padded-bra. "You look hot, Samantha. I thought about our kiss all weekend. Too bad it wasn't more." Lou peeked to the left. Something behind her distracted him. His hands slipped off her hips and his face went cool. "Yeah, so...sorry for that. I should look where I'm going next time." Then, he marched past her and disappeared.

Afraid to look directly, Samantha let the can fall from her hand and land beside her foot. She reached down to pick it up and casually peered over her shoulder. Cooper stood behind her with his hands on his hips. At least she assumed it was him, having never met him before. Also, through her view, he was upside down.

Chapter 6

The overly sweet, cranberry martini slid past Samantha's lips. *Should she just knock it back in one giant gulp?* Lou was meeting them tonight at the Liquid Ambassador, and after two weeks of flirting, her body trembled with anticipation. She downed a shot with Cara, then placed the glass on the counter. She peered down at her black, mini-dress. The shiny zipper reflected the dance floor's lights. Although it easily fit over her head, the zipper extended from her chest to her crotch - more for show than functionality. She unzipped it a little lower as the shot raced through her blood stream.

Cara showed up to the bar already buzzed, stating she had a vodka and orange juice before leaving her apartment, but it seemed as if she had much more than one. When she leaned over to speak in Samantha's ear, her arm slipped off the bar. "So, Cooper kicked me out of the kitchen again. I snuck in to tell Bruce what time we'd be here and he told me he wasn't telling me again. The next time, I'd be sorry." Her head wobbled to the right.

"What an ass. What's that guys problem? I never went in there again after that first time he caught me. Lou's been meeting me near the diet office or the elevator."

"Well, stay away. Or else." Cara chuckled.

"Or else what? What's he going to do? Why does he care?"

"Maybe he's jealous. Fat loser. He probably can't get a girl. Jealous that his boys are grabbing all the hot women around him."

Samantha rubbed her bare legs repeatedly to give them some warmth. "I'm excited, but nervous. It's been a while."

"It's like riding a bicycle. Or shoving a wooden peg through a hole!" She burst out laughing and slapped Samantha on the knee. Her behavior was bordering on obnoxious now.

The clinking of ice in a highball drink caught Samantha's attention. "I think I need another drink."

"Oh, come on. It'll be fine. Lou seems really nice."

"I know. It's just that…I feel like tonight's going to escalate quickly. He's been hinting what he wants to do with me when he gets me alone. I was hoping the first time would be different."

"It's not your first time."

"With him it is." Samantha leaned towards the bin of garnishes and plunked a maraschino cherry into her mouth. The burst of sweetness made her wince.

"What do you want? Flowers? A romantic dinner with wine and candle light?"

Samantha wouldn't admit it, but that's exactly what she wanted. She wasn't sure Lou was that type, though. He appeared smart and caring, but something was missing. She hoped he would've asked her out on a real date instead of just meeting them here.

Cara yawned. "I told my landlord he better get the damn bugs out of my apartment. Did you know, I found dog shit on the stairs the other day? I think that new tenant is just opening the door and letting her dog shit inside the apartment complex!"

"Ew, gross. Why don't you move out?"

"I tried. Everything's so expensive. I have too many bills right now. Maybe once my car is paid off. Or the college loans. Or the credit cards. Maybe I should try stripping. I'd probably be a great stripper and have my bills paid off in no time."

"Yeah, right." Samantha laughed, then scanned the bar for Lou again. Her legs trembled. The skirt barely covered her crotch when she sat. Crossing her legs was impossible.

Cara licked the last drop from her martini glass. "Where's Lou? I need another drink."

"Maybe you should slow down. Have some water."

Cara snorted so loud, the girl behind her shot her a bitchy glare. "What are you saying?"

"I just think you might perhaps be a tad buzzed." That was an understatement. Cara could always hold her liquor. How much did she drink tonight? Did she go somewhere before coming to the bar? The girl behind Cara whispered to her friends. This was becoming way too embarrassing.

Cara wasn't even listening. A huge, steroid-infused beast approached and slid his arm around her. "Hey, Cara. How you been?"

Stale cigarette smoke invaded Samantha's nose. Did Cara know this brute? Something about him made her feel uneasy. In addition to his massive size, his eyes spewed terror and disaster. The mere sight of him shot panic through her.

"Good, Jake. You?" For once, Cara didn't seem to want the company. She looked away and didn't bother introducing Samantha.

When the tension couldn't get any tighter, Lou strutted in wearing a cobalt blue, button-down shirt. His smile lit up the room, and when he caught sight of the two of them, he sauntered over.

"Hello, ladies. How's everyone doing tonight?" He frowned at the beast despite the clear difference in size.

"Great," Cara stammered, "Did you hit a lot of traffic on your way over?" She tilted her head away from the beast and her eyes widened.

Lou tossed her a quizzical look. He only lived five minutes from the bar. His eyes rolled up to the guy and then he smiled at Cara. "Yeah, sorry I'm late. Guess everyone wanted to get the hell out of work as fast as possible. You two need a drink?" Lou ignored the beast, who now edged away.

The beast nodded to Cara. "I'll be seeing you around." He knocked her in the shoulder and sauntered off.

"Who was that?"

Cara tucked her head into her chest and spun on the barstool. "No one important."

"He seemed important."

"Well, he's not!"

"Okay, then," Lou interrupted. "What're you ladies drinking?"

"I need some air." Cara hopped off the stool and wandered through the crowd.

"She all right?" Lou jumped on the now vacant bar stool.

"Not sure. She seems a little off tonight. I'm worried about her."

Lou leaned in and put his hand behind Samantha's ear. His lips smashed onto hers and sent her back into that tizzy from a few of weeks ago. She let him devour her. His hand slid from her neck down her bare arm and then he placed her hand in his. She would make this work. Apprehension spiraled out of control, but she pushed it back down.

"I couldn't wait for tonight. Couldn't wait for the week to end." Lou smiled and cupped her chin.

"Me too." For the first time in a long time, joy returned to Samantha's heart.

"The past two weeks you drove me crazy. Teasing me with all those sexy outfits." His finger sketched her arm, up and down. "I hoped last weekend we'd get together. Two weeks was too long."

"Sorry. I had to—"

He placed his finger over her lips. "Last week's in the past. All I care about is now." Lou's lips brushed against hers gently, but then grew more powerful. His hand found its way behind her neck, and his tongue let her know he couldn't wait any longer. "Let's find someplace more private." He hopped off the stool and led her by the hand toward the back.

Samantha tried to keep up in her painful heels as Lou tugged her arm and weaved in and out of the loud banter and standing-room-only crowd. He leaned her up against the wall next to a plaque that read: "It's easier to forgive an enemy, than a friend." She pondered the meaning, but before it became clear, all of Lou's fingers laced through Samantha's hair as he pulled her back onto his mouth.

His hips nudged her against the wall until her butt smacked into the dark wood paneling. Had anyone kissed her this intensely before? The warmth of his mouth, the spicy taste of cinnamon gum, won her over. She could feel his heart beat relentlessly on top of hers. Or, was it the heavy bass coming from the speakers?

Lou pulled away abruptly. She caught the eerie sight behind him. Bruce mounted over Lou's shoulder. He had to be at least six inches taller than Lou. His boney, lanky frame creeped Samantha out.

"What's going on with you two love birds?" Bruce leered at her, then his gaze transfixed onto her chest. Lou turned to answer and she peeked down. Either her zipper slipped further along its track, or Lou somehow managed to ease it down without her knowing. Her red-laced bra peeked out considerably. She faced the bathrooms and glided the zipper back up.

"Have you seen Cara?" Lou asked with a hint of "leave me alone and go find her" in his tone. Was he giving Bruce the eye?

Bruce looked at Lou and then stared at Samantha. He took a step closer to her, his lips pressed together as if holding back rage. "No. You were the first two I saw."

"She seemed a little drunk. Try to find her. Okay?" Lou spun back to Samantha.

Bruce huffed at his dismissal. "Fine. Drunk can be to my advantage." He raised and lowered his eyebrows.

Samantha flinched. "No. Actually, I'll look for her. She did seem off, and she's my best friend."

Lou grabbed her arm and tugged back.

"I need to find her, Lou. I'm sorry."

His shoulders slumped and his face went slack. Would he get tired of yet another delay?

"I'll be quick. I just want to make sure she's all right." Samantha took off. Thunderous clapping resounded as the band finished their set. With the dance floor all but cleared out, a couple danced to the silence with their hands gripped tightly, spinning each other, and ending with a dip. The crowd cheered.

At the far end of the bar, Cara's arm rested on the counter, possibly to hold herself up. "Cara!" Samantha pushed her way through the final group. "Cara. You okay?"

Cara laughed. "What? Of course. What's wrong with you tonight? Don't throw your fear of being with Lou onto worrying about poor little me."

"I'm not. You're standing in the corner all alone. I was worried."

A guy with short, brown hair turned around with two orange-colored drinks in his hands. He handed one to Cara, smiled, then his view shifted towards Samantha. "Can I help you?"

"She's with me." Cara shook her head, and her red eyes glazed over. "Where's Lou? Shouldn't you be with him? Or did your mom call you to come home and make her some tea?" Cara rolled her eyes, attempted to bring the drink to her lips, but misjudged the distance and smashed the right side of her teeth. Her fingers instinctively raced to her mouth to relieve the pain.

Cara was beyond drunk at this point, but there was no reason to insult her. "Fine. Never mind." Samantha battled the crowd. Obviously, Cara became an angry drunk when she had too much. Years of drinking with her, she'd never become this annihilated. Samantha couldn't help but be concerned, though. She looked over her shoulder one last time and saw Cara laughing with the guy.

Lou had perched himself at the bar. He hailed the bartender over just as Samantha nudged him in the shoulder. Time to have some fun of her own.

The next hour, Lou and Samantha sat at the bar surprisingly without any interruptions. They joked about Roselyn's ineffective management skills and vented about Apollo's horrible cafeteria cuisine. Lou's knees continuously rubbed against hers. After two more drinks, she excused herself to the bathroom.

She exited a few minutes later and Lou's steely gaze caught her by surprise. "Hey sexy." He pushed her against the wall until they melded into each other's curves. Their lips combined - tasting, quickening. Self-doubt crept in.

Lou pulled back and his eyes locked on hers. His finger played with the small, metal zipper and slowly slid it along its teeth. Samantha pressed her fist against her hip and scanned the room, but the rowdy crowd was involved with their own festivities. Two of Lou's fingers found their way beneath the black material and onto the red lace beneath. "So beautiful. What does it feel like to be the most beautiful girl in this room?" He kissed her gently once more. "You have such a nice smile, Samantha."

"Thank you."

"We have great chemistry. Don't you think?"

It had been ages since anyone noticed her. Her heartrate increased, and the room blurred. His dark brown eyes sucked her in.

"Want to get out of here? Go somewhere quiet?" His finger ran across the bottom of her lip. Her mouth - open and gasping for air.

"Yes." The words gushed out. She needed him to take her. Now.

Lou clasped her hand, zigzagged through the crowd and out the front door. He placed his hand behind her back and guided her through the parking lot. Would he take her back to his place? At this point, she didn't care. Forget the flowers and wine. They could do that next time.

A sudden flush of warmth spread from between her thighs, outward. She pictured him easing down that crazy zipper of hers and studying her matching red bra and underwear. Running his tongue over her flesh. Fingers tracing her hills and crevices. Planting kisses everywhere.

They crossed the black pavement riddled with cracks, and turned right, next to a big, red pick-up truck. A flickering streetlight overhead lit the way. Would he drive her back here later to pick up her car? Or would he want her to sleep over?

He passed the truck and stepped onto the grass behind it. *Huh?* Oh no. He wasn't going to lift her into the truck's bed and have sex with her in there, was he? *Don't freak out. You wanted a few adventures, right?* Lou faced her, walking backward, leading her by both hands toward him. Right behind…a dumpster.

Wait, What? Was he serious? She tried to read his expression, but tripped over a discarded beer bottle, instead. A dirty towel and a Dunkin' Donuts coffee cup arranged themselves next to a shredded, kitchen garbage bag and a crushed Heineken box. Her stilettos sunk into the soft dirt.

"Why do you have to be so damn fine?" Before she could process where she was, he yanked on the zipper in one fluid motion, until it revealed her scarlet underwear. He tugged one more time until the dress-halves detached from the silver tracks. His hands moved to her shoulders and pushed the material back. "Holy shit, Sam." He examined her, then panted like a dog. "I like the name Sam. It sounds so fuckin' sexy. Do you like when I call you Sam?"

Her thoughts swirled. Sam? Was Samantha too childish? *Wait.* Were they having sex behind the dumpster? Right here? Her stomach quivered. Before any thoughts processed, he twisted her around and bent her over until her head was only inches from the base of the rusted, green dumpster. Blood rushed through her veins, increasing her body temperature.

She surveyed the metal container and the oozing and dripping of its contents. Luckily, the breeze whisked away any stronger smells than what she currently experienced. She tried not to breathe. A brown paper bag and what looked like a dirty, stuffed Sylvester the Cat doll, sprawled out between her legs near a pile of possible chicken tenders—

Her dress lifted up and her underwear flew down around her knees. This wasn't real. Her pulse froze, then seemed to pound. She heard crackling behind her, as Lou fiddled with what she assumed was a condom. Then, as she peered down at Sylvester again, he plunged into her, awkwardly. Samantha scanned the dumpster for a spot to place her hand to prevent being pushed forward and over. One tiny, clear, green spot materialized, and she placed her index finger on the surface.

When he finally wrestled himself inside, he began thrusting. Was she really having sex behind a dumpster? Is this what she meant by reckless abandon?

"Oh, baby, yes. You're so fucking tight. I love it."

Of course, she was tight. She hadn't had sex in years. Amazed it hadn't sealed itself back up. Her finger ached from Lou's driving force. What the hell was happening? Samantha closed her eyes. Pretended she was somewhere else, somewhere romantic, and tried to enjoy the feeling of a man inside her again. *Calm down. Try to embrace the craziness of it.* When she successfully blocked out her surroundings, and curbed her fear of someone catching them, she let herself go. Samantha released a low moan.

Lou hushed her.

Her eyes snapped open, the vision lost. Sylvester the Cat, with its pink tongue, ogled her like he wanted in on the action, next. Samantha swallowed hard and waited for it to be over. Was she supposed to be enjoying this quickie? Did he think she wanted this wild romp out in the open as much as he did?

Lou thrust hard one last time, then rested his chin on her back. With his breaths pouring out, he pulsed inside her. Then stopped. Abruptly. "Shh," he warned. Footsteps approached, stumbling perhaps, and then the distinct sound of someone puking behind them. Samantha peered over her shoulder. Cara stood there in only her bra and miniskirt, throwing up behind the dumpster.

****

Samantha half-carried, half-walked Cara up the flight of stairs to her apartment. The smell of urine filled the stairwell. Dog? Human? She hated to think about it.

After unlocking the door, she flicked on the light switch, but the room remained dark. She led Cara to the couch and then wandered in the dark to a small kitchen area. She found a light switch over the sink that barely illuminated the living room. Kitchen cabinets hung uneven above outdated appliances. Piles of bills lined the counter top. College loan. Car payment. Electricity. Visa bill. Rent envelope.

Samantha removed the only remaining clean glass from the cabinet and filled it with water. The faucet continued to drip onto the piles of dirty dishes in the sink. She handed the glass to Cara who reached for it as if she were a two-year-old holding a cup for the first time. Amazing how people turn into useless creatures when they get sloshed.

Once Cara took a sip, Samantha made her way through the darkness and searched for a light in the small apartment. A gold table-lamp rested on the wood floor. The bulb had smashed and dispersed itself around the table. "What happened?"

Cara attempted to place the glass on her coffee table and missed. Samantha rushed to her side and guided the glass to the center of the table. The table that was covered with Burger King bags, a condom wrapper, and The New York Times from three days ago. Piles of dirty clothes littered the floor. "Cara. What's gotten into you tonight? You've been so...so—"

"So what? Just say it. I'm a mess."

"Please, tell me. I want to help."

"You go out of your way to help everyone so they'll like you. Maybe you should try liking yourself first, Samantha."

"Obviously you're mad at me. I'm not sure what I did, but just get it off your chest already." Samantha rustled all the garbage together from and around the coffee table. She squashed the debris, cradled it in her arms and lugged it across the peeling linoleum floor to the garbage pail that had no bag. "Do you have any garbage bags? God, Cara. You're such a slob. Your desk at work is immaculate." She found a bag under the sink and transferred the garbage to it. "I thought we were friends. You never tell me anything personal. Only a bunch of crazy stories."

"Fine. You want to know? I'll tell you. Then you'll wish you never asked." Cara curled into a ball and rolled her shirtsleeve around her fist. "My mom married *Steve*, okay? Mr. Incredible. And had two dashingly handsome sons. Then...she repeatedly cheated on him." She clutched her hands together into tight lumps. "Steve promptly bolted."

Samantha, unprepared for the confession, stopped cleaning.

"Then the drinking began. When my brothers were about four and five, she went to some bar and had a one-night stand. Which made me. How romantic, don't ya think?" She leaned her head onto the couches armrest.

Samantha threw her hand over her mouth. "I'm so sorry. I never knew."

Cara held up her hand. "Yup. I was a big, fucking mistake. My mom didn't even know the guy's name. Just some cheesy, car sex, then finds out she's pregnant. Steve took care of his boys, but I wasn't his. My mom continued to drink and attempted to cook dinner. In and out of jobs. You know. The classic shit stories. When I was twelve, she started dating this asshole and sent me off to hang out with my brothers at night. They were annoyed at first. Who'd blame 'em? They were sixteen and seventeen. I tried to fit in. Look cool. I had my first cigarette at twelve. My first beer, too. Had sex when I was thirteen. With one of my brother's friends, no less. Great brothers. Great looking out for your little sister.

My mom bitched all the time that because of me, she was broke. But, she lost jobs because she couldn't finish the day without sneaking a drink. She made me get a paper route at twelve. I Babysat. Forged my working papers when I was fifteen and got a job cleaning women's bathrooms. Rode my bike there every day. The bike I bought myself. I was lucky if my mom remembered my birthday."

Samantha sat next to Cara and placed a hand on her shoulder.

"I bought a piece of shit car later on, then worked two jobs. Schoolwork came easy to me. Made honors all the time. I guess things I learned in school were fascinating. I actually liked doing homework. My life at home revolved around canned Spaghetti-O's and T.V." Cara laughed.

"You'd never know with the way you carry yourself. I envy your independence."

"Had no choice," Cara grumbled. "I applied to college. Had to get the hell away from everyone. Got financial aid, took out loans, whatever I could get. My crappy car died driving back and forth during breaks. Not that I wanted to go home."

"You did really well in college, though. You told me your grades. And you have your own apartment. A new car. Everyone at work loves you. Something had to change for the better."

Cara looked up at the wall clock. Tried to focus. Her eyes closed and squeezed tight. She sucked air in through her nose - slow and deep. Was she going to cry? She'd never seen Cara cry before. Watching such a strong women crumble made Samantha sick.

Cara pushed off the armrest, steadied herself and wobbled a few feet to her left. After taking two or three steps and grabbing hold of the back of the couch, Cara raced to the bathroom. Retching echoed through the apartment. Samantha waited for her to return. She glanced around at the barren, unfriendly apartment. No picture frames decorated the room. No plants. No life.

Five minutes of silence passed, then Samantha took a few steps toward the bathroom, glided open the door, and found Cara asleep on the floor.

Chapter 7

Roselyn leaned back in her chair and sighed. "Cooper has informed me that the two of you are in the kitchen frequently and without reason except to converse with the staff. The boys to be exact."

Here we go. In trouble again. "I only went in there this morning to...bring in a call back for lunch." Samantha lied, but didn't need another write up. Her palms grew clammy and she wiped them on her skirt. In the corner of her eye, she caught Cara yawn and turn away.

"Cara, you especially have been named. Cooper mentioned this previously, but I told him to handle it. Obviously he cannot." Roselyn clobbered her stapler with her fist fastening a pile of papers, then twisted to reach for something in her bottom drawer.

Samantha and Cara glanced at each other. Samantha widened her eyes warning Cara to knock it off. Cara let out a low snicker.

Roselyn popped her head back up and glared at Cara. "Cara, do you have something to say?"

Cara huffed like an eight-year-old sitting in the principal's office for shooting spitballs at the teacher's head. She folded her arms in her chest and it sounded as if a low, snoring noise exited from her gritted teeth. "I will never, ever, go in the kitchen ever again."

Her sarcasm tore through Samantha. She had to fix this. "I'm sure we had no intention of disrupting the kitchen's workflow. It's just a silly misunderstanding. We promise it won't happen again." Samantha stood before Roselyn had an opportunity to respond to Cara's rude behavior. Or, write them up. She was in no mood for this.

They exited the office and once down the hall, Cara glared at Samantha. "Must you always be so nice? We did nothing wrong. We were allowed in there before Cooper started. Can't you ever speak up for yourself? What the hell are you so afraid of?"

A sudden coldness hit Samantha's core. After sticking up for Cara, this was her gratitude? "I'm not afraid. I just won't speak that way to her. It's not right. She's our boss."

"Oh, please. I have no respect for that woman. Stop caring what everyone thinks and speak your mind, will you?" Cara looked away and stomped down the hall.

Samantha entered the elevator at the end of the corridor and attempted to ride it up to her floor. Her body tensed and she felt her toes curl in her shoes. The elevator stopped on the first floor, however. *Dammit.* She had to get out of this confined space. She inhaled every drop of air in the enclosed space.

The doors screeched and squealed as metal scraped against metal, but the deserted lobby taunted her. Samantha jabbed the stupid door-close button. Before the doors sealed shut, a hand appeared through the crack. Bruce. *Yay. All alone in an elevator with the true embodiment of high-class and charm.*

He stepped in, sneered and pushed the button for the fifth floor. As if the day couldn't get any worse, Bruce sauntered over, placed both hands on the wall above her, and bent in until only two inches remained between their lips. "You know, baby, I can give you something, too. I got that hot Latino blood racing through this body of mine. Mmm, mmm." His breath reeked of hard-boiled eggs.

Samantha turned her head, then ducked under his arm. He took a giant step to the right and closed his arms around her again.

"Smile, baby. It's the second best thing you can do with your lips." He opened his mouth wide to demonstrate.

"Look. I'm dating Lou. And plus, you're married and—"

"Dating?" Bruce snorted and released his arms. "Baby, I can share. Everybody cheats."

"I don't."

"Everybody," he snarled. The elevator lurched and the doors staggered along their tracks. He dragged his tongue across his vile mustache, squeezed his crotch aggressively, and sped down the corridor.

Chapter 8

Samantha met Lou at the far end of the hallway, but could see the kitchen entrance from where they stood. Another weekend approached. Would Lou have something special planned this time? Last weekend ended with sex in his car. It was awkward and juvenile. Was she sixteen again? Although they had chemistry – Lou certainly was fiery when it came to that – Samantha knew something was missing. Cara told her she was being picky, and after three long years, she should be grateful.

"Did you like the chicken salad I made you? I added dried cranberries and walnuts to give it a bite." Samantha beamed, her blue eyes twinkled with pride.

"Yeah, um. It was great. So, you going tonight?" Lou inched closer to Samantha until his groin implanted itself in her crotch.

She faked a smile and twisted slightly away. "Why don't we go someplace else? Try something different?"

"Where?"

"I don't know. Out to dinner? A movie? Someplace nice? How about—" A squeaky wheel from a passing kitchen cart sliced through her words.

"What's wrong with the bar?"

"Just tired of the scene. Thought it'd be fun if we went some place where we could hear each other talk. Have some privacy, you know." *Why were guys so clueless? Couldn't they come up with ideas of their own?*

"Oh, yeah? Wanna get your groove on without all the interruptions?" He slid his hands up her back.

"Well, kinda." Instead of turned on, uncertainty rolled through her stomach.

"I don't have my own place, though."

"I assumed—"

"How about your place, baby?"

"I live with my mom still." Her face raced with warmth as the statement sounded more absurd now than ever. She felt like a seventeen-year-old sneaking around to have sex.

"What about a motel? We can have a lot of fun there. I'll promise you a night you won't forget." He leaned in for a quick kiss.

A motel sounded sleazy, but then again, she'd never been to one. They could be alone, though. No loud music. No keeping track of Cara. They could talk without Bruce interrupting. Plan a real date. Maybe grab something to eat afterward.

"Sure. Why not." Samantha glanced at her watch. "I get off at four-thirty."

"I can't leave 'til five." He looked over his shoulder, as did she. Cooper strutted from one side of the kitchen to the other. Luckily, they went unnoticed. "Look, I better go before we get in trouble again. Let's do this." He took a pen out of his chest pocket. "You have something to write on?"

Samantha pulled a stack of green Post-its out of her lab coat pocket. Lou scribbled across one, then handed it back with an address.

"Meet me here. I'll come straight from work and get there by five-fifteen. Get us a room…"

Samantha made a face.

"I'll pay you back." He shook his head, annoyed. "Park near the front entrance and leave the room number on your car's windshield. I'll meet you at the room and knock four times. Be ready. I can't wait to see what you're wearing under your dress today." Lou arched in and sucked on her earlobe. "Tonight will be all about you. Pleasured from head-to-toe. You won't walk for days." With that, he strutted back into the kitchen.

Samantha left her nurse's station and hopped into the elevator a half hour early to prepare for the night. Excitement of the unknown stirred her interest while creating nervous anticipation. Not wanting to ruin her good mood, she delayed telling Cara her plans. Eryn had stopped showing up to happy hours all together due to her new job and new boyfriend. Without Samantha, Cara would have to go it alone or go home. Either way she'd be pissed.

Samantha's purple shirt caught her eye. *Where was her lab coat? Not again.* The elevator's brakes squeezed its wires. She jumped out on the fifth floor and hurried across the newly waxed floors over to the stairs. Before she could open the door all the way, thunderous laughter burst from the stairwell and Dr. Chambers flew out in full-on hysterics. Samantha held the door, but the egotistical jerk ignored her courtesy without a word. *Asshole.*

More giggling and footsteps echoed below. She peered down. Cara.

"Cara!" She chased after her, catching her on the fourth floor.

Cara's eyes met hers and a huge grin flashed upon her face. "Hey, toots. What's up?"

Amazing. She was in a good mood. Samantha stepped closer and squinted. "Were you eating powdered doughnuts or something? You have white sugar under your nose."

Cara wiped the powder away and laughed further. "Yup. My floor just had a baby shower for one of the nurses. What's up?"

For the first time, Samantha felt an awkwardness between them. After her revelation a few weeks ago, she wasn't sure what else Cara was hiding.

"Don't kill me, but I'm not going to happy hour tonight."

"What! Why not?" Her voice ricocheted off the walls.

Samantha redirected her view to the railing. "Lou and I are going out. I want to be alone with him."

"And not me? How can you blow me off for a guy? Didn't I teach you anything?" Cara slammed her fist against the concrete wall.

"I go out with you every weekend. All the time. I just want to be alone with him. A real date."

Cara huffed and folded her arms in her chest. "Where?"

Samantha's voice weakened. "Well, we might grab a bite later, but…first, we're going to a…motel."

"Nice date. I'm sure he's going all out for you."

"He promised tonight would be all about me."

"Ha! When will you learn? It's never about us. It's always about them. They might make you think it's about you, but somehow it ends up being about them."

"That's not true. And look who's talking. You pick up anything that buys you a drink!"

Cara snickered and shook her head. "That's different. I'm in control. I choose them. They do whatever I want. Then I dump 'em."

"How's that okay?" Samantha raised her palm only to let it fall back to her side. "Did you ever think of actually dating someone? Having a real boyfriend?"

"Not discussing this. You want to go out with him, go." Cara snatched the door handle and fled down the hall.

Chapter 9

The Heineken bottles clinked together as Samantha placed them in the backseat of her car. Lou had asked her to pick up beer before she hit the motel. She drove to the Harbor Motor Inn, parked in the front and stared at the small office. What was she doing? This was getting out of control. She rubbed her face and then tilted her head onto the steering wheel.

This is what she wanted? The life of a bad girl? Partying all the time. Having sex in random places. Clubbing and drinking? She had more fun singing to kids. *Was that weird?*

This was living life to the fullest? Why'd she feel so empty then? Why'd she miss singing at the library? Why were her visits to the Pediatrics Unit the past few months disheartening? At least she'd done something meaningful. Something that brought joy to others. How could she like herself when she wasn't doing anything constructive or positive with her life anymore?

Samantha thought of Cara partying every night, meeting different men. Did she do it to forget her past and take away her pain? Did she too wear a mask?

Samantha glanced at her watch. Five o'clock. Lou would be here in fifteen minutes. She climbed out of the car and held her breath as she hurried inside. A man in his late fifties, unshaven, overweight, hair all greasy, leaned on the small, glassed-in windowsill that lead to a back office of some kind.

"I'd like to rent a room, please."

The guy eyed her as if she were Goldilocks and snickered. "How long?"

"Huh?"

"How many hours?" He pointed to the sign on the left side of the window.

Four hours was fifty dollars! Did she even have that much money on her? She rifled through her wallet and flipped through fives and singles, and one twenty. Her ribs compressed as if someone had their knee on her chest. Samantha piled the bills in front of him. "I only have forty-seven dollars." She looked away and shoved her hands in her jacket pocket.

Body odor and sweat filtered through the small opening in the window. *Man.* What it must smell like back there. He huffed and smirked, grabbed the money and then counted it. Samantha gazed up at the clock. *Would he let her in?* He slid a key under the counter window. C42 was engraved on the maroon key chain.

"Thank you." She ran back to her car, scribbled the room number on a napkin and slid it under her windshield wiper. With five minutes left, she jogged in her heels to the room on the opposite end of the parking lot with the six-pack, inserted the key and then gasped at the site of the impersonal, soulless room. Beige walls, brown comforter and a small brown desk. The iciness reminded her of Cara's apartment.

Samantha dashed into the bathroom, removed her clothes and then, after ditching the scratchy comforter, arranged herself across the bed. She caught her image in the hazy mirror and became lightheaded. Something just didn't feel right. This wasn't her.

Knock, Knock, Knock, Knock, came in a slow, disturbing rhythm. She slid her body off the bed. Her legs wobbled as she moved unsteadily toward the thumping. The lock clicked open. Samantha peeked through the two-inch opening and at the site of Lou, her racing pulse thrashed within her ears.

Lou pushed the door open and Samantha stepped behind it, hiding her body. He glided it back towards the doorframe in a gradual reveal, and gazed at her, from her hesitant eyes, down to her purple, satin underwear.

She could do this. They were alone now. Privacy. No interruptions. Then why was she more nervous? Maybe the constant interruptions and having to rush through their trysts calmed her, knowing it wouldn't last long. Now she had four, long hours with him. Shouldn't that be a good thing? Why wasn't she excited to be alone with her boyfriend?

Lou grabbed both her hands and squeezed. Did he say something? Her mind clouded and the pounding of her heart made her hands quiver. She gripped Lou's hands tighter, hiding the sense of foreboding that passed through her. His fingers coasted down her temple and along her neck. His lips brushed lightly against hers and then he eased her onto the bed. He kissed her tenderly for the first time. It was calming, romantic and everything she wanted.

Her nerves settled and the cold sweat dissipated. Safe in his arms, her tension released. Lou climbed onto the mattress and crawled to her. He smiled, kissed her one more time, and then slipped off her underwear.

"Tonight's all about you, baby. How's that sound?"

As aroused as she should be, her body continued to compete with panic and peacefulness. He reached behind, unhooked her bra and slipped it off the bed. The bra hit the Berber rug with a plop, as if they soundproofed the room from any outside noise. The eeriness lingered.

Lou repositioned her until her head faced the far corner of the room and her legs pointed toward the door. He inched closer and glided his tongue lightly across her nipple. Samantha inhaled through her nose and attempted to relax. He ran his hand over her eyes and closed them, forcing her to settle down.

It helped. Blocking the unfriendly room from her view, and picturing him pleasuring her in a luxurious Caribbean hideaway, drifted Samantha off as if floating on a cloud through a brilliant, blue sky. Her body responded to his light, wispy touches. His fingers meandered over her nipples, lightly cupped her breasts, and then coasted down to her belly button.

Lou's fingers skimmed the inside of both her thighs, caressing the sensitive area, teasing her. He carefully inserted one, long finger and worked it around, applying fluid strokes. With one hand on her breast and one between her legs, she let his soothing rhythm heighten her arousal. When his finger threatened to drive her over the edge, his mouth replaced it, and his heavenly lips and powerful tongue took over.

Samantha clutched the blanket beneath her and savored the forceful way he sucked on her throbbing flesh. She spread her legs wider. His tongue dipped in.

Then, warm, soft lips kissed her on the mouth. The taste of garlic, overpowering.

Her eyes sprung open. Lou's head was still between her legs. Kneeling at the head of the bed, was Bruce. He grinned, innocently. Samantha's stomach churned. Her rapidly accelerated breathing shot her heart into overdrive. She tried to bolt from the bed, but Lou's mouth continued with its mission. She shoved him harder, then twisted away.

Lou smiled like he had bestowed her with a birthday present. "What's wrong, baby?"

Samantha covered her breasts with her arms, then crossed one leg over the other. Her clothes were nowhere to be found. Despite the chill in the room, her body engulfed with a flash of intense heat. "What the hell's going on? Why's he here?"

"I told you it would be a night you'd never forget. This is all for you. Two guys pleasuring you." Lou stood and displayed his palm like a game show host.

"How could you do this to me!" She scooted off the edge of the bed. *Shit.* Her clothes were in the bathroom. Her undergarments tossed on the other side of the bed. Next to Bruce. While keeping her legs somewhat locked, she hobbled over to her bra and underwear. Both near Bruce's feet.

With one arm still wrapped around her breasts, she grasped at her underwear, then swatted at her bra. Before she could turn, Bruce threw one arm around her waist, brushed his other hand down her face and cupped her chin. He kissed her on the lips again, forcefully, and then extended his hand between her butt cheeks, down and under, until his fingers stroked the moistness between her legs.

Samantha yanked herself away. "Stop! Stop!" She fought back tears, then stumbled over her feet, tried to catch herself, clutched the desk chair, and dropped her undergarments on the rug. She panted, trying to compose herself.

"Baby, what's wrong?"

Her mind raced, but her thoughts froze in place. She squeezed the chair's headrest, feeling detached from her body. She could see herself standing completely naked in the room while Bruce and Lou slowly, and calculatingly, edged closer to her, ogling her exposed breasts.

"Stay away!"

"I don't understand. What's the matter?" Lou barked. "You had no problem fucking around in an open parking lot. Now in a private motel room, you're suddenly shy?"

"Shy? Shy? Is that what you think?"

"Well, yeah." Lou moved forward until he stood a foot away. "What's the problem?"

"Why is he here?" She pointed at Bruce. Her body heaving as if the room had lost all its oxygen.

"He's your surprise. I figured two guys are better than one. You've done so much for me. I thought I'd repay you."

Cara's words reentered her mind. *It's always about them. They might make you think it's about you, but somehow it ends up being about them.*

"How could you think I wanted this?" she screamed.

Lou's expression turned as cold as the room. "How could I not? Are you for real?"

Samantha's stomach buckled. Had she done something wrong?

Had she misunderstood him? Anger flashed over Lou's face. The two of them stared at her in disgust.

Lou shook his head. "You show up to bars half-naked, tits hanging out. Skirts so damn short I can see your pussy calling me. You wear fuck-me boots to work and talk to me in that sexy, deep voice. You thrust your cleavage at me while I'm working and give me constant hard-ons. You have no problem fucking me wherever I ask you to. You enjoy it and moan so loud I have to silence you all the time. How could I not?"

She no longer tried to cover herself. She stood there stiff, arms dropped to her sides. There was no way she could feel any lower than she did now. Even Bruce, still gawking at her breasts, didn't matter anymore. Nothing mattered. She was back in middle school, during recess, with a dozen kids laughing at her and calling her names.

Lou was right. The way she carried herself at the hospital, the way she dressed, how she constantly teased him. Then tonight she acted all prudish? The way she played hot and cold, blowing him off at times, then taunting him at others. She was going through the motions with this new look. Faking her actions. Pretending to be someone she wasn't. She didn't even know what she wanted. How could he? She didn't protest when he had sex with her behind a rotting dumpster, and allowed him to screw her in his crappy car. *She* agreed to the motel.

She swallowed hard, refusing to let them see her crumble. She'd at least retain that. "You're right. I gave you mixed signals."

"You're damn right." Lou narrowed his eyes.

She couldn't look at Lou. Couldn't look at Bruce. And, she definitely couldn't look at herself. Samantha snatched her clothes out of the bathroom, tugged them on her body, and raced out the door.

Chapter 10

Samantha collected the remaining handouts she brought to her Ostomy Club lecture, and tossed them into an empty box. Roselyn had asked one of the dietitians to volunteer, but both Cara and Heather made excuses. They scheduled the meeting today, Friday, 6:30 p.m., cutting into Cara's happy hour.

She closed the conference room door and exhaled, unable to shake last Friday night's disaster from her thoughts. She could picture herself so clearly, screaming like a psychopath, naked and exposed, while they raked their eyes over her body. She always tried to do the right thing, but somehow it always blew up on her like an overinflated balloon. In the end, the least happy was her.

Memories surfaced from eight grade when she promised Jennie Fitcher she would try a cigarette, but chickened out and intentionally walked out of class with Krystal, then hid by the monkey bars during recess. Jennie never spoke to her again.

At 7:40 p.m., she returned the supplies to the diet office, grabbed her keys, then ran to the car for her dress. She told Cara she'd meet her at 8:30 p.m., but she insisted she make it by eight. Cara had found a new nightclub where ladies drank free until nine. She'd never make it in time.

Samantha freshened up in the bathroom, changed into her dress, but immediately had second thoughts. The faux-leather dress made her feel like she was wearing a rubber suit. Like a hot dog wrapped in plastic wrap. *What was she doing? Why'd she think she had to wear something over-the-top to this new club?*

She unclipped the hospital I.D. from her lab coat, then tossed the lab coat over her chair. After snatching her car keys off the desk, she hurried to the clipboard and signed out. 7:53 p.m. *Totally Late.*

Once she parked in the congested lot, she searched the front seat for her pocketbook. Did she throw it in the back? She looked behind the seat. Where was it? She climbed out, scoured the back seats, then again in the front. Didn't she have it in her hand when she went to the bathroom? No, that was her makeup bag. Her pocketbook still hid inside her desk drawer.

8:11 p.m. She removed her hospital I.D. from the console.

Samantha approached the entrance. How would she get past the bouncer? She had no money, no license, nothing. A group of guys lingered on the fringes for a quick smoke, while a line of club-goers waited to get inside. The bouncer proofed the three women in front of her and when it was her turn, she grinned, full teeth. "Hey there. How are ya tonight? Yeah, so… um, sorry, but somehow I managed to leave my pocketbook at the hospital, and ran out without—"

"You work at the hospital?" The beefy guy nodded to her.

"Yup." She held up the hospital I.D.

He glanced at it and smiled. "A dietitian, eh? I could use one of those." He grabbed his belly and shook it up and down.

"Sure! Anytime." The corners of her lips rose. "Just ask for me if you're ever there." She patted him on the shoulder for added emphasis.

Initially, he frowned at her touch, but then snorted at her boldness. "You got it, Samantha. Okay, go in, but don't cause any trouble, ya hear?" He winked, then patted *her* on the shoulder. "I'll be checking up on you."

"Of course." She gave him a high-five, then darted past the masses of women taking advantage of the drink special and combed the bar for Cara. Loud, thumping music clobbered Samantha's chest, as the DJ made his shout-outs and fueled the crowd. Skimpily dressed waitresses flew by with glowing trays of drinks. She didn't feel weird in her rubber sausage dress anymore.

Cara slouched at the bar alone, shot glass in hand. After downing the butterscotch-colored liquid, she smashed the glass back on the bar. *Who had bought it?*

"Hey." Samantha touched Cara's shoulder. "Sorry. I left late and to make matters worse, I left my pocketbook there. I think I should go back and get it."

"What? Are you kidding?" Her teeth grinded. "I've been sitting here for forty-five minutes as it is. You can't leave me here again."

"Forty-five minutes? You said eight o'clock."

"I arrived early. Couldn't sit in my apartment any longer." Cara sniffed.

"You okay? Are you crying?"

"No! Stop hovering over me like I'm some wounded squirrel."

The girl next to Cara left and Samantha jumped on her barstool. "I just feel weird without my bag. I drove here without ID. I have no money. I don't like leaving it in there either. The door's locked, but not my drawer. Anyone with a key could break in and steal it—"

"Would you relax? I never saw anyone so uptight. Get a drink. No, get two."

Bartenders rushed to keep up with orders as they zigzagged behind the bar. Needing to clear her head, Samantha quietly asked for a water. He handed her the glass, then nodded to the man next to her. Air rattled in a keg's tubes letting the bartender know it'd gone dry. Samantha suddenly craved a beer. Cold, thick, and foamy. *Mmm. What she wouldn't do for one.*

"Holy Shit. Check out those two hot guys in the suits by the bathrooms. GQ models or something. I betcha they'd ride me all night." Cara tossed her hair over her shoulders.

Both men were clearly over six-feet tall. One had a pink shirt on under his dark blue suit and the other, a lavender shirt and a bright, purple tie with polka dots on it. They looked like they worked on Wall Street. Expensive fitted suits hugged their tight, firm bodies. Their jet-black hair, perfectly gelled back. Cara managed to locate the two hottest guys in the congested bar.

"Don't get any ideas. They're mine." Cara slid her teeny skirt up higher.

"Which one?"

"Both of them. Just because you blew it with Lou and Bruce, doesn't mean I have to."

"Blew it? Are you serious?" Samantha's eyes bulged. What was with Cara? Ever since Eryn stopped hanging out with them, she mutated into this obnoxious beast. Like she morphed the two of them into one person. And, Samantha didn't like the behaviors Cara picked up from Eryn.

The DJ cranked the music drowning out the chitchat. *Good.* She didn't feel like listening to Cara anymore. Samantha glanced around the overwhelming club. The dance floor - packed. One giant up and down rhythm like The Wave at a ball game. Despite the air conditioning, stuffy air pressed against her skin - sweat and body odor surrounded her.

Cara knocked over her drink and groaned as the cherry liquor flowed down the heavily polyurethaned bar top. Piles of napkins formed a lopsided tower as Samantha helped Cara soak up the puddle. The saturated globs littered the counter. "Fuck." Cara's red eyes glazed over - similar to how she looked at work one day last week. Smelled like alcohol too, but Cara insisted she had just used one of those nasty bottles of mouthwash they gave the patients.

"Bruce asked where we'd be tonight and I told him."

Samantha rubbed her temple. *She did not. How could she?* "I thought it would just be the two of us tonight. To make up for last weekend."

"You're only hanging out with me 'cause you feel bad about blowing me off?"

"No! Not at all."

"Look, Samantha. I got some last weekend, too. Tonight, those two hot, rich men over there are mine. Maybe they'll take me to an *expensive* hotel and spend the entire night with me. Buy me breakfast in the morning." Cara licked her lips and wiggled her eyebrows. "You can have the kitchen crew."

"Oh, now they're just the kitchen crew? Great." Samantha's voice elevated above the crowd. "You know what? I'm going back to the hospital to get my bag. Go flirt with your Wall Street men. Get the attention you crave. I'll be back in twenty minutes."

"You're kidding, right?" She barred her teeth.

"No. In fact, when Lou and Bruce show up, why not take on all four of them? Maybe four men giving you all their attention will make you happy. Maybe then, Cara McCormick will finally let one of them into her heart without using them and dumping them." She huffed, an obvious edge in her tone.

With that, Samantha hopped off the barstool. She pressed against the patrons to move past them, only to have her foot stepped on. When she neared the exit, she glanced over her shoulder. Cara had cut through the mob in the direction of to the GQ models.

Chapter 11

Samantha unlocked the diet office's door, flicked on the light and made her way to her desk. The metal drawer slid on the bracket, and black leather smiled back. *Thank God*. At least one good thing came of this stupid night.

She drew in a deep breath and envisioned the night that laid ahead of her. Bruce leering at her. Cara ignoring her and spending the night seducing those two Wall Street men. Lou continuing with his passive-aggressive comments he'd been tossing at her all week.

There had to be more to this new life. She was miserable. She didn't even like who she was.

Samantha's key turned in the door lock, then she headed towards the back exit. As she neared the end of the hallway, the kitchen's partially opened door caught her eye. Hadn't Angie locked up for the night?

Her fingers slid across the cold, metal door. Light spilled from Cooper's office casting ghostly images in the abandoned room. Despite the sense of foreboding, Samantha crept toward the unsettling disturbance. Had someone broken in? She hesitated, contemplating what she'd do if someone were robbing Cooper's office. Did he store cash in there? Expensive supplies or kitchenware?

Clunk! The rumble of multiple objects falling off a desk echoed in the deserted kitchen. Her heartrate accelerated.

Like drawn to a strange noise in the garage, Samantha tiptoed closer in her high heels. The blinds were drawn around the heavily windowed office, but she could make out shadowy movements from the fluorescent lights inside. Maybe if she peeked in she could get a description of the thief.

Her feet glided across the linoleum, her fingertips gripped the door's molding, and she eased her head around the corner. A half-naked man leaned over the desk with his back to her. He removed his shoes and tossed them into the corner. *What the—* Was this some sex-fiend breaking in to jerk-off on Cooper's desk? Who hated him that much? She could think of plenty of people. She didn't recognize him from any of the kitchen staff, though. His back was broad. Expansive, like he could lift an entire truck with his bare hands. Muscles exploded across his back, rippling like peaks in the sand.

And then, he dropped his pants.

Samantha struggled for breath at the sight of his tight, black briefs and muscular thighs. Even his butt had perfectly carved muscles. Scrumptious one-hundred-eighty-degree curves that defied gravity. Thick hamstrings and solid calves stretched below his…that ass! *Holy crap*. Why was she looking at some sexual predator's ass? She racked her brain for a list of hospital employees that had his frame. But then, the scent of his cologne invaded her nose. The familiar scent. Cooper.

He wriggled out of his pants, kicked them off, then stretched high above his head, rolling the curves of his back in rhythmic waves. Cara was wrong. He wasn't overweight. He wore that giant lab coat because nothing else fit over those huge muscles.

She had to leave. Now. Samantha ducked her head behind the door and turned. She sprinted around the bend as quietly as possible, her heels gingerly clip-clopping across the floor, and neared the exit.

"Hey!" his voice called out, causing her to hesitate.

She winced. *No. Keep moving. It's dark in here. He can't see you.* She resumed her pace and tiptoed through the kitchen. Ten more feet and she'd be out the door.

"Don't go! Wait." Cooper's plea echoed in the dark kitchen. "Samantha!"

At the doorway, one foot from freedom, she stopped. How'd he know it was her? She crooked her head, and even in the dim light, saw Cooper's face sticking out from behind his office. His naked shoulder peeked out, as well.

"I have to run. I'm late. Sorry. I thought someone was breaking in…I have to go—"

"No, please. Just give me a minute. I was just changing. I didn't think anyone would still be here."

"I…but, I really should go…"

"Samantha. Don't go. Come here…I mean, just give me one second. Please."

She glanced at the exit sign and then back to Cooper. He held up one finger and it wasn't the middle one. His muscular bicep, his naked, bulging bicep, begged her to stay. This night could not get any worse. What did he want with her? Interrogate her on why she was here? Write her up for being in the kitchen again? Accuse her of stealing food like that resident someone spotted the other day?

What was *he* doing here so late?

Cooper hopped back into his office and scuffling resumed. She plodded towards the cave of doom and glimpsed at her clothes. As if her four-inch stilettos weren't bad enough, the short, faux-leather dress had hooker written all over it. Her usual Friday night outfits, something she'd finally grown comfortable in, made her feel slutty and cheap in Cooper's presence.

She eyed the exit again. If she removed her heels and ran, she could explain on Monday she was late for an appointment. *In this outfit?*

Before she could escape, he reappeared around the bend. "All done. Come in." Then, he did something she never saw him do before. Smile.

Samantha drifted to his office, but remained at the door. Why couldn't it be winter? Then she'd have a huge coat covering her body. Her ears burned. She tried to control her breathing. "I'm really late and—"

Cooper moved towards her in his dark blue jeans and a shiny-black, thermal shirt that hugged every muscle, groove, crevice and curve, as if someone had painted it on his skin. He was still barefoot, like one of those beach models that had their pant cuffs rolled up while they strolled along the sand.

He caught her examining eyes. "Sorry, I didn't have time to put my shoes on. I thought you might try to sneak out on me."

Samantha flinched, then tried to fake a smile. *Act cool. Just leave before getting in any more trouble.* Cara entered her mind. Twenty minutes had already passed. Not only would she kill her for taking so long, but also for talking to Cooper. Samantha folded her arms. She wasn't sure if was to hide her cleavage or to keep a distance from the dictator that stood before her.

"What do you want, Cooper?"

"So, you do know my name. We were never properly introduced." He held out his hand.

She turned up her tough-girl image and ignored his palm. "Yeah. Roselyn's not big on introductions." That wasn't true. She always made a grand affair over new managers. Why no big introduction this time?

"Here. Have a seat." Cooper motioned to the chair in front of his desk.

"No, I really have to go. Cara's waiting for me."

"Cara, huh? What's her deal?"

"What's that supposed to mean?" She dropped her hands to the sides.

Cooper pulled his chair out and sat. His hands locked behind his head and he smirked. "Just curious, that's all."

Samantha glanced at the chair next to her and plopped into it, half-off half-on, ready to bolt at a moment's notice - mainly because her feet were throbbing. She wouldn't entertain this buffoon for more than five minutes. "What do you have against her?"

"I just don't like her in my kitchen."

"Your kitchen?"

"Yes," he snapped. "*My* kitchen. Every time I turn around she's in here talking to Lou."

"Lou? You mean Bruce."

"No. Actually, I've never caught her with Bruce. Is there something I should know?"

Her eyebrows collapsed. He must be confused. He hadn't worked here long. Maybe he confused the two? They were together constantly. "I'm sure Cara's just getting nourishments for the patients."

"Ha! Yeah, okay. And my name's George Washington." Cooper leaned back in his chair and placed his feet on his desk.

"Nice to meet you, George. I'm Madonna."

"You sure dress like her. Concert tonight?"

Samantha's body temperature rose and threatened to boil her eyeballs out of their sockets. She covered her body again with her arms, hiding her exposed skin, as well as her embarrassment.

"I'm not surprised though," he continued. "It's not much different than what you wear to work."

"Who do you think you are? You can't just sit here an insult us."

"Look. The two of you traipse around *my* kitchen half dressed, and flirt with all the guys in here, disrupting the workflow. I have a lot on my plate and I don't need the two of you screwing it up."

"The two of us? You say that like we're pieces of crap."

Cooper looked at the ceiling and pretended to yawn.

"How dare you." Samantha flew out of the chair. She'd normally never speak to someone like this, especially a manager, but there was something about this guy that brought out the worst in her.

Cooper eyed her up and down. Was he checking her out or letting her know her outfit was completely inappropriate? "Look." He removed his legs from the desk, leaned forward, and pointed to her. "You don't get it. When girls dress like this they give guys the wrong message."

"And since when are you an authoritative on that subject?"

Cooper narrowed his eyes. "Um. I'm a guy."

What a moron. She was babbling uncontrollably now. Like a regular idiot. She sat back down.

"When a guy sees a girl dressed like that, we know that you are looking to hook up. You're desperate. When we see a girl dressed all slutty—"

"Desperate?" She huffed. "I'm not desp—"

"Samantha, we don't take you seriously and—"

"It's Sam." She gave him her best pissed-off look.

His expression puzzled and he rubbed his face in his hands. "Okay, tough guy. Sam. Is that what the guys call you? Sam?"

She didn't answer.

"Or maybe, baby. Do they call you baby a lot?"

Lou called her baby all the time. She crossed her legs to hide the trembling. "Yes. As a matter of fact they do." She smiled, pleased at herself.

"I bet they do. Wanna know why?"

"No. I know why. It's a term of endearment."

"Really? Is that what you think?" Cooper laughed so hard the walls appeared to vibrate. He tried to contain his laughter and fell back in his chair. *Good.* His cologne was annoying her. "Guys call girls baby so they don't get their names mixed up. Instead of trying to remember which girl they're with, they call 'em all baby, so they don't get caught calling the girl-of-the-hour the wrong name."

Samantha's rapid breathing parched her throat. She had enough. He probably didn't have a girlfriend and was jealous that he couldn't snag women like Cara and her. Probably worked out at the gym every night because he couldn't find a date. She scanned his desk. A picture of Cooper with three blondes hugging him sat in the corner. They looked like Vegas show girls. They probably were. Fake picture he took at some friend's bachelor party.

"Look who's talking. Where'd you take that picture? Some strip club?" *Ha!* She got him back. Arrogant jerk.

Cooper lifted the picture. "Actually, this was taken at my mother's house on Christmas. They're my sisters."

Samantha wanted to crawl into a hole and die. When she could feel no smaller, Cooper burst into hysterics. A storm hammered inside her. Never before had someone so-openly ripped her apart like this. How dare him! He didn't even know her. She was nice to everyone, but he triggered some irrational beast in her.

Samantha snapped up and leaned over his desk. She opened her mouth to unleash all the suppressed anger she'd been holding in since that day the library fired her, but before she could speak, his eyes zoomed to her chest. She peered down. Her low-cut dress, and gravity, shot her braless boobs out and close to the opening. She slapped her hand over her cleavage and inched toward the door. That was it.

Cooper jumped up as well. "I'm so sorry. I...It...they...were just there and you lunged at me, and suddenly they were right there in my face, both of them, and I'd never—"

Her cheeks turned impossibly hot. Samantha reeled around and raced from the office. Cooper followed and latched onto her arm. "Samantha, I'm...I mean, Sam. Please, I would never disrespect you—"

"You'd never disrespect me? What have you done all night?" She fought back tears.

"No. I wasn't trying to put you down. I was trying to protect you. You should hear what these guys say about you two. What they say about all women. That's why I tried to keep you out of the kitchen. To protect you. That's why I have a problem with the way you dress."

"It's none of your God dammed business how I dress or what I do with my life." Samantha shook his arm off her and fled toward the exit.

"Come back! Let me explain better."

But, she was off and running down the corridor. His judgment of her crushed her spirit. Her new life sucked. This wasn't what she wanted.

She tripped in her new, uncomfortable heels and stumbled toward the back exit. Her hands plunged forward, smacking the door. She charged outside, feet pounding the concrete.

The howling of the streetcars and the warm June air sent her wandering down the barren road by herself. She looked at her arm where Cooper had grabbed her. Red imprints remained. His overwhelming cologne lingered in her nose. *What was with that guy?*

She peeked at her watch. 9:13 p.m. She pictured Cara, fuming at the bar, drunk. How would she make it home tonight? Would she be safe? Why did Samantha care? She was tired of worrying about everyone.

She kicked a flattened can of Dr. Pepper into the street and watched it careen off the curb. The thought of dealing with Cara's drunken tirade, Bruce ogling her, and Lou convincing her to sleep with him again, poisoned the evening further. Cara probably took off with those two GQ guys five minutes after she left, anyway.

Cooper, ripping apart everything she had worked so hard to

change, put her over the edge. She removed her shield only to be attacked more? In his eyes, she was a desperate, tramp. He only saw her outer shell, but is that the image she portrayed? Was that everyone's impression of her? She remembered what Lou said to her in the motel room, but saw her reflection for the first time through Cooper's eyes.

Samantha removed her stupid, painful stilettos and chucked them in the metal trashcan near her car. She'd gone from hiding under baggy, dark clothing, to traipsing around in slutty attire, and wasn't any closer to feeling better about herself. She collapsed in the driver's seat and turned the radio way up. This wasn't working and she was drained from trying.

She needed a new plan. Maybe concentrate on her career? Go back to school? Bury herself in work? Find a new job? A constructive hobby? Maybe she could be the next roller derby queen. Did they even have that anymore?

This couldn't be all there was in life. Wasn't there anyone that could show her what she was doing wrong?

Chapter 12

Monday morning, Samantha walked toward the diet office while hurried footsteps pursued her. She stole a quick look behind. Cara's pursed lips led the way. *Oh, here we go. Let the merriment begin.*

"Why didn't you call me back?" Cara's puffy face only emphasized her bloodshot eyes.

"Huh? When did you call?"

"Saturday. Your mom said you were weeding the flower beds."

"She never told me."

"I called again yesterday and left a message on the machine."

"There were no messages on the machine." They both stormed into the office.

"Yeah. Okay. Whatever."

Buzz! Karen, the diet clerk, picked up the intercom. Five seconds later, she turned towards them. "Roselyn wants to see both of you in her office. Stat."

Great. Cooper probably reported her.

They trudged toward her office. "My mother didn't give me any messages. Why wouldn't I call you back?"

"Maybe the same reason you didn't come back to the bar Friday. Obviously I'm not enough for you anymore."

"What? I..." The last thing Samantha wanted to do was tell her she blew her off for Cooper. Cara hated him more than Roselyn. "It took longer than I thought. Plus, I saw you walk over to those two guys. I figured you hooked up with them."

"I did hook up. And it was awesome."

Samantha paused before entering Roselyn's office. Any feelings of guilt erased. Cara was starting to get on her last nerve. "What's your problem? Just spit it out already."

"First Eryn blows me off, now you."

"I'm not blowing you off."

The door swung open and Roselyn's eyes sparked fire. "I can hear you from my desk. Come in already. I have an emergency."

When wasn't there an emergency? They dropped into the leather chairs in unison and folded their arms in tight knots as if they were identical twins. She was turning into Cara. Something she desperately wanted at one point.

"Where's Heather?" Roselyn popped her pen on the desk to open it, then scribbled on a note pad.

Cara remained silent, as usual.

"She's off today. She worked this weekend."

"Great! Just great. What else can go wrong?" She tossed her pen to the side and leaned in. "Listen. Over the weekend, Diane went into labor and now I'm short a kitchen supervisor."

"She wasn't due for another month! Is she okay?" Samantha's emotion-choked voice burst out.

"Yes. Both mother and daughter are just grand. But, the early departure has left me short staffed. I wasn't planning on advertising for her replacement for another two weeks."

"Can't you pull a diet clerk until she's replaced?" Her normally quiet nature, gone, as Samantha exploded with questions and suggestions.

"Problem number two." Roselyn flipped her desk calendar to the following month. "Melissa quit."

"Melissa?" Samantha practically fell out of her chair. "Why? She's only been here six months. She's the best diet clerk we ever had. She was fast, knowledgeable, and great with the patients—"

Cara slapped her in the arm to shut her up. "Why'd she quit?"

"She claims to have been mugged on the subway coming to work this morning. She said this job's not worth her life."

"Oh my God. That's terrible. Is she all right?" Melissa needed to catch an early train to get here on the days she worked the five-thirty shift. She couldn't imagine the idiots on the train at that hour.

"She's fine. I asked her to switch all her shifts to the night clerk position, but she said it won't work with school. So...we're down two. Plus, Ryan's on vacation for two weeks. He's in Ireland in case your next question is whether or not he can switch his time off." Ryan was the newest kitchen supervisor - here for a little over a year.

"What do we do?" Samantha chewed on the tired, tasteless piece of gum in her mouth. She meant to spit it out in their office.

"Glad you asked, Samantha. I have no one else to pull to supervise, so I need a dietitian to volunteer in the kitchen until I can replace both employees. They'll be an ad in this Sunday's classifieds, but it'll be a few weeks before someone can start, train and learn the ropes. Which one of you will volunteer?"

Cara leaned forward. Thank God she was finally stepping up. Instead, she snickered. "You told us you never want to see us in the kitchen again. So, I guess we can't."

Samantha's mouth slid open. What the hell was wrong with her? "I'll volunteer." *So much for finding a new job.*

Cara huffed and stared Samantha down. She pretended not to notice.

"Thank you Samantha. I may need you in the diet office, too. I started working out the schedule this morning." Roselyn glared at Cara. "While Samantha's helping me, you and Heather will be covering her patient load on the days she's not on her floors."

Cara ticked her tongue.

Samantha continued to smile, not wanting to annoy Roselyn further. You didn't want to mess with someone like her. Had she really just volunteered to work in the kitchen? *Uck.* Great career advancement. Did they have any choice with Roselyn, though?

"I'll have the schedule ready for you before you sign out today. You can leave."

Once in the hallway, Cara tore off. "You're such a kiss-ass."

"She's our boss."

"She uses people for her own needs and doesn't care who gets screwed in the process."

"She's trying to run a department. What's wrong with you?"

"Nothing. What you see is what you get. People might not like what I say or do, but it's the real deal." Cara abruptly stopped before the diet office. "Unlike you, who constantly puts up a front as to who she really is. Who is the real Samantha? Do you even know?"

****

Samantha exited the elevator and rounded the corner. Shadows from the past three months drifted through her mind. She blinked, expecting the pain and hurt to disappear. Her purpose in life blurred, lost behind a mountain of regret. Did she have any real friends? Anyone to guide her down the right path? Show her what she needed to do?

A phone rang in the distance while cutlery clattered in the kitchen. Roselyn's intimidating voice poured out from her office and into the hallway. Samantha paused a few feet from the partially open door and eavesdropped.

"I don't care. You have a job and it's not done to my satisfaction. I knew I shouldn't have taken a chance with you. I only hire managers with college degrees and you promised to amaze me with your ideas and skills if I gave you a chance."

"I told you I planned to go back once I settled here, but you have me working ten, eleven hour days. Weekends too." Cooper's voice sliced through her, like scraping your nails down a chalkboard.

"That's what managers do."

"And I've been doing it. Solidly. Have I not?"

Dr. Chambers came whipping out of the kitchen. What was he doing in the basement? He gawked at Samantha and took off toward the elevators with a bag of pretzels and a banana. Was he the resident they saw stealing food? *Cheap ass*. Probably thinks he's too important to pay for anything.

Cooper's eyeball appeared through the narrow door opening. Samantha flinched, then took a step back. *Did he just smirk at her?* He slammed Roselyn's door shut, and the shouting between them continued.

Chapter 13

Samantha adjusted the hairnet on her head while the tray of macaroni and cheese with stewed tomatoes shuffled down the tray line. She scanned it making sure all the items on the menu were on the tray, then pushed it down and examined the next tray. Over, and over, and over, again. The plastic apron clung to her wet neck as heat rose from the steam table.

So much for advancing her career. She managed to regress instead. Back to working on the tray line like she had done in college. What was next? A paper route? Maybe Roselyn would notice her hard work and dedication, and give her a huge raise. See her hustling, and recommend her for a promotion in another facility.

"I need a piece of pound cake on this one." Her scowl carried toward the end of line. "Bruce." She knew he was doing it on purpose to get a rise out of her. Something he'd been doing all week.

He picked up a piece and swaggered over to her, gently placing it on the tray, then slanted close to her ear. "I'd love to pound you."

"Get...lost," she hissed through gritted teeth.

Despite the putrid smell from the tomatoes that looked like blobs of bloody organs, the scent of cologne invaded her nose. Cooper. Another one she wanted to avoid.

"Lou." Cooper called from behind. "Where's that order of salmon? They need it for the catering event."

Make that three. Surrounded by three men she didn't want to interact with for eight straight hours a day.

Lou strutted by with an exaggerated hitch in his step like a gangster. "Yo. Got that right here."

Yo? What's wrong with everyone in here? A regular freak show. Samantha asked for another piece of pound cake from Bruce, and then a high-pitched voice resounded behind her. Afraid to look in case it was Roselyn checking up on her, Samantha leaned across the tray line and pointed to the mashed potatoes the entrée person failed to put on the tray. How hard was it to read your section and add what it asks?

The falsetto voice continued. "You told me to meet you here for lunch. I'm here. In this…depressing room."

"It's a hospital kitchen, Tiara," Cooper answered with a touch of sarcasm.

Tiara? What kind of name was that?

"Regardless, it's sickening. And, I only have an hour."

"I told you I couldn't leave until the line was finished."

"When will that be? I'm already ten minutes into my lunch hour."

"Samantha!" Cooper's voice cut through her. "How much longer?"

Finally given the opportunity to sneak a peek, Samantha turned. There stood an almost six-foot-tall woman, with long blonde hair cascading down to her butt like a shimmering waterfall. She had a beige clutch bag hanging from the crook in her elbow and a black, pinstriped suit with a pencil skirt. Large silver-hoop earrings dangled and illuminated her heavily made up face.

After a good thirty seconds of staring, the woman made a face at her. "Well? Can she speak, Cooper? Is she one of *them*?"

One of them? What was that supposed to mean!

"Oh, yes. She can *definitely* speak. Samantha, how much longer?"

Her nostrils flared. "Ten more minutes."

He glanced at his watch. "I told you I'd call you."

"What am I supposed to do now? Stand here in this rancid smelling area?"

"Samantha," the entrée-station employee called to her. "He just put that tray on the cart without utensils." She turned back to the trays and all eyes were on her. Bruce chuckled behind the pound cake positioned in his hand. Lou appeared behind him with a large box of frozen salmon.

"Okay, um, let me see that tray, please." She focused on the trays, but one hundred percent of her hearing concentrated on the argument continuing behind her. Was that his girlfriend? One of his sisters?

The line finished. Cooper and the blonde snob left, and Samantha put in an order for bread and milk with the appropriate distributors. Forty-five minutes later, Cooper returned and Lou met him by his office.

"That was fast." Lou pushed a hand truck in front of him and leaned on it. "A quickie, huh? Nice!"

"Get back to work, Lou. I'm sure you have lots of it." Cooper glanced at Samantha, then away.

Ass. Would it kill him to say hello? Why'd she care, anyway? She looked down at her plastic apron that had red splatters all over it, and then reached up to her hair. *Uck.* The hairnet was still hugging her bun. Her old, black sneakers were outdated and ugly. She had grabbed a pair of black pants from her closet that she could wear with the low sneakers. She couldn't remember the last time she wore pants, and never realized how baggy they were. Were they even her size?

Why *would* he look at her? Demoted, looking like a wreck, and wearing the geekiest clothes she owned. The woman he left with was stunning. Not everyone was photo shopped. Some, obviously, had it all. Including Cooper. How'd he get someone like that? She wanted to share the information with Cara, who suddenly had a million questions for her about everyone that worked in here, but decided it would just stir the pot.

Cooper exited his office and Samantha ripped off the apron and hairnet, then tossed them in the garbage. Her sneakers stood out like clown shoes. She freed her hair from the bun to try to redeem herself.

Cooper stared. He placed his clipboard on top of the boxes of Lay's potato chips and walked toward her. Why was her heart quickening? She remembered his naked skin and huge muscles that hid beneath that stupid, bulky lab coat.

Before the scent of his cologne consumed her, his lips opened. "Samantha..."

The tight black briefs he had worn on his cute little ass erased any intelligent thoughts from her mind. *Keep it together.* She stood straight, propping out her boobs, and angled her head to take in his incoming compliment. "Yes?" She smiled, trying to look as sexy as the blonde.

"You're not allowed to have your hair down and loose like that. You know that, right?" He shook his head and turned to leave. Bruce's recognizable chuckle exploded behind her.

Chapter 14

Lou had been ignoring Samantha all week like she was some decomposing body he buried in the backyard. *The little shit.* Who'd he think he was? Granted she was in his territory now, and working with him was indeed awkward, but he couldn't say hello? Smile once in a while? Shoot the breeze? Was it the baggy clothes she'd been wearing? The clown shoes and floodwater pants? The hairnet and apron?

Samantha waited for Cooper to leave for lunch with his runway model, then marched into the storeroom. She couldn't deal with Lou's childish behavior any longer. She'd be the better person. "Hey."

"Hey." Lou lifted a box of canned yams and tossed it on top of another. Then ignored her.

Seriously? "How you been? We haven't talked in a while."

Lou leaned on the tower of canned chicken noodle soups. "Just really busy. Got a lot of things going on. Important stuff."

"Oh," her voice hitched. "I see." She did sound desperate! Cooper was right. Why'd she come back here? She needed to stop being so nice to everyone. Especially little shits like him.

Lou twisted away and moved another box over with his boot. "Can't talk right now. But, I'll see when I can fit you in. K?"

Cooper returned from lunch, but Roselyn promptly called him into her office. Five minutes later, he stormed into the kitchen and slammed his door. Then kicked something metal. A garbage can? The clamor turned heads.

He exited a few minutes later and his hair looked like he had gelled it up into some punk rock, spiked look. Had he yanked on it? He glanced around the kitchen as if lost, then his eyes focused on her. His angered expression intensified. Now what? Bruce was looking better and better.

With her better judgment thrown to the curb, her hairnet and apron still plastered to her, Samantha's legs nudged her in his direction. With only three feet left between them, her jaw cemented shut. "Are…Is…everything all right?" *Yeesh, Samantha. You sound like a whimpering dog.*

Lou popped his head out from the freezer and glared at her. Did he just give her a dirty look? How dare him!

"Come in. Have a seat." He motioned to the chair she sat in just six days prior. This time she had a lot more clothes on. So did he. "How are you?"

"I'm fine. How are...you?" *Awkward.*

"Good. Sorry I haven't had much time to interact with you this week. I have a big catering event tomorrow night, I'm down two supervisors, and now I'm losing a storeroom guy."

"Losing?" *Did Lou quit? Was it because of her?*

"Yeah. Lou is leaving for some pre-planned vacation he booked months ago. It appears I have to do Lou's job now, also." He reached for his *#1 Boss* mug.

Samantha shifted in her seat. Why'd she get involved? She had to stop trying to fix the world.

"Roselyn has me doing a hundred things as it is. I stay late every night. I'm shot. I can't do this, also. I had all these exciting projects I wanted to work on. Not doing everyone else's job."

"Why don't you tell her?" She tried to look concerned.

Cooper huffed. "I did. She says there's no one to help." He lifted the coffee mug to his lips and took several long gulps. On the bottom of the *#1 Boss* mug, it said: *I'm a Moron.*

Samantha's head jerked back, then she bit her lower lip to keep from laughing. *Who had given him the mug?* "Um, what about Apollo? Shouldn't the cafeteria manager help out?" Apollo's office, located on the second floor, was near the cafeteria allowing him to stay on top of the chaos, change out the cashier's drawers, and inform the kitchen when they were low on food. By phone. He never came down to the basement to chat or help any of them.

"Oh, please. That ass?" He sucked in air. "Sorry. Don't repeat that."

She shook her head.

"He only helps himself."

Another one.

"I recommended some great ideas for the meals up there and he snubbed me. Told me to mind my own damn business. He's an arrogant, self-absorbed, conceited..."

Geez. Tell us how you really feel. Why was she here? Why was he sharing his private thoughts with her? "What about Kenneth?" she interrupted his rant. Kenneth was the Assistant Director of Nutrition. Roselyn's right hand man. Rumors floated around that the two of them were hooking up despite her being married. Bruce's comment about how "everyone cheats" entered her mind.

Cooper gave her a knowing look. Did everyone know they were sleeping together? Roselyn would lock her door at the end of the day and tell the diet clerks and her secretary, that they didn't want any interruptions or phone calls. Every day. What were they doing in there? Having sex on Roselyn's desk?

"Well, there must be someone. Surely, Apollo and Kenneth can help a little bit."

"I don't want Apollo anywhere near me. I'd rather work sixteen hours a day. He gives me these bizarre looks like he wants to hump me."

Samantha let out an unexpected, loud snort, then couldn't help but laugh wildly in a hysterical fit, causing Cooper to jolt back. This man somehow brought out her deepest feelings of rage, misery, and now hilarity. She had felt numb for so long.

Cooper's grin grew high and wide. "I never heard you laugh before. Or, smile for that matter."

"Me?" She wiggled her eyebrows. "I smile all the time."

"When? Every time I see you, you look grumpy."

"Maybe it's just around you." She tilted her head and winked.

Cooper smirked. "I make you grumpy?" He tapped his chin with his fist as if trying to get in her head.

"You... aren't very nice." Her heart fluttered, unexpectedly. *Huh?*

"Me?" He pointed to his chest and widened his eyes, like a three-year-old accused of stealing his sister's toy.

"What's the matter? Don't like it when the tables are turned?"

Lou sauntered by in a slow calculating manner, giving them both the evil eye, then sucked on his straw overdramatically until the last of his McDonald's shake *gurgled* and *slurped* into his mouth.

Cooper ignored him. "I'm extremely nice. When I'm not here."

"Me too," her voice rose into some silly love-struck tone.

"Ha! I find that hard to believe."

Her mouth dropped open. *What an ass!* No. A *moron.* Before she could respond, Roselyn made an uncharacteristic appearance in Cooper's office. "You just told me how busy you are, and I find you sitting here gabbing with the person you said disrupts your work flow."

He complained about her? What the—

Cooper's fingers released from their knots and he stood. "No. She was just going over the...bread and milk order with me. Weren't you?"

Roselyn glared at her like the evil stepmother in Cinderella. In her peripheral vision, she could see Cooper pleading with her. He tossed her the cutest puppy-dog face, then pretended to sob. What was with this guy? Roselyn looked back at Cooper and he grabbed the mug again, pretending to drink.

Out of nowhere, a giggle bubbled up from her belly. She swallowed it, wondering how many other people knew about the mug. Feeling sorry for the poor guy, she sat up straight, and grinned at Roselyn, "Yes. Just finished taking inventory and confirming that nothing more is needed for the special catering event."

Roselyn's face scrunched, obviously not believing them. "If you're both done discussing *bread*, I need to speak with you Cooper. Privately."

Chapter 15

Cooper

Cooper rushed into the kitchen the following morning at eight o'clock. Roselyn had spent another afternoon belittling him and he wasn't sure how much more he could do for that woman. Kenneth just seemed to follow her around all day to keep her company. What exactly did an assistant supervisor do? With Apollo running the cafeteria, and Cooper running the kitchen, it left little for Kenneth to be bothered with. Department finances, maybe? How long could that take?

At the end of breakfast service, Cooper discussed scheduling, sick calls and missing items from the breakfast meal with Angie. He grabbed Lou and double-checked everything he ordered made it onto this morning's truck for the Men's Health Awareness event in the main conference room at noon today.

By 12:30 p.m., the catering event was well under way and Cooper headed to his office, leaving his staff to restock the appetizers and desserts, then clean up afterward. He collapsed into his chair. *Grrr!* his stomach grumbled. Had he eaten since his morning cup of coffee? He strolled toward the tray line, avoiding the cafeteria and Apollo whenever possible.

Angie, donning an enormous, yellow, plastic flower where her hairnet ended, slapped his hand away. "The line's still going." Then she tossed him a playful nudge.

Cooper reached for a plate anyway, throwing a piece of the Chicken Saltimbocca onto it. The aroma of prosciutto and sage hit him, letting him know it'd soon be in his stomach, but as he turned to grab a packet of utensils, Roselyn loomed in the doorway.

"I have a problem." Roselyn held up a single slip of white scrap paper, and handed it to Cooper in his free hand.

When didn't she have a problem? His stomach let out a fierce and aggravated groan, but Roselyn ignored the sound and the meal in front of him.

"This patient complained that his mashed potatoes had a hair in it and I need you to go up there now, with a new tray and apologize." Her face remained expressionless, as if turned to stone.

"I was about to…" Cooper glanced at the piece of chicken. "Why do I have to go?"

"Because obviously, Angie's busy working the line and this patient is a VIP. It needs to be done immediately." Roselyn continued her vacant stare. Only her nostrils flared in and out. "Seriously, Cooper. If you want to succeed in this industry, you have to give one-hundred percent."

"When have I not? I stayed late again last night and came in an hour early today."

"Is that a problem?"

"No. I'm just letting you know that I'm doing everything in my power."

"Well. It's not enough. At least not to my standards."

"Is this about my degree again?"

Before he could finish, she spun on her heels and exited the kitchen. Cooper covered the now cold piece of chicken with tinfoil and dumped it on his desk. He grabbed the slip of paper, and took the elevator upstairs.

"VIP my ass. Why should certain people get special attention? What is this, the Titanic?"

"Excuse me?" A nurse standing beside him in the elevator made a face.

"Sorry. Just talking to myself."

"That's okay. We all do it." She laughed and was out the door.

Cooper exited the peaceful elevator and turned down the bustling hallway. The overhead intercom buzzed with announcements as the repeated *ding* of an IV pump echoed in a nearby room.

He located room 614, entered, and headed for the B bed on the window side of the room. An elderly man slept in the A bed under a mountain of covers. He looked just like his grandfather, only much thinner. Cooper tipped his head near the edge of the mustard-colored curtain that separated both beds. "Hello, Mr. Semiramide Buttacavoli?" Hopefully, he'd get one of the two names correct. "Hello?" Maybe he got both names wrong. "Mr. Buttacavoli?" He peeked around the corner and then stepped into the space.

Empty. The bed unoccupied. The tray of hairy food still on his bedside table. Cooper lifted the cover and found a long strand of red hair. *Red?* No one had red hair in the kitchen.

"Hi, Mr. Hall?" A voice drifted from behind the curtain.

Of course, *that* patient had a simple name.

"Mr. Hall? It's me, Samantha. The dietitian."

Cooper froze. He took a step back and away from the curtain. *Of all rooms!* Cooper fidgeted, and then raked his hand through his hair. There was nowhere to go, nowhere to hide. What if she came in here next? He should just leave now. Quickly make his exit before it became awkward.

"Oh, hello. Sorry, I must've dozed off." Muffled creaks floated over the curtain as the patient adjusted himself in the bed. "How can I help you, my sweet?"

"They said you weren't really eating well and I was concerned. Can I help you fil out your menu?"

Awkward. Cooper slowly slid toward the edge of the bed and then back near the window. He placed the new lunch tray on the bed and looked out at the streetcars flying by. Why didn't he leave when he had the chance? *Wait.* Why was he hiding?

"I met you the last time I was admitted, didn't I?" the patient's frail voice mumbled.

"Yes. You remember me? Wow, I'm flattered."

"Of course I do. Can't forget a face like that."

"Oh, stop."

"No, no. I'm serious. And I'm not just saying it to get an extra piece of chocolate cake."

Samantha tittered. "You know the menu well, don't you?"

"Too well. This has become my second home. Nothing personal against you, my dear. People like you make me want to come back."

"You're too kind. Thank you. And, patients like you make me appreciate my job."

"Looks like we make a great team then!"

"That we do. Let's go over your menu so I can figure out how I can help you."

Cooper leaned over the bed, removed the old tray and then replaced it quietly with the new one. There'd be no way to get out of this mess now. He was screwed. The new tray cast off the aroma of that delicious Chicken Saltimbocca. His stomach growled ferociously, and he turned toward the window, covered his stomach with both arms, and bent over to hide the noise.

"Someone sure sounds hungry in there," Samantha called out. "I'll be in there next to see how you're doing, Mr. Buttacavoli."

Shit. He was beyond dead. It figured she pronounced the damn name right. Think. Think. What could he use as an excuse? Minutes passed as Samantha read the menu to the patient. Sweat built up on

Cooper's forehead and he unbuttoned his lab coat to bring in cool air.

"Are you ready?" a voice called out.

Should he answer? What the hell was he going to do? He fidgeted and decided it was best to come clean. He took a few steps toward the edge of the bed and—

"Sure, Cara. I'm coming now."

Cara? What was she doing up here? Oh, lunchtime.

"Okay, Mr. Hall. You're all set. I'll check up on you before I leave today."

"Thanks for your time, Samantha. I didn't realize I could choose alternate foods from what's on the menu. Looking forward to dinner tonight, now."

"No problem. Just make sure you eat it all and I'll be more than happy."

Footsteps clip-clopped out of the room. Saved for the time being. Cooper exited the room with the old tray and Mr. Hall shot him a blank stare. He smiled back and ran down the hall as fast as he could, but not before passing a nurse's aide with long red hair. *Figures.*

Cooper peeked around the corner, then took off towards the elevator. Thoughts about the cold chicken sitting on his desk switched to Samantha's demeanor in the patient's room. Her sweet voice and caring nature stumped him. Maybe he *had* judged her wrongly. Mysterious. Accommodating. Different from the usual women he met. Not the needy, materialistic, and self-centered ones he dated. Was she really that compassionate, or was it some act?

He rescued his abandoned chicken, plopped some broccoli on the side, then microwaved the entire plate. He reclined in his chair, back aching, and... *Ring! Please, don't let it be Roselyn again.* He tossed his fork onto the plate and snatched the receiver. "Cooper Timmons. How may I help you?"

"It's me. Your girlfriend. Did you forget about me?"

Cooper glanced at the clock. One o'clock. Had he forgotten a lunch date? "No. Of course not."

"Then why haven't you called me back?"

"Back?"

"Yes. I left several messages. What's going on with you lately? You don't return calls. You show up late. You cancel plans. Are you seeing someone else? So help me if you are, Cooper!"

"No. No. I told you. I've just been so busy. Work is killing me. It's affecting my whole life. I haven't even had time to run to my sisters after work."

"Your sisters need to get their own men. I'm tired of hearing that, too. You're not giving me the time I deserve. Anyone would be dying to date me. I have no idea why my mother set us up."

"I'm sorry, Tiara. I'm just trying to prove myself here. If I put in extra hours, take on extra projects, maybe there'll be a promotion in the future. Or, a transfer to another facility with great growth potential. I thought you understood how important this was to me."

"Huh! More important than me, I suppose."

"I didn't say that." Cooper dragged the plate back to him, speared the chicken breast with his fork, and lifted the entire piece into his mouth taking one massive bite.

"Then make it up to me. Buy me something."

Cooper clutched his forehead and massaged his temples. "I just bought you that bracelet," he mumbled, as the cold chicken lodged in the pocket of his mouth. "Besides...college, remember? I have to finish if it kills me."

"That's not my fault. You should have finished when you had the chance. Why do I have to suffer?"

"Suffer? Look, I have to go. I have work to do and I'm starving. Can we discuss this later?"

"Oh, we will. Trust me. You have a lot of making up to do and I expect an extravagant weekend of sucking-up to happen." The phone clicked off before he could reply.

Cooper crammed a pile of broccoli in his mouth - the over-peppered clump made him grimace - then he thought of the chicken salad sandwich Samantha promised Mr. Hall tonight. He thought of his own grandfather, and then of his dad. Samantha's kind voice and cute giggle resurfaced. Was that some fake personality she put on for the patients, and then made fun of them behind their backs? He thought about her high heels that popped out from beneath the patient's curtain - another gold-digger using her body to get what she wanted. They were all the same.

Or, were they?

After taking another large bite out of his chicken, he left the kitchen and hurried down the hall towards the diet office. He asked Karen for 614B's menu, then gave a slow, disbelieving shake of his head. Next to tonight's desserts, Samantha had written X2 near the chocolate cake and added a cute, smiley face with a heart.

Chapter 16

Two weeks coasted by and Samantha found herself disappointed that Ryan would be returning from Ireland on Monday. He'd take his supervisor shifts back, leaving Samantha with only a few here and there. The new supervisor they hired began training, which meant her time in here would soon be over. Shouldn't she be glad? At least she wouldn't have to deal with Lou for the next two weeks. She caught him sneaking out for his vacation like a thief that just pickpocketed an old lady.

On Samantha's way to the bathroom, she crashed into Roselyn exiting through the same door. Her puffy and bloodshot eyes led the way. "Are you okay?" Samantha instinctively put her fingers on her shoulder. Roselyn recoiled, and she rapidly withdrew her hand. *So much for trying to get close to this woman.* Hadn't she helped her out of her bind? Shown her dedication?

"Yes, just allergies." She dabbed her eyes on a tissue and tossed a meager smile. "I'm glad I bumped into you. With Ryan back, I need you in the diet office more. Those girls are drowning in there." She sniffed, then wiped her nose.

She only worked in the diet office twice in the past two weeks, but they had yet to fill Melissa's diet clerk position.

"When will that start?"

"I just hired someone, but they can't start for another week. I made up a new schedule this morning."

Of course you did.

"You can pick it up now if you like. No one's in my office."

Where was Kenneth? Wasn't the little puppy dog following her around? *Hmpf.* Surprised he hadn't accompanied Roselyn to the bathroom to help her blow her nose and wipe her ass.

Samantha dawdled down the corridor. Roselyn's secretary had her desktop radio on full blast. The upbeat song made its way into the hallway and had Samantha singing along. Then, as if by impulse, she started shaking her hips.

With her head twirling around, hair falling in front of her face, she rotated her hips, stepped to the right, front, then spun on her right toe.

She flipped her head back and, at the end of the corridor, was Cooper, staring at her as if she'd lost her mind.

Samantha ducked behind the wall in the adjacent hallway. She leaned her back against the concrete and closed her eyes, then tried to slow her breathing. *Oh my God.* He must think she's the most bizarre person he ever met. A regular wacka-doodle.

****

Today, Roselyn scheduled Samantha to work as the evening diet clerk, starting her day at eleven in the morning and ending at seven. Working these late shifts allowed her to sleep until nine some mornings. Couple of good things about that. One, her mother left for work before she woke up, and two, she only saw Cara when she came in here to get her things. She had no idea who Cara ate lunch with every day. Happy hours, luckily, had stopped. Cara was in no mood to wait around until eight o'clock at night for Samantha to get off work and entertain her. Or, babysit her. She had no clue what Cara did with her nights, either.

At five o'clock, Samantha brought a stack of callbacks to the tray line and spotted Roselyn and Kenneth leaving together. Roselyn tittered like a silly schoolgirl. What did Kenneth see in a married woman that was at least ten years older than him? Money? Power? Was he sleeping with her to get a promotion?

At 6:28 p.m., Samantha turned up the portable radio in her office and sang along to No Doubt's "Hella Good". The newly released song was one of her favorites and the feel-good message brightened her mood. She increased the volume as loud as it would go, then whacked her pen against the table in violent bursts. She swayed back and forth, then pulsed. Her voice intensified when Gwen Stefani belted out the chorus. Her pen tapped the shelf above, then she grabbed a pencil with Easter eggs on it, and her other hand joined in for the drum solo.

Samantha whipped her hair around like Gwen in the music video. During the rebellious musical interlude, Samantha made up her own lyrics, continuing with the beat.

"Oh, yeah, yeah. You need air…

Just like photosynthesis…

But, we're not plants, no…

We're humans that wear pants. Oh, yeah, yeah."

She flung the chair away with the back of her thighs. *Slam!* It banged into the giant file cabinet behind her. She extended her butt and wagged it back and forth. An image appeared in the doorway.

Samantha jumped, as did her heart, then she reeled around toward the massive figure. The pen and pencil struck the counter simultaneously. Cooper stood there with wide eyes. All the blood drained from her face.

Was he stalking her? Trying to catch her screwing up so he could report her to Roselyn, again?

She switched off the radio and then, due to a complete lack of words for her behavior, nodded. Without his lab coat concealing his body, his muscles pushed the seams of his powder blue, button-down shirt to their confines. His black pants hugged those thigh muscles she saw only a few weeks ago. Black briefs flashed in her mind, as if she were Superman using x-ray vision. She looked away before he caught her staring.

"Um...I'm out of here. Thanks for the last few weeks." Cooper's expression remained impersonal.

Now he thanks her? "Yup. Just a half hour left." She wished the phone would ring. Alone with Cooper in a quiet office with no work to occupy themselves, gave her a fluttery feeling in her stomach. His ferocious body distracted her from his obvious malicious intent.

"Are you back with me tomorrow?"

Me? Samantha grabbed her schedule from the drawer. "No. I actually get to be an early diet clerk tomorrow. Leave here at seven tonight, return tomorrow at five-thirty in the morning." Her sarcastic tone echoed in the empty room. *Why'd he always bring out the beast in her?*

"Lucky you." His face, deadpan.

What was up with him? If she did something wrong, just get it out of his system already. *Phone, ring.* Cooper planted himself at the door and the silence continued. They both opened their mouths to say something, anything to end this staring contest, when the phone finally rang.

"I have to get this."

He crinkled his nose. "Okay. See you—"

Before he could finish, she answered the phone with her greeting. He quickly fled.

"Samantha?" A voice whispered into the phone.

"Lou? Is that you?" Her body relaxed. Maybe he felt bad for ignoring her all this time and leaving without saying good-bye.

A chuckle rippled through the phone. *Oh, God.* Please don't let it be Bruce. "No, Samantha. It's me. Apollo."

Apollo? Why was he calling her? And why was he still here? She glanced at the clock. 6:34 p.m. "Um...yes? Can I help you?"

He let out a long, drawn-out sigh and chuckled again. Was he drunk? "I need you to come to my office for a second."

"What for?"

"Excuse me?" His brusque voice sliced through her.

Idiot. He's a manager. "I'm sorry. I meant, I'm the only one down here and I have to answer the phones." *Good recovery.*

"Let the answering machine pick up. That's what it's there for, right?"

Was it about Cooper's catering event? Or had she ordered the wrong amount of bread for the cafeteria? *Dammit.* "I'll be right up. Your office is near the cafeteria, right?"

"Third door on the left."

Samantha climbed the stairs to Apollo's office. *Now what?* Her heart beat rapidly, throwing off her rhythm, causing her to miss the top step, stumble, and fall forward. She brushed off the dust and filth coating her hands and stood back up. The stairwell door felt heavier than normal as she pushed it open.

She walked the final ten yards down the dark corridor - the lights dimmed for the night. She took a deep breath and knocked on his door.

"Come in." His regal appearance as he sat behind his desk, reminded Samantha of the principal's office in kindergarten when she tried to escape from recess through the back woods. A boy had teased her about her pink, ruffled dress while others looked on and laughed. She took off and hid behind a bush until a lunch aide found her.

Apollo hurled himself out of his chair toward her, leaning completely over the desk. She gasped like some frightened teenager in a horror movie.

"Are you okay?" His face puzzled at her ridiculous reaction. "What's wrong?"

"Nothing, I'm fine."

His five o'clock shadow, way past its time, made him appear filthy. His big thick forehead frowned with frustration. His tiny eyes narrowed as if she spoiled some plan he had devised. She crossed her legs, then clenched her biceps.

"Why are you so nervous?" He grinned, slaying her with uneasiness.

"I'm not nervous. What do you want?"

Apollo tossed his pencil to his right. It careened off the side of the desk and tumbled to the floor. Samantha stepped to her left to pick it up as if by reflex. Exactly what he wanted.

He lunged over to her. "Nothing in particular. Just wondering how everything's going."

"I told you, fine. Everything's fine. Nothing's wrong." She picked up the pencil and chucked it back on his desk. What was wrong with this idiot? Cooper was right. He *was* creepy.

Before she could return to where she previously stood, Apollo plopped down on the far end of the desk. He lifted his legs, planted his feet on the wall opposite him, and circled her body with his dark, blue pants.

"Then give me some of that good lovin' you have."

"What! What the hell are you talking about?" Samantha's pulse soared, slamming her heart against her ribcage.

He constricted her with his powerful thighs, squeezing tighter. "Lou's not giving you anymore of that hot sex. You haven't gotten any in a while. So, I'm here to satisfy your every need. I know what you want."

"No, you don't." Samantha tried to unhook his legs with her hips. They wouldn't budge. Her breath hitched - uneven and labored. Had Lou overheard Cooper and her talking about Apollo in his office? Did Lou tell him what they said? Or, maybe Lou liked sharing his stupid slut with everyone. Her throat tightened preventing enough air from entering.

He ran his hand down her blouse and stopped where the first button positioned itself. He flipped it open as if it was a snap. His thighs tightened around her hips. "You're going to like what I do to you, Sam. Lou's going to be an old memory after what I show you."

Images of her and Lou flew past her like shuffling a deck of cards. She pictured herself behind that smelly dumpster. His crappy car. Bruce and Lou clawing at her naked body. She felt dirty, vile. Like some used, piece of shit prostitute. What had she become? What had Lou told him to do?

Another button released and he tugged her in closer with his legs. "Sam. You like being called Sam, right?"

Only Lou called her that. How could Lou do this to her? Was he punishing her? What a fool she was. Why'd she ever get involved with such a dirt bag like him? Her gaze darted around the room, looking for a way out. It all made sense now. As soon as Lou left for vacation, he had Apollo take his turn. No wonder he avoided her. The scum couldn't even look her in the eye knowing what would take place after he left. "Please," she whimpered.

"Oh, I will. Don't worry about that. I know how desperate you are to get fucked. I won't disappoint you, Sam. I heard what you like and I aim to please. I even brought some rope to tie you to my chair."

He didn't wait to open the last button. He ripped the blouse open with both hands, popping the button off. She watched it roll into the corner.

He followed her gaze. "Why you looking in the corner? You like being in the corner? Want to be a bad, bad girl and be sent to the corner? You like to be spanked?" He placed both palms on her breasts and squeezed - flashes of pain shot past her eyes. "Oh, yeah, Sam. I'm gonna fuck the shit out of you and you won't remember Lou's name anymore."

Her neck stiffened. She mindlessly scraped her nails into the wall behind her. She had to find a way out. No one was in this abandoned corridor. No one would hear her. Her body shivered fiercely under his grip.

"I make you tremble, don't I? I'm just what you need." Apollo slipped his thumb under her bra. Her nipples hardened from his ice-cold hands. "Turning you on already, eh?"

How did Cara pick up strange guys every night? Wasn't she scared? Samantha choked with fear. *Be brave.* "Apollo, I left the phones unattended. I need to go."

He laughed out loud as if it were part of a game. "You're hot when you role play. Who are you now? The disobedient secretary? Ooh, I can play too." He grabbed her shoulders and yanked her toward his lips.

Samantha mouth clenched and she refused to part her lips. Their teeth collided.

"Don't like kissing? No problem. We can just move on to the good stuff." His ominous eyes held her in place. He would win.

Her breathing increased. Loud panting poured from her mouth.

"Yeah. That's it. I'm turning you on, aren't I? I want to hear you scream." He dropped his legs to the ground and rotated her, then bent her over and against the wall. His hand reached for her zipper. "Ohhh, yeah. I'm going to…"

This was her only chance. Panic turned to rage, then adrenaline surged. She shifted, spun, and ran toward the door.

"Nice! You want to play tag? Want me to chase you around the office? Sounds like fun. But, you have to remove one article of clothing each time we circle my desk, okay?"

This guy was clueless! She found new energy as she clutched the door handle and darted into the stairwell. Samantha spilled down the stairs skipping several of them. Too many. She lost balance, fell and landed on her side. It was only then she noticed her shirt was wide-open, her black bra exposed.

She hoisted herself up, no time to register the pain in her hip, and tore down the hallway with her blouse clutched in her fist until she reached the diet office. The door slammed behind her and she quickly locked it. She rushed to answer the ringing phone, hopeful to use it as an excuse when Apollo tried to get her to unlock the door. Did he have a key? Samantha stared at the door while her heart broke through her ribcage.

Her words sputtered into the phone, incomprehensible to the caller. She babbled her greeting, gasping in between words. Samantha waited for Apollo's face to appear at the door's window.

"Samantha? Are you there? It's Cooper. You okay?"

"Yes." Her eyes remained on the door. The pounding of her heart slowed with each word Cooper spoke, but there would be repercussions for tonight. Definitely. Apollo would have a story concocted by the morning, and she could do nothing. Employee vs. manager.

"Samantha? Are you all right? Hello?"

As much as she despised Cooper, Samantha couldn't control what came out of her mouth next. Everything gushed out as if she were projectile vomiting. Tears poured down her face while she recounted to Cooper what just happened.

Her gaze refused to shift from her only means of exit. The other phone line hummed and the answering machine's red light blinked, alerting her to the countless messages she had missed. Her life was out of control. This was all her doing. Cooper was right. The image she portrayed let men believe she was desperate for sex.

Chapter 17

At five-thirty the following morning, Samantha hesitated before entering the hospital after her long, restless night, unable to bear the day that awaited her, like dark clouds and cold mist lingering outside a window.

When Karen, the other diet clerk arrived, she sensed Samantha's unusual jitteriness. It was only a matter of time before Samantha spilled her guts. More shocking - Karen revealed how Apollo put on the very same performance a few weeks ago. With Melissa.

"Melissa? Why didn't she tell anyone? Why…" She stared at Karen. "Wait a second." Then, the puzzle pieces fit together. It was instantly clear. "She didn't get mugged on the train, did she? Apollo attacked her and she quit."

Karen nodded.

"What happened? Why didn't she tell on him?"

Karen closed the door. "He called her up there. Same story. Managed to lift her skirt up and put his hands in her underwear. She kept hitting and punching him. He just laughed. Laughed in her face. She said when she finally scratched his face with all ten of her nails he backed away in pain. She drew blood." Karen snickered. "Good for her. She didn't show up for work the following morning. Angie called her at home, but she didn't answer. Melissa called later and told her she'd been mugged on the subway."

"Why didn't she tell Roselyn the truth?" She covered her mouth, her breathing uneven.

"Apollo called her on the phone when she got back in here. Threatened her. Said it was his word against hers and she was still on probation. He'd say she'd been flirting with him for weeks, then came up to his office after everyone left. That he told her to leave, but she refused. That she was drunk. The lies went on and on."

"I remember the scratches on his face. He told everyone he'd been cutting down bushes in his backyard." Samantha remembered how the phone kept ringing while she was on it with Cooper. She let the answering machine pick up for the remaining ten minutes of her shift. Was it Apollo? Would he have said the same thing to her? What would he say this morning? Roselyn wouldn't believe her. Especially since Cooper complained about Cara and her flirting with the guys in the kitchen. She'd be fired for sure if she tried to blame it on him.

An hour later, the diet office intercom buzzed. It was Roselyn. She wanted Samantha in her office immediately. Her tone - angry and disgusted. Samantha was disgusted with herself. She had thrown on one of her old, baggy blouses today to make her look less provocative than she had over the past few months. Apollo would use that against her for sure. The short skirts. Spiked heels. Low-cut shirts. What a fool. She dug her own grave.

What had Apollo told Roselyn? Samantha should've said something to her right away. A swirl of thoughts ran through her head. Apollo must've told her some awful account of it all. She struggled to compose herself. She tried so hard over the past few weeks to make Roselyn like her, with the hope of a promotion in the future, or a job referral to another facility. All ruined now. There went her career advancement. Back to square one.

Her body strained as she walked toward the office. She knocked, and just as she turned the doorknob, she caught Cara running into the diet office. *Late again.*

Samantha spewed the stale air from her mouth, then slowly opened the door. Roselyn sat with her hands clasped rigidly on her desk, leaning forward as usual. Before pushing the door fully open, Samantha caught sight of men's black trouser pants to the left of Roselyn. Could she face Apollo?

"Samantha. Come. Sit down."

Her heart scrambled to stay in control. She extended the door all the way and glanced to the right. It wasn't Apollo beside her. It was Cooper. Samantha blinked rapidly. His unsympathetic expression persisted. She should never have told him. She should've known he'd rat on her. He tried to warn her about her actions last month. Now, the price would be paid.

Afraid of the thunder, but it was she who caused the storm. She inhaled deeply. Obvious. And, tried to exhale more discreet. Unquestionably, Roselyn would believe Apollo. She told her to stay away from the guys in the kitchen after Cooper's many complaints. And now, this. Was this Cooper's revenge after all his warnings?

"Samantha, I brought you in here this morning because I was informed of events that took place last night. I am unaware if any other events have occurred, but one is too many. I sincerely apologize that you had to go through this and there will be a thorough investigation, immediately. As you know, even if this was consensual, I have a strict no-dating policy for my managers. They're forbidden from dating any employees in our department. "

Samantha glanced over at Cooper, who gave her a tiny grin. At least it looked like a grin. Maybe it was gas. She began her story, recounting everything she remembered, leaving out anything that had to do with Lou. Would Apollo use that against her? That Lou and her had slept together? Would Roselyn question why she left that part out? Roselyn repeatedly shook her head while taking notes. Several times, she plopped her head into her hands.

Roselyn continued to write everything on her yellow-lined pad. "I apologize again. No one should go through this. This is unacceptable at all levels. Thank you for your cooperation. I'll let you know how this resolves as soon as I do. I'll have to ask you to keep this matter confidential until then. You can go."

"Wait." Samantha knew she had to say one more thing. To acknowledge Melissa's encounter, and broaden the evidence against Apollo. She tucked her chin to her chest and played with the skin around her thumbnail. She told Roselyn what she knew about Melissa, embarrassed to look into Cooper's eyes as the words stumbled out. When she finally did look up, Cooper's eyes were on the wall to the left of him. *Idiot.* Was she boring him? Two people were almost raped and he was daydreaming.

Samantha finished answering Roselyn's questions and then retreated into the hallway, expecting Cooper to follow. The door slammed behind her instead. She took a few steps toward the diet office, but bumped into Cara's collapsing eyebrows instead. *What now?*

"What were you doing in there? More brown-nosing? More kissing ass?"

"What? No. We were just...I just had to..."

"Can't think of a good lie fast enough? Didn't expect to see me? Hoping to avoid me all day again?"

"No! I'm not avoiding you. They're using me all over the place."

"You volunteered." Cara's eyes tightened, as did her lips. Her whole body tensed as if under a vise grip.

Samantha huffed, remembering what Roselyn said about keeping the confidentiality of the meeting. She took a few more steps toward the diet office. Why couldn't she think up a legitimate excuse? She didn't like lying to Cara though, but her job was also important to her.

Before a ridiculous lie spilled out, Apollo bolted down the stairwell on the far corridor, turned left towards Roselyn's door, but before rotating the knob, he caught sight of her. Apollo bared his teeth slightly and squinted at Samantha. Then glared at Cara. Did he think Cara stood up for Samantha? What a mess.

Samantha let her face mellow. She had to make a choice. Friendship came first. "Cara, I have to tell you something. Privately. Let's hide somewhere."

They snuck outside into the humid New York temperatures, and headed down the street until they reached the end corner of the hospital before the abandoned alleyway. Stacks of water-stained, wooden crates piled ten high, laid beside hundreds of cigarette butts.

Cara leaned against the chain-link fence. "Go ahead, speak. This should be good. Are you being promoted? Quitting? Found a better job away from me?"

"Stop. No one is leaving you. They just asked me to help out until they replaced the two positions, that's all. I'll be back doing dietitian stuff in another week or two."

"Then what's the big secret? Did you get a big, fat raise?"

Samantha's mouth worked, but only noises came out. As difficult as it was to speak to Roselyn about this in front of Cooper, for some reason it was more difficult to tell Cara she couldn't handle herself with a man. Cara would've kicked him in the balls, flipped him over the desk with some karate move, and then pinned his head, tying him up with her stockings. What did she do? Run away with her blouse wide-open and trip down the stairs. Class act.

"I…when I worked last night, Apollo called me up to his office, and well, he…" She fidgeted in her own body. "He tried to rape me. I was so scared, Cara, but—."

Cara tossed her a dazed look. "What?"

Samantha paced a few feet towards the street, then back. The intense heat worsened the stench of car exhaust and rotting garbage. "I know. I couldn't believe it myself. I didn't understand why—"

"Rape you? He didn't rape you. Are you serious?" Cara shook her head.

"What? How do you know? Did Karen tell you?"

"Karen? Samantha, I told Apollo to show you a good time. You know, since Lou had been blowing you off. I told him you hadn't gotten any in a while. To show you some lovin' and to—"

She drew back sharply. "You did what! You told him to attack me?" Not knowing where to look, Samantha's gaze landed on a rust-pitted garbage bin beside her. She rubbed her collar-bone trying to calm herself.

"Stop. He didn't attack you. He was supposed to call you up there and give you a quickie. Although, knowing him, it'd definitely be more than a quickie."

Samantha became breathless. "You sent him to do this to me?" The dizziness continued to swirl. "Knowing him? You know him? What—"

"Yeah. I ate lunch with him in the cafeteria a few weeks ago, and then he rocked my world that night. Holy Shit. The things he did to me. I've been dealing with amateurs all along." The gleam in her eye paired perfectly with her satisfied grin.

"What are you talking about?"

"I was leaving work that day. You know, one of the Fridays you blew me off. And, he walked me out. Asked me if I wanted to grab a drink. The next thing I knew, we were hooking up in his apartment, doing it in his kitchen. That cafeteria manager definitely knows his way around a kitchen, if you know what I mean." Cara nudged her in the shoulder.

The disorientation persisted. Samantha flickered her eyelids - for that's all she could do - unable to fit the pieces together.

"So, the other day we were talking about you and I asked if he would give you a freebie. He said sure."

"Toss me a freebie? You told him to attack me?"

"He didn't attack you, Samantha! Knock it off. Stop exaggerating." The chain-link fence clattered as she moved away from it. "You didn't fight him off, did you?"

"Of course I fought him off. I had no clue what was happening."

"You're impossible. You still don't know what you want. You ask to change, but you fight it every step of the way. You lost Lou from your own doings. You can't get any guys yourself. I throw you one and you mess it up."

Samantha's fingers combed her sweaty hair into one giant clump, removing it from her drenched face. "Throw me one? How is this okay? He attacked Melissa, too." She tied her damp hair in a messy pony tail with the elastic band around her wrist.

"Oh, please. Where'd you hear that? Karen? You knew how flirty Melissa was. She teased Apollo every day in the cafeteria and then when he went to act on it, she reneged. Really?"

"You knew about Melissa?" She looked away and watched a pigeon peck at invisible crumbs.

"Apollo told me. That's why she made up that ridiculous lie about getting mugged. She was embarrassed. It was her own fault."

"Her fault? Are you kidding me?"

"If she felt the need to quit, that's her loss." Cara flapped her hand at her.

"He lied to you. She wanted no part of him. Those scratches on his face were from Melissa clawing him. I truly have no words for you, Cara. You're so delusional right now. He tried to rape two women and you're saying it's our fault."

"I'm delusional? You're clueless. You wander around not knowing what the hell you want. Make up your damn mind! And the next time—" Cara paused. She stared at Samantha long and hard, her eyebrows collapsed. "Why…why were you in Roselyn's office?"

Samantha took a step back.

"What did you do? What did you tell her?" Cara's face reddened.

"I…I told her what happened."

"You didn't! She'll fire him, you idiot!"

"I didn't know you sent him to me." Her breath caught in her chest. "How's this my fault?"

"If you fuck up the only good relationship I've had in a long time, I swear to God, Samantha." Deep red crept across her face.

"Relationship? You asked him to have sex with me. What kind of relationship is that?" Her muscles tensed.

"I was doing you a favor. Again!"

"I don't need your favors." Her fist tightened into a ball – the sudden urge to punch something, surfaced.

"Fine. Have it your way. I send you a great guy and you fuck it up. I'm done. You're on your own." Cara charged up the street toward the hospital.

"Don't you dare walk away from me. I don't understand any of this."

"You don't understand a damn thing."

Chapter 18

Samantha ate her lunch in the cafeteria. Alone. Cara had called in sick. She poked at her dry, pork chop not caring about life in general. Not even the horrific smell of burnt microwave popcorn joggled her.

Cooper entered through the rear door - Angie by his side. He pointed to the cash register and then to the grill. Angie smiled and tittered like she just won a Ms. America pageant. Her new eyeglasses - red and pointy – matched the clown-like, red lipstick. *What was going on?* Cooper caught Samantha's surveillance. She averted her eyes back to her pork chop and began cutting it into tiny pieces. *Don't come over. Don't come over.*

He didn't take the hint. Cooper plopped himself in the seat in front of her. "Hey. How are you?" He tapped his pencil on the table making Samantha more nervous.

"Good," was all she could muster.

"Feel better that Apollo was fired?"

Better? How could she feel good about getting someone fired? She couldn't help thinking Cara was right. Apollo was supposed to 'show her a good time' and she turned around and got him fired. He must be reeling! Maybe Melissa did tease him. She *was* a big flirt. Samantha would never know who was telling the truth. All she knew was Apollo lost his job, and Cara refused to speak to her. She kept quiet.

"Um. Not sure if you heard yet, but Roselyn gave Apollo's job to Angie."

Samantha perked up. "She did? That's wonderful. I'm happy for her."

Cooper scratched his head. "Yeah, sure. Hopefully she can handle it. I think Ryan would've been better suited for it."

"Why? Cause he's a man?"

"No! Not at all. Angie's just a tad *slow*."

"Huh?" Samantha pushed her pork chop away.

"Let's just say...she's as sharp as a spoon. A lot of trays go upstairs that're missing items. She can't order bread and milk to save her life. And, she's terrible at math. I gave her a fifty and four twenties and she counted it five times, still unsure how much was in her hand. I saw her walk away and ask one of the tray line employees to count it for her. She also doesn't know how to group foods. I asked her to help me change Thursday's patient menu and she came up with chicken breast, white rice and cauliflower. All white. How appetizing is that?"

Why was he always confiding in her? Did she look like she wanted to know all his private thoughts?

"One problem though. Now we're down a supervisor again since Angie has to train in here. Lou's on vacation for two weeks and I have to train Angie, watch over the newly hired kitchen supervisor, and do the storeroom." He tossed her the most sarcastic grin she'd ever seen. His grin resembled that of a game show host with huge white caps smiling to the audience.

Samantha bit down on her lip to keep from smirking.

"Yeah. Exactly. I'm drowning again. Any chance you can help? I'll ask Roselyn. The new diet clerk starts Monday and Karen agreed to work overtime to help out in there."

"Supervising?"

"Actually, I can use help with the storeroom."

"Storeroom?"

"Yes. Remember, I mentioned it two weeks ago? Lou will be out for the rest of this week and next week. Angie will be up here training in the cafeteria in between tray lines. Ryan will pick up the extra supervising shifts, and well, if you can help with the inventory and ordering it would be a huge relief. I can get a bunch of the guys to unload the boxes of food. I'll help you, of course. Maybe pay you overtime if you need to stay late?"

"I..well..."

"Please." He leaned his elbows closer and his damn cologne wafted past her nose.

She envisioned a week and a half of hell as he ordered her around, yelled at her for not counting inventory correctly, and watched her like a hawk.

"I can even have Bruce help you do the—"

"No!" She leaped from her seat. "I'll do it. I don't need any help from Bruce."

Cooper sighed and eased back in the chair. "Thank you. I really appreciate it. I'm losing it."

He was losing it? When would the madness end?

Just then, Roselyn sauntered into the cafeteria for lunch. Kenneth following closely behind. Cooper called Roselyn over and

Samantha quickly resumed pushing her food around the plate. He told Roselyn the plan and she gawked at Samantha.

"You certainty are one to volunteer for everything thrown at you, aren't you?" Her gaze was lifeless and stale. Like the pork chop. *Could she ever say anything nice?* "Very well. If she can manage doing all four jobs, so be it. I'm off to have some fun." She spun on her high heels. Her skirt twirling as she went.

Roselyn, have fun? What *did* she do in her office with Kenneth?

Chapter 19

The following morning, armed with a clipboard and pen, Samantha took inventory of all the canned goods in the storage room. You have no idea how unappetizing six-pound cans of diced beets or mashed potatoes look. Cooper pointed out various tips and tricks to make her job easier. He had the staff unload the trucks with incoming goods. Before the dinner meal began, he gave her a tour of the refrigerators, with a new sheet of paper for her clipboard. Somehow, before her day ended, she completed inventory in both areas.

Friday morning, she wandered into the kitchen at 9 a.m. Cooper planted himself outside his office, leaning against the wall, arms folded in his chest, eyes fixed on her. Was he waiting for her? "Good Morning," he sang.

"Continuing with your happy-go-lucky personality, I see."

"And you too. You must've had an excellent evening last night."

A flush of heat tingled through her body. "Yes. It was good. How 'bout you?"

"Wonderful. Simply splendid," he teased in his best British accent.

The porter rolled a platform hand truck loaded with overflowing garbage bags past them. She snatched the clipboard from Cooper. "What torturous event am I in for today?"

"Has it been torture?" Cooper pouted, laying it on thick.

"Such a nice, sweet person as myself is not used to such harsh conditions."

"Ha! Really? That's not what I heard." He rolled on his heels and continued his arrogant stroll toward the back of the kitchen.

What was that supposed to mean? Samantha glanced down at the sheet on the clipboard. The word FREEZER typed across the top. *Fantastic.*

Cooper gave her a quick review of the form, then entered the refrigerator that lead to the main freezer. When he opened the freezer door, glacial winds burst out like icicles piercing her flesh. It hit hard. She could feel snow building on her eyelashes. Samantha hated the cold. Why wasn't she born in Florida? She tried to hide her trembling.

"Are you cold?" Cooper detected anyway. He removed the snorkel coat from the hook on the outside door and threw it around her shivering body. She glided her arms into each sleeve, and then looked up. He was staring at her. She met his gaze, unable to pull away. His chestnut eyes seemed to twinkle.

Then, his expression changed. His eyebrows collapsed as if displeased. Did she put the stupid coat on wrong or something?

Before the mood dampened, a rush of frozen air exited the freezer and pushed the scent of his cologne toward her. Images of a smoky campfire in the forest, framed her thoughts. She inhaled as if wanting to bring him inside her.

Cooper reached down, grasped the zipper, and led it up in a slow, calculated manner. When it reached Samantha's neck, he flicked his eyebrows once and then whisked it up past her nose, leaving only her eyes visible. The coat, made for a six-foot tall, three-hundred pound man, hung on her. He laughed uncontrollably, but for the first time in her life, she wasn't embarrassed. Samantha chuckled as well, and slapped him in the arm with the extra twelve inches of material that hung from both wrists.

Chapter 20

Two weeks later, life returned to normal. The new diet clerk became more acquainted with her job, needing less direction from Karen. Roselyn hired a kitchen supervisor to replace Angie and she began training. Angie struggled through her cafeteria tasks as Cooper suspected, requiring him to check on her often, but luckily that wasn't Samantha's problem.

After enduring two weeks of Cara ignoring her, followed by excessive moping, they made up. Samantha wanted her old life back. Cara wanted their friendship to return to the way it was. And, they both wanted the past four months of drama behind them.

On Monday, Roselyn scheduled Samantha to supervise the evening shift. She hoped this would be her final week in the kitchen. Lou returned to work today with skin so tan, his teeth blinded everyone when he smiled. Her stomach rolled. She had blamed the whole Apollo thing on Lou, when it was Cara.

Ryan asked Samantha to take over the lunch tray line as soon as she entered the kitchen so he could help order supplies that Angie needed for the Employee Appreciation Day they had planned in the cafeteria next week. At least her afternoon would fly. She threw on an apron and hairnet, and quickly focused on the trays already streaming down the belt.

While scanning the menus, a packaged dinner roll smacked her in the side of her head. She glared at Bruce, but refused to acknowledge his immaturity further.

In the corner of her eye, Lou rounded the corner with a platform truck loaded with cases of juice. Not missing it either, Bruce motioned to Lou and then laughed like the total jackass he was. She pretended not to notice and asked the cold beverage person to toss her a skim milk.

"Sure had a great time on vacation," Lou shouted, as if the entire kitchen was deaf. "All those babes in bikinis, throwing themselves at me."

"I need a utensil package, Terrance." Samantha kept her head low.

"I'm lucky I can walk today. So sore. Too much action."

"I bet," Bruce joined in. "I need to come with you next time."

"Nah. I already shared with you. That was a disaster. I work alone from now on."

Samantha cringed, then leaned to her left and squatted down, pretending to look for something on the metal food truck that held all the completed trays. She stood back up and seven packaged rolls were arranged on the tray in front of her. She removed six of them and placed them on the table to her right.

Lou paused, as if thinking of something else to say. Without Samantha's response, his jokes became old, even to him. He continued around the tray line behind her, then back towards the refrigerators. The kitchen grew silent. Only the faint sound of a knife chopping vegetables resounded in the large room.

"Miss him?" Bruce whispered, but loud enough for her to hear.

Stupidly, Samantha glanced at him. He licked his lips in a repulsive, poor attempt at being sensual. *Ew!* She stole a quick peek towards Cooper's office. With the manager nowhere in sight, she grabbed the pile of dinner rolls in the crook of her left arm, then hurled all six of them at Bruce, one after another, not missing once. They bounced and pinged off his head and chest as if caught in front of an automatic tennis ball machine. Bruce ducked under the tray line like a five-year-old boy shielding himself with his arms. *Yup.* All talk. Big Baby.

"Afraid of a little dinner roll, are we?" Samantha quirked her eyebrow. The tray line burst into hysterics.

Fifteen minutes later, the last tray slid by. Samantha tore off her apron and hair net, then charged towards the loading dock's door. She kicked it open and clenched her fists. Light drained from the sky, and streaks of clouds took over as the sun made its descent. Fresh air entered her nose, but her stress-release was ruined when a passing taxi cab blasted its horn while distant police sirens roared.

"Why do you let them get to you?" a voice from behind startled her. Cooper lounged against the brick wall, drinking a cup of coffee.

The last thing she needed was a fight with Cooper. "I don't have to discuss anything with you."

"No, you don't." He took a sip of his coffee and kept his eyes on the lights spilling from nearby apartments windows.

"You don't know the first thing about me."

"Right again."

Samantha's chest heaved from angered breath. She didn't know who to trust anymore, but knew Cooper wasn't one of them. His constant picking on her drove her crazy. Had Cooper used Apollo's attack on her to get him fired? He had mentioned how much he hated Apollo.

"But...you do have a good throwing arm. Nice pitching. Ever play softball?"

Samantha swallowed hard. As if the July humidity wasn't bad enough, embarrassment burned under her skin. Her aggravated feet tore down the sidewalk. How did he see her? Was he peeking through his office blinds? Spying on her?

As she reached the end of the block, the alleyway she and Cara had argued near came into sight. She turned right instead and stepped off the curb, heading up the next block. She snuck in between two parked cars, then out onto the busy street as a large delivery truck came barreling down. It screeched to a halt, narrowly avoiding impact. She sprung back, covered her heart with her hand, then ran across the street hoping Cooper had finished his coffee and returned to the kitchen.

When she was a good twenty-feet down the next sidewalk, she peered over her shoulder. Cooper was shaking his head and laughing. God, she hated him!

****

The phone slammed into its cradle after Samantha placed her final order for bread and milk, thankful it was her last day in the kitchen. She had spent the rest of the week avoiding Cooper. Bruce and Lou continued to taunt her, but she refused to acknowledge them. Why *was* she letting them get to her?

On Friday, Lou approached her at the supervisor's desk. "What's going on?" He sat on the desk and nodded his head waiting for her reply.

Seriously? She shuffled the papers in front of her, rejecting him. Now he wanted to talk? On her last day? "Nothing. Just counting down my final minutes and hoping I never have to work in here ever again."

"That bad? I heard you had a lot of fun while I was gone."

Her head shot up. Lou's eyebrows rose and dove. "What's that supposed to mean?" Had he heard about Apollo and her? Of course, he had. The whole, damn kitchen was talking about her.

"Guess you don't need me anymore. You didn't come back to the bar that night. You got Apollo hitting on you. Then you and Cooper are hanging out, flirting—"

"Cooper? Aside from training me, there's no communication

between us."

"Not what I heard."

"Well, it's a lie. And, *you* left without saying good-bye. You've been ignoring *me*."

Lou's eyebrows slanted in as if he was concocting some devious plan. "You play games."

"What exactly do you want from me?" She was tired of proving her worth. And, sick of everyone playing hot and cold with her.

Lou looked over his shoulder at the abandoned kitchen and then back at her. He streamed his finger down her neckline, over her pink shirt, and whispered in her ear. "I think you can come up with something. Haven't I kept you entertained? If you really missed me, then I need proof. And, I think you know what I mean."

Was he freakin' serious? He was interested in her again? Was it because of Apollo and Cooper? Was the little prick jealous? She clenched her jaw and responded through gritted teeth. "Who said I missed you?" Samantha relaxed her mouth trying to remain calm. "Look, Lou. Not sure what you're getting at, but I'm in no mood."

"You never are." He hopped off the stool and strutted off to the far storeroom.

Before she could reply, Cooper appeared from inside his office and leaned against the door jam, glaring at her. His expression was a toss-up between alarmed and irritated. As much as she'd grown to hate happy hours, she suddenly needed a drink.

****

Samantha pushed the final tray down the line towards the loader, placed it on the truck and let out a long, relieved huff. Thank God, this was over. She couldn't wait to return to her floor and avoid all the drama down here.

She tossed her protective gear in the trash, while the rest of the employees broke down their stations. The pot washer's pans and cooking utensils clanged together in the large, tub basin behind her. Before she could leave the area, Lou materialized in the center of the room.

"Bruce. You going out tonight?" he screamed, since Bruce apparently became hearing impaired while he was away on vacation.

"Yo. Totally getting my drink on tonight," he screamed even louder, since Samantha was hearing impaired, as well.

"Yeah. Me too. Maybe we'll find some hot ladies. Ones that aren't so frigid under the sheets, you know?"

Samantha froze. The condiment station employee whispered

something to Bruce and laughter broke out among them. Well, she wanted to be noticed. She got her wish. She glanced at the clock. There was still an hour and a half left of this crap. She wanted to jump in her car and drive home leaving the doors unlocked. Who cared anymore?

She stormed into the hallway, towards the diet office. Everyone had left for the day except the new diet clerk who lacked any social skills. With no one to talk to, she grabbed her keys and fled outside. She'd sit in her car for five minutes.

Luckily, someone had pulled away from the curb just as she arrived at work this morning. With her car only thirty-feet from the loading dock door, she jammed the key into the lock. Before she opened the door, a tap on her shoulder jolted her body.

Cooper stood behind her. *Great.* Now she'd get in trouble for abandoning ship. Leaving the animals to destroy the place without proper supervision. "What, Cooper? What now?"

"Cutting out? Quitting? Leaving the animals behind to trash my kitchen?"

Her mouth fell open. "I...no. I was just getting something from my car."

"Oh, yeah? What?" He folded his arms over his chest. Then something grew on his face that she hadn't seen all week. A smirk.

She peered into her back seat. An empty, crushed water bottle, a wool scarf left over from the winter, an umbrella, and three McDonalds French Fries arranged themselves on the backseat's floor. *Awesome.* "Cooper. What do you want?"

"Just trying to get into your head." He squinted to let her know he had the hidden talent of mind reading.

"There's nothing to see in there."

Cooper laughed out loud. Samantha squeezed her eyes shut at her own insult. This guy had the power to rip her mask off and see the fool she was underneath.

"I beg to differ." He nodded. "I think there's a whirlwind of activity in there. Too much for you to handle, I'm thinking."

She let the car keys dangle in her fingers. "Don't think then," her sarcasm rang out. "Sometimes it's better to go with the flow." She flicked her head back at an attempt to bring her tough persona back.

"That's the problem with you women. You think with your heart, not your head. It gets you in a lot of trouble."

"Excuse me?" Her neck and ears suddenly felt unbearably hot. "Again, you know nothing about me."

"I hear a lot. That's for sure. I see a lot, too."

Samantha's mouth went dry. A breeze slid through the leaves on a tree beside her. "What do you hear? From who?"

"Why do you care?"

"If people are talking about me, I want to know."

Cooper turned to leave.

"Tell me!" Samantha's voice reverberated off the brick building. A couple strolling by glared at her.

"If what they say is a lie, and it comes from a crappy source, you shouldn't give two shits about it. If it's true, then you should reconsider your life choices."

"Now you're telling me how to live my life? First my clothes, now my life?" She took a step closer as the wind picked up again. A trampled coffee cup scuttled in between them. "I want to know right now. I find it impossible that you heard anything. You're just saying that to make me—"

"I hear everything in that kitchen." Cooper leaned against the lampost. "My door's always open and those thin, wall-to-wall windows surrounding my office let all those gossipy conversations flow through."

Samantha's patience wore thin. She folded her arms over her chest.

Cooper smirked. "Did you know Nadia's getting divorced? Did you know Karl's daughter was in a bad car accident? How 'bout Sabrina? Did you know she's pregnant? Two and a half months. Yup. It was a shock to her, too. Especially since she doesn't know who the father is. And then there's Felipe, who recently…"

His words spilled out as if he was a radio DJ dishing the latest dirt on celebrities. This guy, who sat in his office ignoring everyone, burying his head in his work, knew everything about everyone. Some of the stories he blurted out were complete shockers. Almost two months of working in that kitchen and she knew nothing about anyone.

"…and then there's you." A playful grin appeared on his face, as he looked her directly in the eye.

"What…what do they say?" *Did she really want to know?*

"I'm sure it's just talk from a bunch of guys trying to outdo one another. Guys that have nothing going for them, so they make things up."

"Tell me." She knew who he meant. What was upsetting her more, though? Hearing what they had to say, or grasping that Cooper knew all this time. No wonder he hated her. "Tell me. I need to know"

"I think you already do—"

"Why are you playing with my head?" she shouted over him.

Cooper huffed, as if disgusted. "Fine. You want to know? I hear ridiculous stories about threesomes and dumpsters. I hear…"

Nausea rolled in Samantha's mouth. They talked about these things? The details spewing from Cooper's mouth answered her question. She was just some plaything to them.

"…also the binge drinking and cocaine and everything from bondage to—"

"Wait! Hold on." Samantha held up her hand.

"I told you, you wouldn't want to hear it."

"No. I mean…" Okay, the first half was true, but the second half was blatant lies. If she admitted the second half was lies, he'd know the first half was true. "They're lying. Exaggerating. That never happened."

"Never? Seemed very descriptive to me." He tossed her a side-glance. "Then the stories of you and Apollo. How the whole incident was set up previously and you reneged on it."

"No! They must've known you were listening. Making things up."

"Sounded believable to me."

"Well, it isn't. None of it. Now if you don't mind, I have to finish my shift. This will be the last time I ever help you." She charged off, back in the direction of the loading dock.

"Don't get mad at me," he yelled. "Just remember. You asked."

Her body felt like it was collapsing in on itself. She snatched the door open and sprinted into the bathroom. She was the laughing stock of the kitchen. Of the entire department. Had Roselyn heard as well? Had Cooper told her what he knew?

Her blotchy skin marked the truth on her face. Her hand slammed into the soap dispenser until a pink mound of liquid coated her palm. She smeared the runny fluid across the mirror until her reflection disappeared. She wished she could disappear. Why'd she promise to meet Cara at the club tonight? She wanted to fade away.

Chapter 21

The rowdy, bass beat from the DJ, something she normally loved, annoyed Samantha tonight. The whole scene annoyed her. Scouring the room for hot guys, morphed into hiding from a room full of pimps that thought you were one of their girls. Dancing close to a sexy number, transformed into sleazy guys grabbing you in places you'd rather not be touched. Hoping a few guys would buy you a drink, mutated into serial killers trying to get you drunk so they could kidnap you and hide you in their trunk. Samantha didn't care if she stayed single the rest of her life.

Cara stumbled off the dance floor and back to the barstool. Her red dress looked more like a negligee. In the dim lighting of the club, it passed for a lacey dress. However, up close, it was thin and transparent. Cara twisted behind for her drink, and her left nipple twisted with her, until it popped out beneath a tiny piece of lace. She was braless. As if she was witnessing a bad car accident, Samantha's eyes traveled down to Cara's crotch. The material thickened toward the bottom, covering the top portion of her thighs. She wouldn't be surprised if she had no underwear on either.

"Your dress looks like a negligee." Samantha found the words tumbling out. She promised to be back to her old self again tonight, but questioned who that even was anymore. A mango margarita and a shot of tequila weren't helping either.

Cara leaned in. "It is actually. I was hoping it looked more like a dress, though."

Samantha also questioned Cara's sanity. Her actions became more bizarre with each passing day.

The more Samantha drank, the more irritable she became with the whole situation. She couldn't help thinking about the way Cooper egged her on today. As if he was in on the joke with them. Had the three of them gone out drinking and shared stories?

"I have a surprise for you," Cara slurred. "You can't guess. No, no, no." Her little-kid talk she'd been doing all night, aggravated Samantha to the core.

Please don't say Lou and Bruce were showing up. She needed

time to process what Cooper had said. Sure, some of the stories were lies, but a lot of them were true. "What's the surprise, Cara?"

"I got Eryn to come tonight!" She flapped her legs up and down as if practicing her kicks for swimming class.

"Really? I thought she stopped returning your calls."

"She's having dinner with Russell, but then promised to swing by after nine-thirty. The old gang is back!"

Samantha glanced at her watch. 8:56 p.m. Then looked back at Cara. That huge, steroid-infused beast from two months ago, had parked himself in Cara's personal space. His giant thighs encircled her left thigh, pushing her dress hem up. She *wasn't* wearing any underwear.

"Mmm," he moaned. "My favorite dress."

"Shh. Be quiet." Cara looked away, but there was no mistaking the enormous, steroids-gone-wrong, hulk that deposited his chest in her face.

"I bought you a shot. Your favorite." He held the golden liquid against her lips and helped her guide it in and down her throat, like an abusive father forcing his child to drink poison.

Cara had shown up buzzed again and after an hour and a half of drinking, the alcohol had more than caught up with her. Who was this ass? Wasn't Cara hanging out with Apollo? Did Apollo dump her after he was fired? Cara needed to find a better caliber of men.

The beast leaned close to Cara's ear and whispered. Then stepped back, ogling her. "See you Tuesday." He turned without noticing Samantha, and strutted away.

Tuesday? Samantha waited for Cara to explain, but as usual, she remained silent. Instead, Cara asked the bartender for another martini. Samantha raised her hand to protest, but knew Cara would explode.

"Want to grab something to eat? I could go for some mozzarella sticks." Samantha dug into her bag for a twenty. Maybe the fat would absorb all the alcohol.

"Since when do we eat when we go out? Wanna have garlic breath? Food stuck in your teeth?" Cara tried to point to her mouth, but missed. Her finger flew past her teeth and into her ear.

"I think we should go. We can go to the diner and grab some food. Did you eat?" Cara had lost a considerable amount of weight over the past two months. Too much. "Have you eaten at all today?"

"What's that supposed to mean?" Cara carefully tried to move the martini glass to her lips without spilling any liquid. Her over exaggerated relocation of the glass with her other hand escorting it, was too much for Samantha to watch.

"You're drunk. That's what it means. By the time Eryn gets here, you'll be passed out on the floor. I'm calling her to tell her not to bother. Come on. We're leaving." Samantha hopped off the barstool. Cara ignored her and took a sip of the drink. Half of it poured down the side of her cheek and into her cleavage.

****

The drive to Cara's apartment became all too familiar and never ended well. Samantha tried to walk Cara to her bedroom, but her legs gave way, and dragging her to the other side of the apartment wasn't happening. Samantha directed her to the couch instead.

She wandered over to the kitchen sink once again, switching on the light. Surprisingly, the lamp she had found on the floor months ago, stood upright on the end table. She hurried over to it, but wasn't too surprised to find it still lacked a light bulb. That's when she saw it.

On the coffee table, next to a bottle of Frank's Hot Sauce and a condom wrapper, was a rolled up dollar bill, a razor blade, and remnants of white powder on a rectangular mirror. The vision of Cara flying down the stairs with white, doughnut powder under her nose, resurfaced.

Samantha dropped onto the couch liked she'd been shot. She looked over at her co-worker, who was unaware of her discovery.

"You're such a good friend, Sam."

"Don't call me that. It's Samantha."

"Sam I am. Sam I am. I will not eat green eggs and ham." Cara let out a stream of laughter that bounced off the walls. She grabbed her stomach and curled into a ball, continuing the wave of giggles. Samantha threw a sweatshirt that smelled of warm beer, over Cara's lower half to avoid seeing her butt and other body parts.

"What's going on with you, Cara? I don't even know you anymore."

"You don't know me? I don't know you. Who are you Samantha Hart? Are you a nerd? A grunge chick? A closet nymphomaniac? A prude? A secret spy for Roselyn? Will the real Samantha Hart please stand up!" Cara pushed herself up on the couch, but then fell back and clutched her head. "This is gonna hurt in the morning! Who's working this weekend anyway? Heather?"

"No. Me."

"You? How the hell you gonna to wake up in the morning?"

"Exactly. But, if I blew you off again, I'd never hear the end of it."

"That's why I love you Samantha Hart. You're a good friend. Did

I ever tell you that before?"

"Yes. About three minutes ago." Samantha slipped off her shoes and tossed them by the front door. "What's going on? You never told me what happened when you went to college."

"That's a crappy story! Who wants to hear that one again?"

"I never heard it the first time!"

"It's a very bad, sad, mad, lad story." Cara covered her eyes with the sweatshirt.

Samantha rose, filled a glass with water and handed it to Cara. She took a sip, but then guzzled half of it. "So good. And cold. Mmm. Water's so awesome. And cold." She finished off the rest. "Yeah, so, I met this guy...Leo..." Cara jerked as if punched in the stomach. "...the beginning of my junior year. He was a senior. I met him in the library, actually. Go figure." Cara laughed and her voice echoed in the empty apartment. "Leo kept looking at me from the next table. Only two inches taller than me. Blonde hair. Not like the tall, dark and beefy I go for."

Samantha shifted on the couch, finding a comfortable position. *She might as well make herself cozy for this one.*

"After an hour, he shoved his Economics book under his arm and pulled out a chair next to me. Starts wowing me with his talk about forecasting financial trends and consumer spending habits, and I was blown away by the intelligent conversation. He invited me to coffee the next day and that weekend we went to this tiny Italian restaurant right outside of town and had a nice breakfast. I mean dinner." Cara giggled. "He walked me back to my dorm and kissed me. Said he would call me first thing in the morning. And he did. We started dating and it was...I can't explain it. It wasn't real, Samantha. I kept thinking this isn't happening. I don't deserve someone like him. He was totally out of my league." She attempted to lick the last drop of water from her glass.

"Do you need more water?" Samantha interrupted.

"Yes, please." Cara grasped at the smelly sweatshirt and slipped her arms into it. "So, at the end of the year, he graduated. I had another year and wanted to find a school back home to be closer to him, but he said I couldn't screw this up so close to the end. When I came home for Christmas break, we looked for an apartment together and found the cutest place. Right before I went back, he moved his stuff in and I cooked our first meal. It was some chicken thing. It sucked, Samantha. It was so dry and gross."

Samantha filled the glass again. "You're a great cook now, though." Discarded plastic cups and an empty bottle of vodka laid scattered across the floor. Paper plates smeared with food stains, dirty utensils and a spilled cup of water occupied the end table. A 7-11 coffee cup, with half its contents still living in it, and what appeared to be men's white, knee-high socks, positioned themselves by the couch leg.

Samantha returned with the water and Cara took another big slug. "The morning before I left, he told me he loved me and when I graduated we'd get engaged." Cara paused and leaned her head back on the couch.

"Engaged? Wow, Cara. I never knew. You never told me."

"I don't like to talk about my past. Can't you tell? It's all bad." Cara rubbed her eyes and bent forward until her elbows touched her knees. "Do you want to hear the rest of the story or not?"

Samantha nodded.

"I came home that March for spring break and slept at Leo's. That week with him in his apartment, showed me what my life could be like. Two professionals taking on the world. We'd be successful and have money. We'd have each other. I thought about that cute apartment all the time. I thought about our engagement. Our wedding. Thoughts of the wedding scared me, though. Would my mom be drunk? Start a scene? Would my brothers show up all high, and fucked up?" Cara shifted in her seat, shook her head.

Samantha licked her lips. Now she was thirsty. Her parched throat and the stifling air in the apartment made her drift to the sink again and grab water for herself. She couldn't relax in the gloomy apartment. The sight of the drugs in such close proximity made her more edgy. She glanced toward the bedroom. A garbage bag, only a quarter of the way full, spread itself across the floor near the hallway. Cara apparently gave up cleaning after the first three minutes.

"The next two months couldn't come fast enough." Cara continued.

This story couldn't come fast enough.

"They had promoted Leo in March and he loved networking with all these big wigs. A month before I came home, though, he started acting weird. Weird! Said work was really busy. I tried calling at all times. He never seemed to be home. And, when he did answer, it was a short conversation. Always with the same excuse about work."

Cara leaned to her side and grabbed the green Tupperware bowl on the floor. She kept it near her chest. Was she going to throw up again? Maybe Samantha gave her too much water to drink.

"What was wrong? Why was he acting weird?"

"Two days before I came home ..." She swallowed. "...he

answered. Said he was fine. But, I knew something was wrong. He hated telling me bad news. What was he hiding from me this time? Had he lost his job?"

Samantha shifted on the couch, feeling the sharp point of a spring. She glanced at the clock. Her eyelids started to droop.

"I planned to leave Oneonta first thing Saturday morning, but I couldn't sleep. Friday night, I got out of bed and drove straight to our apartment. His car was parked in his usual spot. No damage." Cara knocked back the rest of the water.

"I left all my crap in the car and ran inside. I had to know he was all right. The lights were off. I flipped on the living room one, but the room was empty. I ran into the bedroom and..." Cara's breathing intensified. She gasped out breaths like she was hyperventilating.

Samantha jumped up and plopped down next to Cara. Their thighs touched. Then, she placed her arm around her. "What happened? Did he get fired? Was he sick? What? What?"

Cara shoved her off her. "Get off me. Are you a lesbian? Is that why you have a problem with men?"

"No! Just finish the damn story!"

"God. What's the hurry?" Cara stood up. She steadied herself with the arm of the couch. "No! There was some fucking blonde girl, with that short, Rachel haircut in our bed! She was on top of him with her boobs dangling in his face."

"Oh my God. I wasn't expecting that at all." Samantha covered her mouth.

"Neither was I!" Cara paced the room, stumbling as she went. "I started flipping out. Told her to get the fuck out of my apartment! She jumped out of bed and tried to grab the comforter. The one I bought. I snatched it out of her hand and she ran into the living room naked. Leo ran after her. Her. Not me. That tramp tried to find her clothes, but I opened the door and told her to get the fuck out. She had the nerve to start crying. Then, as if it couldn't get any worse, Leo said he drove her and she had no way of getting home. He needed to give her a ride *back* to her house."

Cara wandered toward the kitchen sink. "I waited and when he returned, he sat next to me with that stupid face he always had when he needed to tell me something bad. He said he wasn't expecting me tonight No! Really? He said he was planning on telling me tomorrow when I came home!"

"When you came home? But you packed up all your stuff and were going to move in that day."

"I told him he was a coward, a liar, and a cheat. I started

gathering up all the stupid plants and pictures I bought him. He tried to talk to me while I ripped things off the wall, but I couldn't listen to him anymore. I ended up just leaving the shit and running to my car."

"What was he saying?" Samantha stood now, too. She held out both her hands to catch Cara in case she fell.

"Who the fuck knows. Something about meeting her a few months ago at his new position. They worked on a project together. A bunch of them went out for drinks a few times and, you know, 'it just happened.' He said it was lonely in his apartment, and it was getting to him. Being with her made him feel less lonely."

"But you were coming home in May. He couldn't wait?"

"I guess mommas boy was used to being taken care of. He initially thought it would be cool and we would have a place to be alone, but, alone was too much for him. That slut knew how to calm him down, especially with the stress of the new job."

"But, wait, was he planning on giving the girl the boot after you came home?"

"No. That's the thing. They'd been fucking around in our apartment for two months. He said he fell in love with her. How do you fall in love with someone in two months? He met her family, and his family adored her. She came from a good home. It went on and on. Either he or his mom thought I came from trash. Miss 'Rachel-haircut' was from a well to do family and worked in his office. She made him feel important and…they fell in love."

"But when was he going to tell you? I don't understand."

Cara plopped down on the couch again with her legs spread wide. "I don't really know. He apparently hates confrontation and couldn't tell me, so he stopped calling, stopped answering the phone. He had no plan. I guess…who knows, maybe he'd let it go on all weekend, maybe he'd let it go so far that I'd start moving in before he told me. Who the hell knows."

"So, what happened?" Samantha's voice echoed in the room.

"Well, I wasn't going home to my mom, that's for sure. I drove to an apartment complex near my house and slept in the parking lot. Then I did the same thing I did with Leo just months before. I withdrew my savings, filled out the paperwork, bought a few pieces of furniture. I didn't have much. Plus, my car had died again on another road trip and I knew I needed a new one. I got a job waitressing, then started the internship. Not sure how I made it through that first year. Worked until midnight some nights. Tips were good. The apartment was a shitty, studio apartment, but once I started working here, I bought a new car, then moved into this new shit hole. I didn't tell my mom for a month. She thought I was still in school. She didn't realize I graduated. Can you believe that, Samantha?"

"I can't believe anything you've told me this year. You'd never know. You're one of the most organized, independent, intelligent people I know. To get where you are today after all you've had to overcome. That's huge. It makes me feel like a loser for being afraid to put myself out there. You just go for it. You don't think. I have to think about things for days before I act on them."

"I have nothing, Samantha. I'm alone. No friends. No boyfriend."

"That's not true. You have a mountain of friends at work."

"Friends? No. They just use me for laughs and a good story. They never invite me out. I hear stories of pool parties that happened over the weekend. Baby showers or weddings that I wasn't invited to. Girl's nights and dinners. No one invites me. No one wants the disaster showing up."

"That can't be true. And, as for boyfriends, you pick up guys all the time."

"I use them like I've been used. It's my revenge on men. For all of them that have used me or screwed me over."

"I don't believe that. You're just going to sleep with strange men for the rest of your life? You must want what you had with Leo again."

"What I had with Leo? What? Lies? Deceit? Cowardliness?"

"No. The deep love you guys had initially. Surely, you want to find that again. Sleeping around can't be fulfilling that need."

"It decreases my anxiety of being all alone. Fear of abandonment. Being hurt again. Feeling hollow every time I leave work. I'll never let another man rip my heart out like that again. If I just keep all my free time occupied, fill every minute with something, I…" Cara's eyes widened as if realizing she just revealed her deepest secrets to Samantha. "I have a huge headache. I don't want to talk about this anymore. Please go. You have work in the morning."

Chapter 22

Samantha returned to work on Tuesday refreshed from a day of soul searching. Cooper pointing out how others perceived her, and Cara's revelation, put her life in perspective. The path she'd chosen was not only disgraceful, but destructive. Although she was no longer working in the kitchen, she needed to set Lou straight. Samantha wanted to move on, and his renewed interest and requests had to stop.

"Lou." She caught him as he was signing out for the day. Nothing like waiting until the last minute. "Can I talk to you for a second?"

He eyed her up and down like some blow up doll. "Yeah, baby. What's up? You change your mind? You gonna give me what I want?" His fingers slid down her back and over her ass. The sensation sent chills through her. He leaned in. His breath flashed across her face. For a brief second, her body responded.

Samantha closed her eyes and shook the thoughts away. "Look, Lou. We obviously want different things. It's not going to happen."

Lou drew back. Had she hurt his feelings? He squinted and held up his palms. Just when she thought he was going to beg for forgiveness, "Girl? You serious?"

"Yup. Don't see this going anywhere."

"Going anywhere? You having delusions, girl? We were just fucking around, baby. You think you're the only one? I got girls day and night. In Mexico, I had a new girl every night. As for you…" He pointed up and down at her torso. "You were willing and able. Accommodating. Looking for some action. I gave you some. But that's all it ever was, baby. A quickie to get us through the week…"

Even before he finished speaking, her entire body engulfed in heat. Her ribs squeezed together as if to crush her to pieces. The word baby repeated, over and over again in her head, along with Cooper's explanation of the term. Her mind became numb as she closed off the rest of what Lou was saying.

She actually thought Lou would take her out to dinner? Bring her flowers and presents? No. He brought Bruce instead, and…Oh, God. He never paid her back for that damn motel room. *Wow.* She was beyond blind and stupid.

Samantha turned away and wandered down the corridor in a daze. Painful memories from seventh grade returned. Visions of Randi, her bully entered her mind.

"Why are you sitting at my table?" Randi demanded.

She wasn't at Randi's table, but it didn't matter. Samantha would take her tray and leave, but tomorrow would bring a new threat.

"Answer me, you terd." *Randi wore a black T-shirt with a giant skull on it that said Grateful Dead. Samantha wished she were dead.*

Samantha wrapped her fingers around the edges of her tray. With her head hung low, she eyed Randi's blue and white Adidas sneakers, and trembled as she made her way to a table on the other side of the cafeteria. She caught sight of the clothes her mother made her wear for picture day: orange Danskin skirt, white tights, brown leather shoes with laces, and a white ruffle blouse - the one with the sizeable bow tied under her neck. Pathetic. Randi's laughter continued while Samantha ate her burnt pizza square alone.

****

Once home, Samantha changed out of her work clothes and stared at her reflection in the mirror. Nothing had changed. She flipped to the magnified side and all her features seemed to explode in front of her. Pale lips. Splotches of makeup. Big pores. Frown lines.

She shoved an Oreo in her mouth and a handful of Bugles, and as the sweet and salty mixture crunched between her teeth she pulled out a roll of tape from her drawer. After ripping off large pieces, she taped up her face. Long, gluey strips stretched from her eyebrows to her cheek, covering her lips. She stuck a final one across her face horizontally, giving herself a pig nose. "Oink! Oink!" She laughed.

"Did you call me?" her mother yelled from her bedroom.

"No." she mumbled, her lips still stuck together. Then she chuckled. "Yes, I called you. Oink, oink. Here piggy, piggy," she whispered behind the tape.

Ring! The phone snapped her out of her gloom. "Hullooo?"

"Samantha?"

She ripped the pieces of tape off one by one, tearing off hair and skin in the process. "Hello? Hello? Cara?"

"What are you doing? Are you insane!" Cara's voice screeched into the phone.

"Huh? What do you mean?" Was Cara spying on her from the bedroom window? Could she see her disfigured face?

"Hello?" A weak, sickly voice moaned.

"Mom. I'm on the phone. It's for me."

"Who is it?"

"It's Cara. Please, hang up."

"Don't be rude to me, young lady. It's my phone and I have a right to know who's on it."

"It's a serial killer, okay? He's calling to let us know he'll be showing up tonight around eleven. Will you be available?" Samantha squeezed the phone in her hand, wishing it were her mother's neck.

"Don't you dare sass me. Who do you think you are? I'm expecting a phone call. Hang up."

"You're not expecting a phone call. And, I just got on the phone."

"I don't care. Hang up. Now."

"No! I have the right to talk to my friends. You hang up."

"You have five minutes and then I'm yanking the phone out of your room."

The click of the phone sent Samantha tossing her Calvin and Hobbes book hard against the wall.

"Are we free to talk now?" Cara's sarcastic tone poured through the receiver.

"Sure. You have all of four minutes and fifty-two seconds. Go for it."

"Unbelievable. How can you put up with that?"

"Four minutes forty-six seconds."

"Why don't you just move out already?"

"You're wasting your own precious minutes. Speak fast and tell me what I did wrong now."

"Lou. He told me you didn't want to see him anymore. Is there something wrong with you?"

"Me? It's the first sensible thing I did all year." *That was it. She made her decision.* Samantha pulled open her makeup drawer and dropped her case of cosmetics on top of the desk.

"Sensible. You're nothing but. He was willing to give you another chance."

"Give *me* another chance?" Samantha put her black eye shadow back in the case. "He used me for his own needs."

"You had the same needs. He was giving you what you wanted."

"That's not what I wanted. I wanted a boyfriend, okay? I wanted someone that actually wanted to be with me. Someone to go to dinner or dancing with. Someone that would listen to my stories and be interested. Maybe someone that would tell me what the hell I'm doing wrong with my life. You know. A friend. Someone with character, and integrity. Someone I could trust and spill my guts to." Her black eyeliner bounced off the side of the case as she tried to fling it back in.

"There's no one out there like that. Get over it."

"I won't. I won't settle. I shouldn't be dating trash like Lou and having to put out to Bruce to prove my worth and devotion to some guy that just wants to get off, and then moves on to another *babe*. I want to be myself and laugh and joke and be silly and not care that I might be turning someone off."

"You tried with Dr. Chambers and look where that got you. You're going after guys that're out of your league."

"Out of my league? Are you saying I'm only good enough for players and cheaters?"

"Speaking of which, Lou told me you've been chatting up a storm with that fat, idiot, Cooper! Are you insane?"

"He's not fat…" The words flew out before she could stop them.

"What?"

"I mean…I only talk to him when I have to. God, I'm working for him. What do you want me to do? Ignore him? Run away? Hide?"

"Just stay away from him before we get in trouble again. He's an asshole and is looking for an excuse to rat on us."

"I think I can handle myself, thank you."

"Fine! Try to get your own guy then. I'm tired of helping you. I send two guys your way and you fuck it up."

"Two?"

"Yeah, duh. Apollo. Lou."

Samantha gasped, her lipstick fell from her hand. "Liar. I got Lou all by myself. A whole bar full of women and he approached me. He could have chosen anyone, but he—"

Loud cackling hit her. "You think you got Lou by yourself? Yeah, okay. A bar full of women and he just walks right up to you, can't see you from behind, and just starts talking to you. Sure. That's how it happened."

Samantha hands curled into balls. "What're you saying?"

"Lou and Bruce entered the bar. They asked where you were. I pointed you out to Lou and told him to show you some love. Told him you hadn't had sex in years."

"You told him that! How could you?"

"I didn't tell you because I wanted you to think you could get your own guy. After months of watching you leave bars alone, it was ridiculous. I threw you a bone, okay? Two bones."

Samantha dragged her brush through her hair in violent bursts. How could this be? She couldn't even get Lou on her own? *Wow*. How freaking sad. He only approached her because Cara asked him for the favor? Told him she was hard up for sex? This was some bizarre nightmare. This seriously could not be happening to her. How did her life go from boring invisibility, and spending weekends at the library with children, to this insanity? Her thoughts were snarled, like the clump of hair in her brush.

At times, she felt sorry for Cara, at others, she wanted to cut ties with her completely. Obviously, her drinking and drugging clouded her judgment considerably. She was out of her mind. Couldn't make rational decisions anymore. Completely deranged!

Samantha surveyed the short, tight skirts and slutty dresses in her open closet. The ones Cara picked out. None of this was her. It never was. No amount of partying, sex, drinking and bar hopping would change that.

She needed to get away from all of this. Breaking it off with Lou, even though there apparently never was anything between them, was her first step. Bruce would stay away now, too, and of course, not having to work in the kitchen anymore would save her from all the drama. Including Cooper.

"Are you listening to me, Samantha? Before our time runs out?"

"You know. I really don't need this right now. I had a crappy day and I don't need you yelling at me that you *tried* to help me with your fabulous help. You should've become a therapist instead of a dietitian."

"What's that supposed to mean? You ask for help and then have an attitude?"

The familiar creak outside Samantha's door, alerted her to the intruder. She casually turned her head to the right, and let her eyes drift to their corners.

"I've had enough with you, Samantha. You can fend for yourself for now on!"

The phone clicked off, leaving Samantha alone in her room with the phone still pressed to her ear. A shadowy figure hovered near the two-inch crack in her door. Eavesdropping at its worst. This was the last straw. With the phone against the side of her head, she twisted ever so slightly to the right and raised her voice.

"Cara, I will not sell cocaine for you. I told you already. The sex club was bad enough, but I'm not getting involved with illegal transportation of drugs."

In less than two seconds, her bedroom door flew open and her mother, donned in light blue flowery-print pajamas, shook her fist at Samantha, seething. "I knew that damn Cara was no good! You're forbidden from seeing her anymore, you hear! Drugs. Sex. What's next? Prison?"

Samantha tossed the phone onto her bed, strolled to her armoire, and pulled out a pair of jeans. She eyed her favorite Led Zeppelin T-shirt, snatched it out of the drawer and tugged it on. Then she reached into the closet for her sneakers, all while ignoring the spit flying from her mother's mouth. She plastered her lips with the hot-pink lipstick she wasn't able to apply earlier, then strolled past her mother as if she were invisible.

"Are you listening to me, young lady? Where do you think you're going?"

"A place I feel comfortable at." She snatched her car keys and unlocked the front door. "A place I can do what I've wanted to do for a long time. Just didn't have the courage 'til now."

Her mother chased after her, but then hid behind the open door, refusing to let the neighbors see her at her worst. "Where? I need to know."

"It's not about you, mom. It's about me. For once."

Chapter 23

Cooper

Cooper left Tiara's home and drove two blocks before pulling over and parking in front of an unlit house. He rubbed his face, then reclined the seat. Six weeks had passed since the kitchen returned to normal with full staff, and he had spent every free moment with Tiara. Making up for his busy months, catching up with her news, treating her to extravagant dinners, shows, and clubs. They resumed their bi-weekly lunch dates and tried every restaurant near their jobs.

He bought her a gorgeous pair of earrings last week to celebrate their one-year anniversary. They went to Evangeline's restaurant in the city and took a carriage ride through Central Park, then finished their romantic evening dancing the night away at the posh, and hard to get into, Club Lavender.

She wore a clingy, white dress - one of those that flows out when you twirl - the earrings he bought, and these clear shoes that looked like glass slippers. Her tall and firm body made others look on. Her sultry dance moves aroused them further.

It was the perfect night. The perfect anniversary.

After returning his seat to an upright position, he continued down the road toward the busy intersection. He turned left, not wanting to go home yet, and traveled along the main road that swelled with cars and bright lights from the storefronts. His car, practically on autopilot, wandered through the town of Westlake Village, and passed both Olive Hill and Huntington Woods. When he entered Cairnbrook, his taste buds craved a nice, cold beer.

The time flashing on a bank's exterior sign caught his eye. 8:37 p.m. A large parking lot with grand opening flags flapping in the wind came into view. The red, white, and blue triangles hung above a store on the far end where a good twenty cars had parked. He missed the first entrance and continued to the next light, making a left turn into the parking lot.

Unfamiliar with the area, he surveyed the stores, most of them closed for the night. A stripper club, Vamps & Vixens, had at least a dozen cars parked near the entrance. A bagel store - four of five. The grand opening banner hung from a streetlight, then toward the brand new Dunkin' Donuts. Although several cars parked near the storefront, the remainder of them were at the far end occupying every spot in the first two rows. He neared the front entrance and looked up at the neon sign: *Déjà Vu.* A typical bar, but why so much buzz for Tuesday? He drove further, pulling alongside the curb. A sidewalk, chalkboard easel positioned itself next to the bouncer at the door.

Déjà Vu Mini Acoustic Night
Tonight 8-11pm
Two for One Tap Beers
21 and over
$5 Entry

Wanting that beer more than ever, Cooper parked his car in front of Dunkin' Donuts and made his way to the entrance. The bouncer stood near a heavy, wooden, strap-hinged door, collecting money and checking I.D.s. Cooper pulled out his wallet as loud applause erupted inside. The faint sound of an acoustic guitar played while a man with black, uncombed hair, three spots ahead of him, fumbled for his wallet. He removed his I.D., a five-dollar bill, and entered the bar. Pat Benatar's "Invincible" floated out through the opening.

A guy in front of Cooper, barely of age, wrestled with crumpled, torn, dollar bills from his back pocket, front pocket and his jacket's pocket. Impatient, and craving the beer, Cooper tried to peek into the bar to catch a glimpse of the singer. Her voice surged and made its way out into the street. The bouncer nudged him back in line. *Seriously?*

The kid with only four dollars tried desperately to find the final bill.

"Do you have the five bucks, buddy, or what?" The bouncer folded his arms over his huge chest. Heftier than Cooper, but only because he had a good thirty pounds to lose.

"I think I have one more somewhere." The scrawny boy reached in his back pocket again.

Cooper opened his wallet, pulled out a crisp one-dollar bill, and handed it to the kid. "Here, take this already."

"Thanks, dude." He flipped a smile towards Cooper, but his heavy eyelids made him wonder how much weed he smoked before coming. "I'll totally buy you a beer once we...oh, heck, I don't have any more money."

"It's okay. Can we just get inside already?" Cooper handed his license to the bouncer and the kid opened the door, stumbling in. The singer's voice drifted out once again. He handed a five to the bouncer and finally entered the packed bar as the song ended. Cheers and banging exploded from within.

Rows of tables and chairs took over the decent sized room. A modest stage, way in the back, held two bar stools, one for the guitar player and one for the singer. The next song began, one he didn't recognize, but her voice exploded with raw power and emotion, drowning out any chatter as Cooper headed for the bar. He ordered a Heineken on tap, not familiar with any of the other choices, and hopped on one of the stools.

Waitresses crisscrossed one another with platters of deep-fried chicken fingers and spicy Buffalo wings, while others carried trays of beers and assorted drinks. He took a long swig from his cold beer and frowned when the bartended handed him the free one also. *Great.* Now he'd be forced to drink fast before the other one warmed.

The stage held two large speakers on opposite corners like bookends. A guy in his late thirties strummed an all-black, acoustic guitar. His tall frame covered most of the high-back, bar stool, while the microphone covered his mouth and most of his nose. He turned toward the singer and a full grin spread across his face. He looked at her with such adoration, then appeared to chuckle in awe, as she belted out the second set of lyrics.

She *was* really good. Her voice climbed and intensified until it struck Cooper. An eruption of goosebumps flooded his arms. Or, was it the cold beer? The singer's faded, brown T-shirt had what looked like a pie on it. A pink pie? Ripped blue jeans covered her legs and ended where the black Converse high tops began. Her hair hung in low pigtails. Her eyes were obscured by thick, black eye makeup and both hands grasped the microphone tight against her lips. The Fedora hat hung low, veiling her forehead.

The final verse left her lips, and raucous whistling drowned out the applause. After the guitarist leaned his guitar against the stool, he clapped high in the air. The singer bowed, replaced the microphone in its holder, but instead of some arrogant countenance, she tipped her head until the hat concealed her face completely.

The guitarist devoured her with his eyes. Cooper had never seen someone that lovesick before. Enamored by her talent. Proud to be a part of her life. He flung his arms around her, swinging her in wide circles.

Man, he was lucky to have such a cool girlfriend.

Both performers left the stage and headed to the bar. As she approached, Cooper stole a better look at her T-shirt. A pink pie with eyeballs, sat in the middle of her chest, grinning. Above and below read: *Wanna Piece of This?*

Cooper snorted. *What a nut!* The singer took a few deep breaths, whipped off her hat and pushed the sweaty hair away from her face. He instantly froze. It was Samantha.

Despite all lack of motor coordination, his heart sped up. What was she doing here? She could sing? Who *was* this girl? Breathless, he turned away and grabbed his second beer. Samantha, still caught up in the excitement, rushed to the bar with the guitarist and leaned over the counter. Directly next to Cooper. He panicked, remembering the day he hid in the hospital room while Samantha spoke to that patient. He couldn't let that happen again.

With one last exhale, he rotated on the bar stool and faced her with his beer held high. "Wow. That was some performance. Who would've known?"

Without looking, Samantha wiped her forehead with a napkin. "Thanks. It's so scary the first few seconds, but then—" She twisted, then gaped at him. Her mouth fell open, but no words came out.

"Cheers." Cooper raised his glass again.

She remained speechless until the guitarist tapped her on the shoulder. He handed her a glass of water and after guzzling half his drink, strolled toward the bathroom. *How long had they been dating?*

Samantha intentionally prolonged the drinking of her small glass of water until it became obvious. Then, as if she composed herself, redirected her attention to him. "Hi. When did you get here?"

"When you began singing this song."

She looked away and took another sip. "Why…why are you in Cairnbrook?"

"I was leaving Tiara's house and decided to take the long way home. You live here?"

"No, two towns over, but why'd you…?"

"I was in the mood for a beer. Want one?" Cooper held up his beer.

Samantha stared at her water. "I have to work tomorrow."

"So do I. And I'm sure I have to be there a lot earlier than you." Before she could answer, he called over the bartender. "Another Heineken on tap."

"No! Not Heineken. The summer ale they have's really good. It's imported from…" Samantha's eyes widened. "I…I like beer. It's really good here, too."

Cooper smirked, then nodded his head to the bartender. "Summer ale it is." *Was she some beer expert? What else was up this girl's sleeve?* The bartender brought two beers again and Cooper frowned. "Looks like you better drink fast. Before they get warm."

She pushed the second beer over to him. "Looks like you'll have to drink one, actually."

He pushed it back. "This is my second. And, I just started it. You have to catch up."

She frowned, then took her first of many sips.

After fifteen minutes of uncomfortable small talk, Samantha's boyfriend returned. Cooper turned away and let them talk. Five minutes passed. Would the guitarist think he was hitting on Samantha? Cooper directed his attention toward the solo guitarist that sang and strummed to The Stone Temple Pilots "Plush". He finished, a small amount of applause rang out, and then Cooper felt a tap on his shoulder.

Samantha smiled and held up her empty beer. "I guess I *was* a little thirsty." She giggled.

She looked cute in her pigtails. He wanted to pull on them. *Wait, what?* He pushed the second beer closer to her. Her boyfriend disappeared again. "Where's your boyfriend keep running off to?"

Samantha glanced around the bar, then back at him. "Roger? He's not my boyfriend. He's just a guitarist that helps me out."

He gave a slight headshake.

"Yeah. Um, so my first night here, I tried to just go up and sing. Alone. It was a little weird, and, well, Roger comes here a lot so he jumped on stage and started playing his guitar. Winging it, but at least I didn't look so awkward singing without music."

"Not dating, though?" *Why was he asking? Why'd he care?*

"No. He's married with a four-year-old son. His wife comes occasionally. When she can get a babysitter." She plopped an ice cube from her water glass into her mouth. "I'm not dating anyone."

A sudden tingling swept up the back of his neck and across his face. He needed to change the subject. And, quickly. "So, a singer, huh? I never knew."

"No one does. You won't tell anyone, will you? Please don't."

"What?"

Samantha took a large slug of her second beer, squeezed her eyes shut, and then slouched down in the barstool. "I always liked singing. Thought I could, but my mother said I sounded like a dying sheep. Or an injured ferret. Or a beaten ostrich."

Cooper looked on, not fully understanding.

"Anyway, because of her, I never sang in public."

"But, you can. And, very well."

"I know but...you know when you're little and you sing to your parents, or play the guitar, draw, whatever, and they say, "Oh my God, you're amazing!" and you believe it?"

He nodded.

"But, then one day you get an F on your art drawings. Attempt to play the guitar or sing in front of your friends, and they let you know how *truly* awful you are."

Cooper bit his lip to keep from laughing. "Or, you tell everyone on the bus you still believe in Santa because your mother never got around to telling you the truth, and the whole bus laughs at you? One of those parental lies?"

"Exactly." She pouted her lips at his pathetic story. "Well, my mom told me from day one my voice was horrible. And, why wouldn't I believe my mother? So, I never sang in public. Then one day in college I got a little drunk at a party. Okay, I got *a lot* drunk, and this great song came on the stereo and I couldn't help myself. I started singing. When I finished the first chorus, I realized the room had hushed. I was mortified. I didn't have a lot of close friends in college and I thought, oh man, I blew it now. But...some guy sitting on the couch screamed out, "Holy shit, that girl's got some pipes!" They all started howling and carrying on, then asked me to sing something else, but a commercial came on, thank God, and I hid in the kitchen the rest of the night."

"And, that started your singing career?"

"Career? No. I met my Ex, Glen that night. I thought things were looking up for me. In all avenues. But...well, he broke up with me six months later and it did a number on my confidence. I needed to get out of my funk so I started singing to children at a library last year. But, then...I got fired." Samantha buried her head in her hands. "Why am I telling you all these embarrassing stories!"

"Embarrassing? Please. I wouldn't be surprised if I was fired soon. At least I'd know it wasn't my fault, though. Some people you just can't please. And, I can't picture you doing anything bad either. What'd you do? Sing out of key?"

Samantha's eyes widened as if he hit a nerve. *Damn*. He could never say anything right around her. He wished he didn't down those two beers. He had no problem talking to Tiara with all her sophistication and class. But, hanging with Samantha, alone in his office, or even here at a bar swigging back a few beers, he felt nervous as hell.

"Look. Forget the past. You're here tonight and you were incredible. Something changed for the better."

Samantha clutched her beer with both hands. "I've been doing a lot of changing this year. Good and bad. One night, I found the courage to come here and watch. I've actually seen Roger play quite a few times. He's really good. I watched others sing, play guitar, one girl sings and dances her ass off. I couldn't go up there, though. So I just watched. For weeks."

"Then..."

"I had a bad day. A bad weekend. Oh, who am I kidding? Everything just came to a head and I lost it. I couldn't continue down that path anymore. I had to start doing things for myself, and stop putting so much thought into everything."

Cooper looked at her second beer. It was almost empty. Her words flew out and the babbling continued. He had no idea what she was talking about, but wondered if all the gossip he overheard was true.

"I got really pissed off one night, about a month and a half ago. With a bunch of people. I knew it was time. Even if I failed, I had to do it. Okay, well, no one ever failed on stage. Some aren't that good, but no one ever boos you or anything. Anyway, I watched for a good hour, forced myself to write my name on the signup sheet, and had a beer. I was afraid to drink the second one in case I got too buzzed, so after the first one, I handed my second beer to the guy next to me. Asked him if he wanted it. That guy happened to be Roger."

Samantha finished off her glass and pushed it away. The MC announced the next act and applause took over.

"Want one more?" Cooper glanced at his watch. "It's only nine-thirty." She hesitated, but before she could say no, he ordered the summer ale. The bartender handed him both, and Cooper slid one over to her.

"Thanks. If I can't function tomorrow, I'll be marching into your office."

"Good. I'm looking forward to it." Cooper winked.

Samantha sat up straight and avoided his eyes. She took a large gulp of her beer and the foam speckled her upper lip. Her tongue licked it off slowly, and then it was Cooper's turn to look away. *Mental note:* never drink with your co-worker. Especially one that intrigues you so damn much. He had yet to figure this woman out.

"So, I sat at that corner table counting down the three people ahead of me. As the girl before me finished, I thought I was going to be sick. My fingers were trembling." Samantha held out her left hand to demonstrate.

Her black nail polish triggered heated, sexual thoughts, reminding him of the black leather dress she wore in his office that night. "Then they called your name." His words soared out, attempting to mask the images in his head.

"I was so scared, Cooper." She let go of the beer and her cold hand gripped his forearm. "I could barely walk to the stage. There was no music, but I knew the song by heart. I started singing John Mellencamp's "I Need a Lover," and in less than thirty seconds, Roger jumped on stage and started playing his guitar. Seeing him next to me, supporting me, I instantly calmed down. I sang that song and then another and, Cooper, I can't even begin to explain what it felt like when everyone started clapping and screaming!"

Samantha sounded buzzed now and he felt bad. Had she had anything to eat? "I'm glad you had the courage to go up. You were amazing." He smiled, but her face turned cold.

"Why are you being so nice to me?" She shook her head. "Are you drunk?'

"I...no. I'm always nice."

"Not to me. You pick on me."

"No, I don't. When?"

"Every single day."

Cooper casually pulled the beer away from her. "Name one time."

"You told Roselyn on me. Gave me dirty looks whenever I went in the kitchen. You insulted me that night in your office. The whole time I was supervising you either teased me or completely ignored me..."

Cooper raised his eyebrows. He had no idea. Did he come off that callous? He thought back on the stress in his life over the past year and wondered if he acted like an ass to everyone? "I'm sorry if you thought that, but it wasn't my intention."

"What was then?"

"Roselyn puts too much pressure on me. Makes me feel like I have to prove myself 24/7. No matter how much I do, it's not good enough. I guess I came off as unfriendly, but—"

"You did. No matter how much I did for you, you were cold. Even laughed at me!"

Cooper finished the last of his beer, and more clapping thundered around him. Obviously, he'd done nothing right in life. "I'm sorry. I am. Not sure if you know, but since you guys were without a kitchen manager for five weeks, Roselyn was desperate and gave me the job reluctantly. Said she only hired managers with bachelor's degrees, and, well, I only made it through my third year. I never finished."

"I didn't realize that mattered."

"To her it does. She said she'd give me the job, but I had to prove myself, otherwise when my probation was over, I'd be out. I've worked long hours, weekends. It never seems to be enough. Like she wants me to fail."

"I'm starting to think Roselyn only cares about herself. I worked fifty different jobs and she never said anything to me. I better get a huge raise."

"Kenneth's like a God to her. When he helped in the kitchen before she hired me, I heard she bragged about him."

"She did. Every day we had to hear how he was busting his butt for the department and we should follow his lead. Meanwhile, I have no idea what Roselyn does all day."

Cooper opened his mouth—

"I'm not saying she doesn't have a lot on her plate, but we're her backbone."

"Agreed, but she doesn't see it that way. I'm surprised I'm still employed."

"Why didn't you finish college? If you don't mind me asking." Samantha glanced down at her pink pie.

He wished he had ten more beers in front of him. "Family."

"Huh?" Samantha reclined in the stool and folded her arms. The eyeballs on the pink pie popped above them. They looked like they were giving him a seductive look.

Cooper leaned his left elbow on the counter, his head in his hand. "My father...he died when I was ten."

"Oh, I'm so sorry. That must've been awful. I don't even know what to say."

She looked genuinely concerned so he continued. "As you saw, I have three older sisters. My dad was my life, and after three daughters he was thrilled to have a son. We hung out all the time and he took me to all my baseball games. Whenever we went somewhere as a family, it was always the two of us and we'd run off and leave the ladies to do their girlie stuff. When he died, I was...I can't even explain it. Just devastated."

Samantha placed her hand over his. This time warmth radiated from her touch and traveled up his arm, comforting and protecting him.

"I was much younger than my sisters and I knew I was an oops, but at that moment I realized why I was born. To help out after my father died."

Samantha shot him a blank look. "You can't really believe that can you?"

"Sure. It made perfect sense. I became the man of the family. My mom and my sisters' lives became my responsibility."

"At ten-years-old? Cooper, I really don't think that's why you were born. I feel we all have a purpose on earth. Not sure what mine is yet, but I doubt that's what yours is. He wouldn't make a ten-year-old take care of his entire family. If that were the case, you'd have be born first."

"No. You're wrong! That's why."

"How does a ten-year-old take care of four older women?"

"I did everything I could. Learned to fix things and mowed the lawn. Cleaned. I even became a whiz at helping them with their problems during dinner. *Shit*. Girls have so much drama in their lives."

Samantha laughed. It was a rarity. He wished he heard it more. That he could be the one to make her laugh. The eyeballs on her shirt appeared to wink at him.

"What does that have to do with college though?"

"I was almost through my third year when my older sister, Jasmine, told me she was getting divorced. Her husband just picked up and left. Left her with a house and a three-year-old. I was there all the time. Then my second sister, Lindsay, got pregnant. Not married. 'Daddy' was a big loser and after their daughter was born, split. My mom tried to help Lindsay, but she worked full time and had her own house to take care of. Lindsay had a hard time keeping up with work, her apartment, and her daughter. My youngest sister, Hannah, is getting married next year. In Jamaica. One of those destination weddings." He shook his head. "It's a nightmare. Don't ever do one."

She squinted and sucked in her lips. "Again, what does any of this have to do with college?"

Cooper played with the damp napkin. The crowd grew silent at the sweet voice of the young singer. "I didn't have the time. Fixing things at Jasmine's house. Helping my mom. Lindsay always needed someone to watch her daughter. Helping Hannah with the wedding…"

"Why's this your responsibility? They're grown women. You're not their husbands."

His body tensed. "I just told you. I'm responsible for them. I have to help."

Samantha recoiled. She rolled her eyes and looked at her watch. *Shit*. There he was being an ass again. "Sorry. Let's just drop it."

"Look, I really need to go." She hopped off the barstool and pulled the T-shirt down over her hips.

"No. Wait. I'm taking my anger out on you. I'm Sorry."

"You do that a lot. Try taking it out on them. Obviously they're causing your stress."

"Please don't go." Cooper stood, tossed a few bills on the bar, and then grabbed her arm. Samantha scowled. He pulled away just as quick. "I want to know more about your singing. About you."

Samantha removed the rubber bands from her hair and raked her fingers through the pigtails. "Don't you have to run home to Tiara? I'm sure she needs you, too."

His breath hitched. The eyeballs on the pie appeared to frown now. "Tiara and I aren't together anymore. I broke up with her tonight."

Chapter 24

Samantha slipped the two rubber bands into the front pockets of her jeans. If Cooper stared at her chest one more time, she'd kick him in the balls. He'd been ogling her chest all night.

The three beers rushed through her bloodstream. Too buzzed to drive, but she had to get away from this ass. Luckily, her initial embarrassment of him seeing her perform had vanished. Singing belonged to her and she wouldn't let anyone ruin that ever again. She chose an acoustic night far from her hometown, far from everyone. Or, so she thought. Of all bars, Cooper managed to find her. What were the chances? Maybe he really was stalking her. Hopefully, he'd never show up again.

For the first time all year, Samantha found something she could call her own. She felt comfortable in the Déjà Vu bar and escaped here every Tuesday to sing. She could be herself and made a few new friends along the way. Friends that didn't care what she looked like, what she drank, or what she talked about.

She enjoyed wearing faded jeans and her funky T-shirts again. Glad to drink beers and not the syrupy drinks Cara made her buy. She loved being silly, and joking around with the other performers. No one laughed at her or made her feel like she had to be someone else. She finally fit in. This is who she was and Cooper was not going to take that from her.

She searched the bar, but most of her friends had left. She shoved her hands into her back pockets, digging for her car key and caught Cooper's eyes wander to her chest again. That was it.

"Do you have serious issues?"

"Huh?" He looked genuinely confused.

"How many times are you going to look at my boobs?"

"What? No! I wasn't...I was looking at your..." He stammered while his hands flew around wildly, pointing at her chest and then making their way back toward his sides. "They're looking at me."

"What! How dare you. They're not things. And they don't look at people, so stop looking at them! You did the same thing that night in your office."

"No. The eyeballs. On the pie. The eyeballs are giving me dirty looks. They're kinda real."

Samantha looked down at her T-shirt. With her hands buried deep into her back pockets, her boobs stuck out like she'd done it on purpose. The eyeballs appeared to be staring up at her. She ripped her hands out of the jean pockets and folded them over her chest. Then glanced down again. The pie appeared to be suffocating under her embrace. This whole thing was humiliating. Why'd he always bring out the worst in her? He never failed to see her at her lowest.

Realizing her mistake, Samantha lowered her hands, and huffed. "I'm sorry. I thought…"

"I'm sorry. I really wasn't…"

"I know. I know. What were you saying, now? You broke up with Tiara?" She found it hard to believe Tiara would let him break up with her. She appeared to be the type to break up with her men. Maybe she had, but Cooper refused to admit it. Damn macho men.

"Can we sit back down? There's an empty table right there."

Samantha looked at her watch. Torn between being too buzzed to drive home, and wanting to run from the one man that caught her making a fool of herself all the time, tugged at her.

"Please. I promise I won't look at your pie again." His eyebrows whisked up and down, as his play on words made her hide her face in her palms. *This was not happening.*

She ducked her head and proceeded to the front entrance. The heavy wooden door resisted her pull. She grabbed with both hands and it suddenly opened with ease. Cooper had both hands around the edge, helping it along.

"Hey, Samantha! Great set tonight!" Chuck, one of the regulars, re-entered the bar and gave her a high-five.

"Thanks."

"You really should try Thursday nights. You could win some serious cash. Hit the big leagues, why don't ya?" Chuck danced away and headed toward the bathrooms. His long, black, curly hair springing off his shoulders.

"Another boyfriend?" Cooper teased.

"No. Another friend." He seemed too eager to rip apart another piece of her life. She refused to engage him.

"What did he mean by coming here on Thursdays?"

The warm, night air sailed a breeze up her arms and lifted her hair. She'd entertain him for ten more minutes under the canopy and then she was out of here. "Tonight's just the mini night. Thursday you can compete for money. There's a much bigger crowd and you can set up with a band if you want."

"Why aren't you doing that, then?"

"Are you crazy? This is just fine. Small crowd, less people performing, no competition. I'm not here to win money."

"Sounds like you're afraid."

"I am not." *What was his problem?* He probably wanted to see her fail. Force her to come and then laugh when she came in last place. The Thursday performers, in her opinion, were trained professionals.

"Samantha. You have talent. You should come. You're really good." He placed his hand on her shoulder and gave it a light squeeze. His touch, surprisingly comforting. His chestnut eyes seemed to smolder as he peered into hers. The breeze returned and sent his persuasive cologne whisking past her nose.

What the hell? No, no, no. It was the beers. She shouldn't have drunk two beers. Or was it three? Had she had three? *Crap.* Cooper still had his hand on her shoulder. Was he planning to kiss her? Oh, God. She had to leave.

She shifted to her right, releasing his fingers from her T-shirt. "I really have to go, Cooper." She maneuvered around the blackboard easel toward the curb, but the person leaving the Dunkin' Donuts caused her to freeze. Cara stepped off the curb with a large coffee in hand. She wore black thigh-high boots, fish net stockings, a short black mini-skirt, and what looked like a black and silver, sequined bodice of some kind. What was she doing in Cairnbrook? Was this the new hot spot? Were there no places left on Long Island for Samantha to hide!

She pulled Cooper back under the bar's dimly lit canopy before Cara entered her car. Why was she here? Another romp in the sack with some guy? In that outfit? Had she no shame? Granted it was a warm night, but a light jacket could've covered up most of the get-up.

Did she buy her cocaine around here? She wondered where she was getting it. All the psychos she hooked up with, she wouldn't be surprised if Cara found a seller. How long had she been doing it?

Was she in the bar earlier? Had she seen Samantha sing? Cara had crushed every glimmering moment Samantha had this year. She wouldn't let her wreck the one thing she'd done by herself.

After Cara exited the parking lot and headed west on the main road, Samantha released a load of bottled-up air. "Whew! Thank God." She turned toward Cooper. With his chin held high, his eyebrows collapsed. He looked pissed. "What's wrong?"

"You tell me."

"I have no idea."

"Wasn't that Cara?"

"Yeah."

"Aren't you guys best friends?"

As much as she hated to think of Cara as the ideal best friend, she supposed at this point in her life she was. "Yes. So?"

"Not sure but, if I saw my friend leaving the store next to me, I'd call out their name, say hello, shoot the breeze."

Her brain scrambled for a logical excuse. She was in no mood to explain their strange friendship, or why Cara might be out here tonight. "I didn't want her to know I was here."

"Obviously. But why?" Cooper folded his arms over his mountainous chest. As fearful as she should be of this brawny man - his biceps enlarging as he tightened his grip and popped out his veins - Samantha suddenly wanted them around her body. His lips pressed together and she imagined them pressed against her own. She etched a Post-it in her brain: *Don't drink around Cooper ever again.*

"I never told her I sang. She doesn't know I come here."

"Ha!" Cooper released his arms and lifted a single eyebrow. "Nice try, but why'd you pull me away from the street lights then?"

Now Samantha was confused. "What're you talking about?"

"Obviously, you didn't want Cara to know we were hanging out. God forbid she saw us together, right? What would she think?" He stormed away and headed to the parking lot.

"Wait! Don't leave."

"Now you want me to stay?" The back of his denim-blue shirt sent her a clear warning.

"No, please. That wasn't the reason." Okay. It was part of the reason. Cara didn't hate anyone more than Cooper, and seeing Samantha with him, would've put her over the edge. What would Cara do if she thought the two of them were hanging out?

She raced to Cooper's car before he could climb in. *Slam!* Too late.

After starting his car and putting it in gear, he squeezed his eyes shut, then released them. Cooper lowered the window and gazed up at her. "Are you sure you're safe to drive home?"

Chapter 25

Cooper hauled his ass down the hall, cracking his knuckles one at a time. His shoes pounded the tile floor leading toward the kitchen. He rolled his shirt sleeves up as heat flushed through his body. Angie had asked him to assist her with something *he* had suggested months ago. Something Apollo refused to do. Now he had to help *her* with it? It was *his* idea.

This place tunneled beneath his skin like a bad case of scabies. A relentless itch, increasing over time, and this was his breaking point. How much more could he tolerate? He needed to cool off before returning to his desk. What Samantha said about his attitude, had stuck with him all night.

Cooper turned right along the corridor leading to the loading dock, when a cute, petite thing floated in through the back door. Samantha sauntered toward him with a lollipop in her mouth and her finger twirling a lock of hair.

Damn. She was the poster child for a Barbie Dream House commercial. Images of his friend's wife dressing as a sexy, little-girl for Halloween entered his mind. This was not a way to cool down. He was only getting hotter.

They both paused and stood less than two feet apart. Cooper, with a loss for words as Samantha spun the lollipop around inside her mouth. Was she teasing him? He deserved it after taking off last night. Seeing her at work today alive and in one piece eased his mind.

"Good morning, Samantha. I see you made it into work. Not too hung over are we?"

"I was about to barge into your office to complain about my roaring hangover."

"Surely, you can handle more than three beers?"

"Was getting me drunk your plan? Want to see me make a fool of myself again?"

"When have I ever seen you make a fool of yourself?" He raised his palms searching for an answer, or a route into that mind of hers.

"Ha! Okay. Now we're into lying."

"I've never seen you make a fool of yourself and I'm not lying."

She twisted a lock of hair around her finger, and licked her lips several times. She *was* teasing him, and it was driving him crazy. No. He couldn't let this happen. Samantha continued to lick her lips forcing Cooper to shift his vision to the wad of blue gum plastered on the cement wall beside him. Roselyn would probably blame him for that as well.

He needed to change the subject before his bulge pushed any harder against his pants. "Hey. I just thought of something. We were actually talking about this a few months ago. Want to help me?"

Chapter 26

Samantha opened the back door leading into the kitchen corridor from the loading dock. Her headache and nausea from drinking too much last night beckoned her to breathe some fresh air. The blue-raspberry lollipop she bought from the gift shop alleviated her need to vomit on everyone.

She stepped into the hallway, but her nausea returned. Cooper. In no mood for his crap, she tugged on a chunk of hair and wound it around her fingers wishing it were his neck. The harder she pulled, the better she felt. To avoid speaking to him, she rotated the lollipop around in her mouth and chewed on it. A piece of hair caught on her sticky lips though, and she tried desperately to remove it with her tongue. She let go of the chunk of hair, and as she reached up to remove the annoying strand glued to her lip, Cooper requested her in his office with yet another task.

Apart from the headache and nausea, she caught Lou's stink eye as she entered the kitchen. What had she seen in that pea-brain? She trudged into Cooper's office and the scent of his cologne in the small, enclosed area, something that normally drove her crazy, made her stomach kink and coil. Maybe she shouldn't have eaten those runny eggs this morning.

"Remember when I talked about redoing the cafeteria menu and putting some healthy fare up there?"

"Yup. And you said Apollo wouldn't listen to you."

"Well he's gone."

"Really? I hadn't noticed!" Her sarcasm echoed in the room. Despite his somewhat kind nature this morning, she still didn't trust him. The room spun. She closed her eyes and inhaled through her nose.

"Angie asked me to help her plan out the cafeteria menu and salad bar."

Samantha leaned forward and quirked an eyebrow. "Why can't she?"

"Remember? Angie doesn't know the first thing about healthy choices, pairing the right foods together, making the plate colorful, choosing fruits and vegetables that're in season..."

"And you do?"

"I was working toward my B.S. in Hospitality Management." He flicked *his* eyebrows now.

"Impressive. Who would have known?"

"That's how I got into body building, eating healthier—"

The charred smell of burnt sausage competed with the distinct scent of fish crisping in butter. With her lollipop long gone, she thought of finishing the meeting outdoors in the fresh air before Cooper witnessed her vomiting. "I was wondering about that." She swallowed the sour taste in her mouth. "How do you have time to work out, but not go to school?"

"Working out for a half hour a day is a lot different than spending hours in a classroom, typing up term papers, studying for exams. And, hey. I have some priorities, you know. Plus, it keeps me sane."

"You're sane?" She rolled her eyes.

"Ha, ha. You're hysterical." A devilish smirk twinkled across his face.

As much as she wanted to punch him in the face, he could be cute when he wanted to. "What do you need me to do this time, Cooper?"

****

A week later, Samantha had plans to meet with Cooper at the end of the day. She stopped in the diet office to dump her books only to find Cara had already left. Two hours ago. God forbid she let her know. Their friendship wavered between Cara ignoring her, to running into work with great news about having paid off her car loan. She never knew what mood she'd be in.

Last week, Samantha asked Cara to borrow her spare calculator. When she reached into her drawer, Cara flipped out grabbing her wrist aggressively. But, not before Samantha saw the tiny bottles of alcohol in the drawer.

She tried to speak to Cara about it when they left work, but she blew up on Samantha and told her to mind her own business. To stop being a nag and maybe if she drank too, she wouldn't be such a bore. Samantha didn't mention it again.

Samantha carried her menu ideas into the kitchen at four-thirty, right when the dinner line began. Despite the hospital's air-conditioning, the humidity and multiple operating ovens, won out. With the staff occupied on the tray line, and Lou getting ready to leave, she slipped into Cooper's office and closed the door behind her.

"Hiding again?" Cooper asked. "Don't want anyone to know you're in here?"

In spite of his playful tone, she knew he was half-serious. She opened the door and pushed the doorknob flush against the wall. Then, shoved an old adding machine with the paper roll still attached, along the bottom of the door for emphasis. To prove she wasn't hiding their meeting, she strolled over to the window, reached up, and yanked on the blind's cord. The pieces of plastic slid up in a wild slapping rhythm, causing Bruce to look up from his position on the tray line. Samantha crossed her eyes and stuck her tongue out at him.

"Are you finished?" Cooper drummed his fingers across the desk.

Before she could answer, her eyes caught sight of the animal on his desk. "What the hell is that?"

"My pet rabbit." He petted the thing as if it were real. There on his desk, was a large cantaloupe with banana halves as legs. His head was made out of a turnip, with two carrots as his ears, olives as eyes.

"I've been slaving away all week creating menus for you while you make vegetable animals?"

"I have many talents." He wiggled his eyebrows.

She was afraid to find out what they were. "Anyway. I created a month's worth of menu ideas."

"Good. I can't stand looking at the food up there anymore." Cooper made a gagging noise.

"I know! What was that for lunch today? It looked like a bunch of chicken legs taped together, and some gross, gelatinous dressing oozing from them."

Cooper laughed at her description, then covered his mouth to prevent pineapple juice from spewing out. "You'll never see it again. Show me what you got, darlin'."

Her insides tingled from his enthusiastic grin. "Um, all items on here are healthy, colorful, and appealing to the eye. A vegetarian option every day. Fish twice a week…" She babbled on while Cooper sat quietly. In addition to her voice trembling, her legs shook. Why wasn't he saying anything? Were her ideas horrible?

Cooper reached over and tapped her fingertips. Was he trying to hush her without the employees seeing? She could hear it now: *This is too much work. This isn't doable. You wasted an entire week on this?*

"I don't get it." He leaned back in his chair and it squeaked.

"Get what?" *How stupid she was? How she could possibly be a dietitian with these dreadful ideas?*

"I've never met anyone like you. You go out of your way for people. Above and beyond, as far as I'm concerned. But, you don't ask for anything in return. You have a good heart, and your passion for things really shows through. With your patients, working on that damn tray line, singing, making up these menus on your *spare time*, I'm sure."

Despite his compliments, her face scrunched up. "And I don't get you. You pick on me every chance you get, but then flip and praise me."

"I don't pick on you. You take everything personally. Joking around with you is not making fun of you. I really admire you. Whether you believe me or not. You're just…different."

Different. Here we go again. She was tired of being different. Why couldn't she blend in with everyone else?

Someone appeared in the doorway and Samantha turned her head.

"I'm done, boss. Need anything else from me?" Lou removed his work gloves and tossed Samantha a knowing look.

Why did he care if she was talking to Cooper? They hadn't spoken to each other in almost two months. Did Bruce tell him she was in here? Was he jealous? According to Lou, he got a new girl every week.

"Nope. Enjoy your weekend, Lou. Catch ya Monday." Cooper trailed his eyes over to Samantha and then back at Lou. "Oh, and thank you for all your help this week. It's greatly appreciated. The storeroom runs incredibly well because of you." Cooper smiled, but it seemed forced.

Lou looked at him like he was on crack, then sauntered away.

"Laying it on a little thick, eh?" Samantha leaned her head onto her palm.

"Just taking advice from you, that's all. Trying to leave my stress outside."

"Good. No one likes to get picked on."

"Especially you, right?" He grabbed his pet rabbit and walked it across the table toward her. All four banana legs fell off.

Samantha let out a bout of hysterics and curled over. Cooper ripped off one of the olive eyes, tossed it in the air and caught it in his mouth. "Yup. Lots of talents."

"I can see that. What else do you have up your sleeves?" *Besides those huge muscles.*

Cooper smirked but didn't answer. "I have a couple of ideas, too. I looked at pricing for several items to see if we can swing it. Want to hear them?" His once harsh eyes appeared gentler now, almost calling her.

"Sure. Of course." Samantha shifted in her seat. Why was Cooper having this effect on her? And, this time she wasn't drunk. His eyes, his touch, his smile, stirred something inside her.

He spread out several sheets of paper and leaned in close. The large open window quickly transformed into a portal to her private thoughts. Could the employees tell what she was feeling as Cooper leaned his shoulder closer to hers? His descriptions blurred as she noticed her beating heart more than what he was saying.

"...complete with theme days. Stir-fry one day a week, and maybe alternate that with a pasta dish made while you wait. Lots of steamed veggies. We can have healthy desserts instead of those mushy doughnuts..."

Images of his almost entirely naked body in this room seemed like years ago. Why hadn't she felt this way about him before? Had he changed? Had she? What about the day he stood outside the diet clerk office staring at her? That tight aqua shirt pressed against his chest. What did he want to say? He called the diet office later on, after Apollo attacked her, but she never found out why.

"Then we can make fresh soups daily. I researched it and the cooks have the time and I thought we could have lots of fiber-rich varieties, with beans and vegetables..."

He protected her afterward by letting Roselyn know, jeopardizing his own job while still on probation. You never knew what reaction Roselyn would have. She could've turned on Cooper and fired him for starting rumors about Apollo.

"I color-coded everything to insure there wasn't a whole 'plate of white' staring back at you. I was also thinking we can..."

Then that night at Déjà Vu. She was too shocked, not to mention drunk, to notice this handsome creature in front of her. Too busy with her own problems to realize Cooper had a mountain of troubles himself. How hard did he have it in here, and at home?

Why had her feelings toward Cooper suddenly changed? Or, were they always there? Buried beneath Cara's hatred for him, too busy trying to win over Lou, and worrying what everyone might think?

And, why had he broken up with Tiara?

Cooper looked like an excited puppy now, as he poured his heart out with his brilliant ideas.

"Why didn't you get Apollo's job?" Her eyes narrowed.

"Huh?"

"She should've given it to you. You helped get rid of that vile manager. You have the background. The great ideas. Why did Angie get it?"

Cooper leaned back and merely sighed.

"I thought you said Roselyn only hired managers with college degrees."

He gave a weak shrug. "She does. And Angie has one."

"She does? Then why's she a kitchen supervisor?"

"She couldn't find a job."

Samantha tilted her head. "What's her degree in?" Her tone uncertain.

Cooper stared at the ceiling. "Philosophy and religious studies."

Now Samantha leaned back in her chair. There was nothing to say. Absolutely speechless.

"Yup. My thoughts exactly. Now, shall we finish?"

"Wait. No. That's not fair. Three years of hospitality management trumps religious history."

"Not according to Roselyn. No degree, no promotion. Oh, and another reason - I was still on probation."

Samantha's mouth flew open. How could Cooper sit there so calmly? His whole tough-guy façade dissolved and she saw the beaten down man.

"Look, Samantha. For whatever reason, she's searching for an excuse to fire me. I won't go down without a fight. I know I'm an intelligent, hard-working man. She'll realize one day."

This was so unfair. Samantha would do whatever it took to ensure the cafeteria menus made Cooper shine. Roselyn would have nothing bad to say about him then.

"Hey. What are you doing next Saturday?" Cooper's eyes lit up and he pushed the dead rabbit aside. The turnip head fell off and rolled onto the floor next to the adding machine. "Are you free? I'm doing the health fair in the Stop & Shop parking lot with a bunch of other departments. One of our cooks is preparing a dish, but I could use help handing out the food, the flyers, recipes, and other brochures for the hospital."

"Aren't you getting sick of me yet?" she teased.

Cooper bent closer, his cheeks seemed to glow. He focused on Samantha without blinking once. "Darling, I'm just getting started."

Chapter 27

Samantha helped Cooper and Jonathan, the head chef, lug boxes of pamphlets and assorted machinery to their assigned tables at the Stop & Shop supermarket in the town of Eastcliff. The late September air, still warm, had a wicked wind that picked up every so often, tossing her hair up and into her face, while flipping the handouts of other departments off their tables and across the asphalt parking lot.

Cooper had provided Jonathan with a wonderful butternut squash and Israeli couscous salad recipe to prepare today. The vivid colors alone could tempt you. The bright cranberries and hunter green of the Swiss chard, along with the feta cheese and splashes of orange from the squash, lit up the bowl.

While Cooper and Jonathan set up the ingredients and cookware, Samantha tackled the brochures and copies of the recipe. Each time Samantha placed a stack of papers down, the wind teased and whipped the corners up. She glanced around at the other departments that were trying desperately to find objects to hold their papers in place, too.

Samantha grabbed several cans of Ensure and placed them on top of each stack, wishing she had something a little more attractive. Luckily, she had the handouts photocopied in various colors to bring interest to the otherwise boring table. She hoped the free food would draw the crowd over. Roselyn drilled it in them that she wanted no one sitting around, and expected all literature to be handed out, otherwise they weren't doing their jobs.

Once Jonathan placed the ingredients in the bowl, seasoned, and stirred, Cooper removed tiny paper cups from the plastic packaging and began filling them with the colorful salad. To see such a huge, muscular man play with such minuscule cups brought a chuckle to her throat. He looked like he was serving expresso at a fancy restaurant.

Cooper looked up. "What's so funny?" His right eyebrow collapsed, squinting at her.

"I'm just surprised that such big, strong hands can play with such dainty, delicate things."

Cooper stood up straight and smirked. "You'd be surprised what these hands could do." Then he tossed her one of his winks. "They can be gentle and rough. Especially with dainty things."

Samantha immediately turned her head to hide her obviously flushed face. She bent over to grab another can of Ensure, when an arm grazed hers.

"Let me help you with that." Cooper reached into the box and grabbed two at a time in each palm. His right arm slid along Samantha's and then he purposely let his face linger only two-inches from hers.

The minty scent of his gum, as he parted his lips ever so slightly, locked her in place. She stiffened, unable to remove her gaze from his amber eyes, suddenly noticing his pouty lower lip. "Thank you," was all she could breathe out.

Samantha placed her can on the purple recipe stack, and Cooper piled the other four cans on top of each other creating a tower. With her right hand she snatched a tiny cup filled with salad and placed it on the top can. "Let's see if you can do a shot of it without using your hands." She raised her chin a few times, nudging him on.

Cooper's eyebrows squished together at first, but within five seconds of the dare, he linked his hands behind him and leaned in, clamping down on the cup with his teeth. He hesitated a few more seconds, contemplating his move, then in one swish, flicked his head back and caught most of the salad in his mouth. A stray piece of squash clung to his closed eyelid.

Before he could unclasp his hands and remove it, Samantha reached up and plucked it off. His eyes opened slowly, taking her in. He moved the salad around inside his mouth, but his eyes remained on her. *What was he thinking about?* As inept as she felt, she couldn't take her eyes off Cooper, as if his hypnotic gaze held her in place. Her heart rate sped up.

"I should have known not to let the two of you work together. It's becoming more and more obvious to me now." Roselyn stood before them with an empty shopping cart in her grip.

Cooper and Samantha both froze in their tracks. *What the heck was she doing here?*

"I thought I'd do my shopping here today to show support, but it appears you two are just goofing off. All the other display tables are up and ready and the two of you are playing with the food."

Samantha waited for Cooper to explain, but the shock of it all kept him silent. "We're all done, as a matter of fact." Samantha bluffed her way through the torture. "All the flyers are out and Jonathan finished preparing the salad. Cooper filled all the cups, and Jonathan's adding spoons to them." Just then, a huge gust of wind blew several handouts off their table. Samantha rushed over to save them.

Roselyn huffed. She was not fooled or amused. She ignored Samantha and glared at Cooper. "I expect to hear big things from our table. I want word to get back to me that is was a huge hit. Do I make myself clear?"

Cooper nodded. "Of course."

Roselyn turned back to Samantha. "As for you, I'm not sure why I keep agreeing to let you help him. Obviously, he can't do anything on his own. That's not displaying great leadership skills."

Samantha opened her mouth, but as Roselyn turned to leave, Cooper seized her arm. "Don't." He let go and walked away, resuming the task of filling the small cups. Their size difference didn't seem that far removed anymore.

Her heart crushed after witnessing Roselyn's criticism of him for the first time. None of Cooper's recounts could accurately describe the way Roselyn had just scowled at him as if he was an unmanageable child. She tried to think of something to say to him, anything, but she was as tongue-tied as he was.

The three of them remained quiet while they finished filling the cups with the salad, sticking spoons in each one, and ensuring the flyers stayed put. At eleven o'clock, the health fair began and store customers, as well as families that saw signs as they drove by, began walking up and down the aisles.

Nurses took blood pressures, while children bounced in the giant bouncy house. A massage booth was set up to do neck massages, as children had their faces painted and ate red and blue snow cones. Physical therapy and cardiac rehab explained the importance of exercise, keeping active, proper stretching techniques, and promoted their walk/jog event in two weeks. Local chiropractors, dentists, and the fire department provided important preventative safety measure for all visitors.

Everyone flocked to the nutrition booth when they heard they were giving away free food, and Cooper and Samantha tried desperately to keep up with the demand, while Jonathan continued to make more salad. When they had filled multiple cups, Samantha persuaded visitors to take free diet literature. They glanced at the nutrition papers, smiled apologetically and grabbed the food instead. Several papers she had given away, ended up tossed to the ground.

If they returned with all this literature, Roselyn would know they failed. She could throw it in the garbage, but the thought of tossing such great information pained her. Cooper glanced at the stack of literature they still had and tried hard to smile. A boy around ten grabbed a can of Ensure and took off with it. Before she could react, the wind soared and set the papers sailing again. This was a fiasco.

An hour later, with the majority of her flyers still in their same spots, a large group of children came skipping down the aisle. Samantha clutched a stack of "Healthy Snacks for Kids" literature and stepped in their way. She began swaying from side to side with the handouts held up to her chest, and then, as if by reflex, opened her mouth.

"Fruit salad, yummy, yummy." The words exploded from her mouth and the children immediately stopped in their tracks. Samantha belted out The Wiggles song she had sung a million times at the library. She pretended to scoop fruit salad out of her imaginary bowl and a little boy on her right began dancing. A girl around five shook her head, jiggling her pigtails. Samantha rubbed her belly and three more kids jumped up and down and wiggled to the song. A boy with a Mohawk started singing with her, and then the parents joined in, too.

Soon, a group of almost a dozen kids and parents were singing and pretending to eat fruit. "Peel your bananas...Toss in some grapes..." She continued to sing and shake her hips while dispensing brochures to the parents, who seemed more than happy to accept them now. Her voice rose and attracted other kids to their booth. Cooper joined in and grabbed information about the hospital, handing it to the fathers in the crowd. Then, without missing a beat, Jonathan grabbed a platter of salad cups and offered them to anyone that approached. With more children joining in, Jonathan, who had a son of his own, attempted to sing as well, while Samantha distributed literature about diabetes and portion sizes to the parents.

Several employees from the hospital left their posts and watched from the edges of the Nutrition tables. They grabbed a salad cup, but then glanced at their nutrition literature and decided some of it was actually worthwhile. They picked a few pamphlets and walked away with them.

"Give everyone a plate and a spoon. We'll all be eating it very soon..."

Cooper, not knowing the words, danced instead. He laughed at her antics and then threw her a smile. A tiny boy, no older than two, bobbed his head back and forth, and Cooper kneeled in front of him and held his hand. The two couldn't be more different in size.

The crowd started to clap, and soon everyone sang the familiar chorus. Then, behind them all, towering over a group to the left, was Kenneth's head. No one else had noticed but Samantha, and her voice faltered. A few children and parents continued to sing, but without Samantha's powerful voice, the singing declined, and soon the crowd dispersed.

Cooper released the little toddlers hand and when he stood, he saw Kenneth as the crowd of at least twenty-five people separated and continued in opposite directions. Jonathan ran back to fill more cups.

What was he doing here? Had Roselyn sent him to spy on them? Samantha took off to rearrange what was left of the diet literature, but Kenneth slid in beside her and tapped her on the shoulder. She closed her eyes, took a deep breath and turned towards him.

What she was met with though, was unexpected. A huge grin spread across his face. "Samantha, that was incredible. I didn't know you could sing."

She gulped, and then faked a smile. Was he sincere? Was this a trick to get information out of her and then tell Roselyn? "Just trying to get the kids to have some fun."

"Don't be so modest. You have a great voice. And, hey. It worked. Your booth's the busiest."

"Good thing there's only an hour left. We're running low on brochures and pamphlets and it looks like the salad's almost finished, too." Good save. Fifteen minutes ago, their table was still full of handouts.

"What salad did Jonathan prepare?" Kenneth sauntered over to the glistening silver bowl filled with the colorful mixture.

"Cooper gave him the recipe, actually. It was a big hit. I had two myself." *Damn.* Was she allowed to eat the food? He'd probably tell Roselyn that, also.

Kenneth scooped up a spoonful of the salad and the mixture appeared to explode in his mouth. His eyes widened and he moaned. "Wow. This *is* good." He turned his attention to Cooper. "Where'd you get this recipe?"

Please, don't let Cooper say anything that'll get him in trouble. She couldn't bear to see him reamed out again. Would Kenneth be mad that Cooper didn't let Jonathan come up with his own recipe? Did Roselyn tell Kenneth they were goofing off and sent him to snoop?

Kenneth strolled over to Cooper and the two of them discussed the recipe. She heard Cooper mention several other recipes that he had tried in the past at various events. Samantha kept busy, attempting to eavesdrop, but the brutal wind picked up and garbled their conversation. *Be careful, Cooper. It's obviously some cruel trick to get you fired.*

After ten more excruciating minutes, Kenneth walked away from Cooper and shook Jonathan's hand. Then, waved good-bye to Samantha. She rushed over to Cooper while he emptied the remainder of the salad into the final cups. "What happened? You didn't get in any trouble, did you?"

"Not sure. It was weird. He asked me a million questions. Like he was grilling me or something. I felt like I was on a job interview."

"Do you think Roselyn sent him here to spy?"

"Seemed that way. He wasn't even asking me about the health fair. Maybe Roselyn sent him to interrogate me."

"That is strange. Maybe she called him at home and told him to get his ass over here to check on us."

"I hope not. It's bad enough I get crap from her, but is he going to ride my ass now, too?"

"Excuse me." A woman with three children stood in front of her booth motioning to the diet literature. "Do you have any handouts on lunch ideas? I give up with these three."

Samantha hurried over and searched through the remaining piles. "Here you go. Anything else?"

"What else you got?" The poor woman looked overwhelmed and desperate.

Samantha picked up one of everything and made a pile. A few other parents strolled over and before long, she had a group surrounding her with questions about after school snack ideas and healthier birthday party options. An obese mother with similar looking children, begged for nutritional advice after their pediatrician had scolded her. Glad the doctor didn't downplay the seriousness of the situation for once, she spent almost twenty minutes with the frantic mother.

Jonathan and Cooper began cleaning up their cooking station. The woman thanked her and hurried off as the wind continued to pick up. Dark clouds pulled in, warning of a possible storm. Jonathan took off with two boxes of cooking machinery and walked toward the van.

"Need any help?" Cooper asked.

"I guess we can clean up. Most of the families left after the drawing for the bicycle." Samantha lifted the box she brought the literature in and placed it on the table. Cooper chucked the eight cans of Ensure back in the boxes without thinking, and the entire display of handouts took off into the air at once. The blowing and looping sheets of paper caused an upsurge of color to fly into the sky, around and over the other tables, creating a rainbow.

Both of them stood in the line of fire. The papers smacked them in their faces and then swirled around like a tornado. Cooper had a look of panic on him, but Samantha exploded into convulsive laughter at the sight of it all. She raised her arms up high and smiled from ear to ear, then twirled around as if dancing in the rain. All Cooper could do was smile.

When the wind died down, Cooper and Samantha rushed to capture the runaway papers and scuttled across the blacktop grasping at each one. Some caught under tables, while others careened into the parking lot, lodging beneath cars. A few landed in puddles leftover from last night's storm.

Samantha's arms held the majority of flyers and then she saw a yellow one under a minivan. She looked to her right to make sure a car wasn't coming or backing out, and then crawled to the back of the van to reach underneath for it. As she leaned in to grab it, Cooper's face appeared from behind the rear tire. He bumped into her shoulder, knocking her back and onto her ass. Directly into a filthy puddle.

Before she died from embarrassment, he raced over and placed his arm gently around her back, guiding her up and towards him. Then his strong hands gripped her firmly and pulled her into his warm chest. With only a few inches between their lips, Samantha breathed heavily, glancing back and forth from his eyes to his mouth. What was happening? She could not be falling for Cooper Timmons.

Cooper stared at her with dazed silence, but refused to release her from his grasp. Her heart beat hard upon her chest, and, by the way he was breathing, his was too. Neither could speak. He let his eyes fall to her open mouth, but before he could react, a father with a toddler in a loaded shopping cart, stopped at the back of the van pressing his trunk unlock button. The van beeped breaking their spell.

"You guys all right?" The father approached, one hand on the cart and one hand reaching out to them. "Did she get hit?"

How embarrassing! Suddenly, other supermarket customers arrived offering their help.

Cooper stared at Samantha one more time, but the magic had ended. "No, I accidentally bumped into her, knocking her down."

"What were you doing under my van?" Now the father looked pissed.

"Picking up all this literature I let fly away." Cooper held up the soiled pieces of paper.

"*I* let fly away," Samantha corrected. She let Cooper lift her up and the two sauntered back to their tables where Jonathan waited for them in his own confused state. Both tables were gone, in addition to all of the supplies.

"I didn't know where you guys went." Jonathan scratched his head.

Although they were innocently retrieving the brochures, Samantha and Cooper avoided each other as they shoved the handouts into the empty box.

"A bunch of papers flew away." Cooper refused to look at either of them.

"Yes." Samantha lifted the box into her arms. "It was a total disaster." As the insensitive words left her mouth, she drew back and her eyes immediately locked on Cooper. "I mean... the papers. All over the place. It was a mess. The papers were a disaster."

Jonathan shook his head. "Look, I gotta run. Are you coming in the van...or...do you have a ride to the hospital?" He glanced back and forth between Cooper and Samantha.

Did he suspect? Suspect what? They didn't do anything. Could Jonathan read the expression on her face? Was she that transparent? If Jonathan saw it, then it was real. This was too much. She couldn't be falling for someone that teased her all the time. She already let Lou and Bruce do that. She'd never let another man treat her that way again.

"If Samantha doesn't mind driving me back, you can hit the road." Cooper looked at her. "Is it okay?"

"Sure," she blurted out. Was she crazy? She couldn't be alone with him in her car. Was it even clean? Maybe if she ran there quickly, she could chuck all her garbage into the trunk.

Chapter 28

Cooper watched Jonathan stroll toward the van with his hands in his pockets, glad the guy read his mind and took the hint. As much fun as he had with Samantha today, he didn't want it to end. They stood in the middle of a surge of hospital employees departing. Cooper reached over, grabbed the box of literature from Samantha and looked into her blue eyes. "Where's the Samantha mobile?"

"This way." She pointed.

She looked annoyed. Did he read her signals wrong? This woman captivated him with her mysterious ways, but never allowed him inside. He wanted to know everything about her, yet, she hid so much. He remembered when they first spoke. That first day in his office. Wearing that dress. She seemed so different now. Who was that other person?

He followed Samantha to her car, but she walked quickly ahead of him despite his long legs. *Great.* Now she was literally running away from him. She *was* annoyed. What would she see in him, anyway? Roselyn made him look like an idiot today, he didn't have a college degree, and he *was* mean to her when he first started. He was only trying to protect her though.

Why was he protecting her? Didn't he have enough women to take care of?

He neared her car but Samantha peered into her back seat instead of opening the doors.

"One second, let me open the trunk for you." She popped the trunk, but then opened her door, grabbed everything from the back seat and tossed it in the trunk, slamming it shut before he had the chance to walk towards it. "Never mind. You can put it in the back seat." Samantha jumped into the driver's side and started her car.

Mystery woman for sure.

He climbed into the passenger seat and watched as she nervously wrestled with her seatbelt, turned the radio on, lowered the blaring song, then attempted to turn the ignition again on her already running car. The screech from the starter cut through both their ears.

"Oh my God. I'm so sorry." She pounded her head into the

steering wheel.

He laughed. "What's wrong? Like I haven't done that a dozen times." Okay, he never did that, but the girl was obviously nervous about having him in her car. Or, maybe he was creeping her out. Why he thought he'd ever snatch a girl like Samantha, was beyond him. She was smart, cool, funny, talented, beautiful. Sexy. What did he have to offer?

They drove to the hospital in silence, except for the '80s songs streaming from her speakers. "This is really good." Cooper leaned his shoulder close to hers. "I haven't heard some of these songs since high school. I don't think a lot of them made it onto the regular radio stations. Mostly B sides, or played on college radio stations. Is it some greatest Hits CD?"

Samantha lowered the volume. "I made it. I have an entire collection of '80s CD's and a bunch of '80s greatest hits from almost every band or singer. I took my favorites from them and made a mix tape."

"You made this? Cool. Any chance I can get a copy?"

"You really like it? Or, are you just saying that, Cooper?"

Obviously, nothing he said was right. "No. I really like it. I grew up listening to this college radio station and this is all they played. It was on station 88.7 I think."

"Yes! All the way at the end of the dial. I listened to that, too. And WLIR."

"Of course, LIR. That was a must. I was obsessed with them. All new wave and punk rock. Some really great songs. And, memories."

She pulled in front of the hospital, but refused to look at him. Both hands gripped the steering wheel as if she wanted to rip it from the dashboard. Her white knuckles emphasized her obvious annoyance of him in her car.

"Thanks for the ride. Sorry you had to go out of your way. I should have taken the ride back with Jonathan. My bad. I just figured—"

"Want to get a cup of coffee?" She glanced at him finally, her mouth open and breathing hard. *Was she hyperventilating?*

"Um, well, yeah, sure. That'd be great." *Did he read her wrong?* Her odd behavior only drew him in further.

"There's one up the road."

As she pulled away from the curb, his phone vibrated. *Now what?* "Hello? Jasmine?.I didn't get any messages. I was working the health fair all day. What's wrong?" He balled his fist up and squeezed until his nails dug into the skin. "Yeah. Fine. I'll be there. On my way." He hung up the phone and turned toward Samantha.

"Sorry, but my sister had a flood in her basement from the storm last night. Apparently, she left several messages this morning, but I never looked at my phone. I have to go. Raincheck? No pun intended." He grinned.

"Yeah, sure. Whatever." Samantha made a U-turn and headed back to the hospital. She said nothing until they reached the curb. "Bye."

"Thanks again for the ride, and…oh! For helping me today. It was a lot of fun."

She sucked her lips in tight, bit down, and smiled. Annoyance burst from her eyes. Cooper hopped out, shut the door, and before he could step back, she sped down the street leaving him with only black skid marks and the stink of burning rubber.

Chapter 29

Samantha trudged into the cafeteria on Wednesday to meet with Angie and Cooper about the new cafeteria menu. She avoided Cooper the past two days and was in no mood to sit across from him now. She knew he faked that phone call in the car. What a shocker. As soon as she suggested coffee, he suddenly gets a call and has to leave? She should've known he wasn't interested in someone like her. Tiara was her exact opposite. Cara seemed more his style.

Angie and Cooper seated themselves in a front booth opposite one another. Samantha had tossed on her tight, blue suit today, feeling rambunctious. She strutted down the long aisle toward them with her head held high. *Screw him.*

Ten feet before she reached them, Cooper glanced up, right when Samantha's four-inch heel wedged in one of the broken cracks in the tile and sprung her forward. Her shoe stayed, she didn't. She leaped onto her good foot, caught herself and then hopped a few steps on the foot with the shoe. Cooper tried to stifle his laugh, then jumped up to help her. More humiliation. She didn't know how much more she could take. Keep laughing, bucko.

"Are you okay?" He let go of her arm and sat back in his seat.

"Yes. Thank you." She retrieved her shoe and slipped it on while hiding her flushed face. With both shoes squarely in place, she made her way back to the booth. Angie and Cooper sat on opposite sides, but Angie was close to the edge. In her own world. With a giant, purple bow in her hair. Samantha had no choice but to sit next to Cooper who didn't have a problem scooting over to the far corner.

"Nice of you to finally meet us." Cooper refused to look at her. "Nice suit."

Was that a compliment? Every tiny thread of body hair stood on its ends. She fought back the impending shiver.

Angie finally glanced up. "Oh, hi, Samantha. These menus look superlative."

Huh? Since when did Angie use such big words? Most of the time she sounded like she had a fifth grade reading level. How she passed college was baffling.

"Okay, so..." Cooper lifted the menu designs and spread them across the table. "Like I was saying while we were anxiously awaiting for Samantha to show up..."

Samantha gritted her teeth. What was his problem today?

"I was explaining how we now have a vegetarian option daily. Wednesdays will alternate with either stir-fry day or pasta-while-you-wait day. No more canned vegetables. Frozen or fresh will be our standard. Samantha informed me that frozen might actually have more nutrients than fresh, since we have no way of knowing how long ago the food was picked, placed in a bin, carted across country and sat in a warehouse before it arrived here."

"Exceptional idea. Radiant!" Angie beamed at them.

Who was she? Wilbur in Charlotte's web?

"Then, twice a week we'll have a fish entrée, and decrease the heavier items like meatloaf, mac and cheese, and chicken wings. Samantha ensured that all groupings of food were colorful. No more of those white chicken, mashed potato, and cauliflower entrees." Cooper flipped to the back of one paper, read the notes he had, and flipped back. "Oh, yes, and our desserts will be changing. No more soggy doughnuts or Danishes in that plastic wrap. All the icing comes off them anyway, and then temps from the steam table melt them into sludge."

"Marvelous."

Samantha had always liked Angie. Usually accommodating, and sweet, but, today she was getting on her last nerve. Was she trying to show off in front of Cooper and her? Trying to look intelligent? It made no sense. What made her angrier was that Angie did nothing to help with this project. Not one damn idea. She thought they were supposed to help her with this, not do it all.

"Finally, Samantha re-worked the entire salad bar. No more mayonnaise covered items. All fresh vegetables, fruits, three different kinds of bright green lettuces, beans, nuts, dried fruit. Colorful and eye-catching."

"Splendid and luminous!"

A hard kick came at Samantha's calf. Did Cooper just kick her? She peeked down and he did it again. She let her peripheral vision slide to the left and caught Cooper hiding a smirk behind one of the papers. He obviously thought Angie was acting weird, too. Now Samantha smirked, while Angie continued to throw her scholarly words at them.

"Fresh soups will be made daily, and will also change quarterly with the season. Why Apollo had spring vegetable soup in the winter, and roasted butternut squash soup in the middle of July is beyond me."

"My point exactly!" Angie raised her finger in the air as if she had just preached the sermon of a lifetime. *What point had she made?*

Cooper's finger glided across their seat until it wandered dangerously close to Samantha's butt. He casually glanced down, noticed where his finger was, and then moved it due north, poking her in the thigh instead. The adrenaline rush made her forget about Angie's silly words, as well as her anger toward Cooper. What's with him and his mixed signals?

"Cooper? You have a call." Eunice, one of the cafeteria employees, called him over.

Still lost in the feeling of her tingling thigh, Samantha continued to daydream.

"Um, I need to get up. To answer the phone. Unless of course you want me to climb on top of you?" Cooper winked hiding his huge grin from Angie.

"Sorry." Samantha scooted up and out. What was wrong with everyone today? Did someone sprinkle their oatmeal with narcotics?

As if the weirdness couldn't get any worse, Roselyn appeared from behind the counter and approached Angie and her. "What are the two of you up to?" Her lips pursed like she had something stuck in her front tooth.

"Just going over the new cafeteria menus." Angie lost her ridiculous speech. *Thank God.*

Roselyn frowned at Samantha. "*You're* helping again?"

What was that supposed to mean? Didn't Roselyn know she was helping? Had Cooper taken all the credit?

"I look forward to seeing them on my desk this evening. Oh, and Samantha. I need to do your evaluation. Meet me in my office at two o'clock." Roselyn turned on her heels, snatched one of the soggy doughnuts, and left.

"I'll bring the menus in later," Angie shouted to the back of Roselyn's head, displaying the biggest, fakest smile she'd ever seen.

Samantha had enough. What was the point of her being here? Couldn't Cooper explain it to Angie himself? Before she could leave, Cooper called Angie over to the phone. Now she was stuck here until one of them returned. Weren't they done anyway? At least she had her evaluation to look forward to. Something good would finally come.

She reached across and gathered the papers together, when she caught Kenneth spying on her from the grill. *Great. Now what?*

He scooted past the employees and strolled toward her. Were

they some kind of tag team? As soon as Roselyn left, she sent Kenneth over to snoop so she'd know what to criticize later?

"Good morning." He scanned the papers.

What a surprise.

"Homework?"

Yeah, right. Like she might fall for that. Act dumb. Sure. "No. They're the new cafeteria menus." *Surprise!*

"Mind if I have a look?"

That's the whole point of your coming over here, so sure. Why not. Spy away. Rip them apart. Go for it. "Of course." Samantha pushed them near him and watched as he read each page.

"You did all of these?"

"No. Mainly Cooper. I helped with the healthy, nutrient, colorful part of it." Now she was babbling. Did that even make sense?

"You were helping Angie?" Kenneth frowned.

Awesome. Her mouth kept getting them in more and more trouble. "We both were." *Good save.* "He came up with the Wednesday specialty stations, the vegetarian items, fresh soups—"

"And what did you do again?"

"I...made sure it was nutritious, healthy, high in fiber, colorful—"

"You came up with the healthier desserts?"

"No. He did that."

"The stir-fry?"

"Nope. Him again." Where was he going with all this? What did Roselyn want to know exactly? Was she going to say he should've been concentrating on his own kitchen instead of poking his head into the cafeteria?"

Kenneth remained silent and continued to examine their ideas. He flipped the pages back and forth. "Is this affordable?"

"He checked with all the vendors and our main supplier and priced everything out. He wasn't sure it would fly at first, but some of the items that we'll be making ourselves were actually cheaper than pre-made foods."

"What about man power?" Now he looked pissed.

"He made a spreadsheet and reworked their stations and it'll flow well with what he came up with. There was, um, some cooks that could use some more tasks to occupy their time. If you know what I mean." *Are you an idiot, Samantha!* Why not just tell him Cooper's cooks goof off all day. Why couldn't she keep her mouth shut? Where the hell was Cooper and Angie anyway? She glanced over her shoulder and they were both gone. *Dammit.*

"Okay. Looks like you did your homework. Thanks." Kenneth

rose and walked back towards the office, but not before he sneered at the mushy doughnuts.

As if on cue, Cooper returned. "Where were you? First Roselyn shows up, then Kenneth."

"They did? What'd they want? You didn't show them the menus, did you?"

Now she was dead. Why Cooper even associated with her was beyond reason. Images of her tripping in front of him less than twenty-minutes ago, resurfaced. "Kenneth saw them. Roselyn looked like she couldn't care less."

"Of course not. Especially when you have an assistant manager to do all the spying for you. What a little rat he is. How can he follow behind her like some baby duckling and do all her dirty work?"

"Well, you said they were sleeping together, right?"

"I don't know that for sure. Just from what I've seen and heard. She won't let him leave her side. He's in her office all day. The door's always locked. Why lock your door? Why tell your secretary not to bother you? They're probably doing it on her desk!"

Samantha grimaced, then laughed. "Ew! Maybe that's why she doesn't have any knick-knacks or picture frames on her desk. Too much to remove every afternoon."

"Ha ha! My point exactly!" Cooper raised his finger, mocking Angie.

"Yes! What was all that about?"

"No clue. Maybe she felt bad for not helping us. I asked her several times, though."

"You did? I didn't realize." Chairs scraped across the floor as several employees cleaned up from the afternoon rush.

"Yup. She kept saying she was swamped and would stop in tomorrow. Then, proceeded to say that every day. I gave up."

"You said she had no background in it. Maybe she felt stupid." Samantha *tsk'd* her tongue and shook her head.

"That's what I figured, too. I didn't mean to embarrass her. I wanted her included in the process. Now I feel bad."

"I know. You're a good guy. When you're not an ass." She bit down on her lip to hide the expanding grin.

"An ass, huh?" Cooper leaned in pretending to gather up the papers, but came within six-inches of her face. Since she was already leaning over the table, it looked like he wanted to kiss her. Samantha flinched, her eyes widened. The adrenaline rush returned. He noticed her uneasiness and leaned back into his seat.

She needed to leave. "I have to get back to work."

"Already?" He sprang up with her.

"Unless...there was something else?"

He sighed, appeared to gaze at her like they were in some romantic movie, eyed her suit up and down and then looked away. "No. I guess that's it. I'll give these to Angie when she returns and have her hand them to Roselyn. I'm in no mood for her to rip my ideas apart again. Let Angie deal with the criticism. That's the least she can do since we did all the work."

"Good idea."

"Watch your heel on the way out." He nodded to the tile she had tripped on.

Could she get through one day without him witnessing some act of shame?

****

Samantha stopped in the bathroom after lunch, then checked in with the diet office before heading to Roselyn's office. Cara sat there playing with the cord on the phone.

"Hey," Cara moaned like a bored child at a pencil museum. "Your turn?"

"What?" Samantha pretended to look for something in her drawer.

"Your eval? I just had mine."

Yeesh. How'd that go? Surprised Cara wasn't fired. "You did? How was it?"

"What I expected. Two percent raise." Cara's cheekbones poked out beneath her skin.

"I'm sorry."

"Why? I barely showed up for work every day. Didn't do much when I was here either."

"Oh." What could she really say? She couldn't help feeling bad, though. Cara had so many bills.

"Good luck." Cara smiled, looking genuinely happy for Samantha's effort and hard work this past year. Where had their friendship gone? She missed her. Missed the support they used to give each other.

Samantha knocked on Roselyn's door, then entered after a brusque "come in." Had Cara pissed her off? She could only imagine.

Not wasting any time, Roselyn shoved her evaluation at her, then continued to rummage through her personal day timer. She penciled in "Hair appointment, 10:00 a.m." for this Saturday.

Not a word. Unbelievable.

Samantha scanned the first two pages, then flipped back to the cover to see if *her* name was written on top. It was. The pain in her jaw - immediate. She skipped to the end, then back to the third page and her throat constricted.

Key words stood out. *Meets* needs. *Adequately* performs functions. Communicates *satisfactorily.* *Acceptable* time management. *Follows orders* and takes direction. *Capable* of working independently. *Reasonable* leadership skills.

Then the final page. Two percent raise. Two…percent? The same as Cara. The paper trembled in her hands and the words blurred. The bottom crumbled under her tense grip.

Roselyn sighed. "Are you done yet?"

"I thought…"

"It's the same one every year, Samantha. You'd think you'd be able to blow through it by now."

But this year was different. "Yes, but…"

"But, what?" Roselyn slipped her arms through her blazer. "Last page. Where it says employee signature. Make sure you write the date, too. I have to hand these all in by this evening."

Samantha swallowed hard. The pen threatened to bend in her quivering fist where all her anger and resentment gathered. Was she that insignificant, even to her boss? She signed her name reluctantly, wanting to tell Roselyn off. Wanting to tell her how lucky she was to have an employee like her. Someone with great ideas, resourceful, reliable, diligent.

But she didn't.

****

Samantha left her patient floor at 4:15 p.m. and made her way to the office, dying to get the hell out of here. She passed the nurse's station, rounded the corner and spied Bruce leaning against a wall with his back to her. An innocent new aide stood in front of him.

"Baby. You're so hot, I could bake cookies on you."

Samantha made an obvious, loud barfing sound and flew past them. She pushed on the stairwell door, stepped in and walked down five steps. She dug into her lab coat. Where was her beeper? She climbed back up the five steps, opened the door, but then let go and reached into her lab coat pockets one more time. Nope. She felt her right hip, thinking she clipped it to her waist when she removed her lab coat earlier, but it wasn't there. After switching her binder to her right hand, she patted her left hip, and there it was. She unclipped it and tossed it into her pocket.

She turned to resume her six-flight descent when she heard a noise. She paused, listened, but when she convinced herself the sound came from the corridor, the noise came again. From above. A low hum. Or moan. Yes, a moan. After looking up the set of stairs that lead to the roof, she listened more intently.

Uhhhh.

It came again. Was someone hurt? A construction worker climbing on the roof? One of their engineering employees? Had someone fallen? Or, had a patient escaped and collapsed on the landing above? She wanted to get help first, but decided to investigate quickly. Samantha tiptoed up four stairs when a low giggle floated down. Then the moan again.

She took two more steps, then froze. Each step took her closer to what appeared to be Dr. Chambers leaning against the wall near the opening to the roof. Was he hurt? His eyes were closed, his hands were by his side. Was he high? Tripping off some meds he stole, along with the food he continued to swipe from the kitchen? Then she thought of all the gossip about the residents doing drugs, coke specifically, to keep awake during their shifts. Was this some overdose of some kind?

Her feet edged up two more steps and then she recoiled. Disbelief locked her feet in place. Her heart beat so hard she thought for sure she would lose balance and fall backwards. She grabbed the handrail as her mouth flung open. No. It couldn't be. She heard so many crazy stories, but to see her in action, proved to be too much. There was Cara, kneeling on the hard floor in her skirt, giving Dr. Chambers a blowjob.

Samantha quietly, without turning, stepped back down the stairwell, keeping her eyes on Dr. Chambers the entire time. *Please don't open your eyes. Please don't look over. Please, please don't see her.* But, before she reached the final step, Dr. Chambers, obviously reaching his high-point, flung his eyes wide-open and caught Samantha moving in the corner of his eye. His head shot in her direction, but once he realized it was just little old her, a devilish smirk grew on his face. What an ass! Did he think Samantha already knew about their little trysts? Why wasn't he stopping Cara? The pig! It was always about them.

When her feet finally unglued themselves, and Samantha proceeded to turn away, Dr. Chambers had the nerve to wink at her, let out a silent exaggerated belly laugh, and then give her the thumbs up! Like she was one of his high school buddies watching him take advantage of some poor sophomore in the back of the gym.

Disgusted, shocked, and angered for multiple reasons, Samantha sprinted down the stairs, opened the door and flew back onto her floor, smashing her index finger into the elevator button multiple times.

She wasn't sure who she was angrier with. Dr. Chambers for being a total dick? Arrogant fuck was right! Who'd he think he was? Did Cara get her coke from him? Was he supplying it? Was this her pay for the coke? Blowjobs every evening; coke every night? How long had this been going on? She thought about that day she caught Cara running down the stairs giggling, with the white powder under her nose. That was months ago. Why hadn't Cara told her? Did she tell her anything though?

And Cara. She knew how much Samantha liked Dr. Chambers last year. He was all she ever talked about. Cara said he was untouchable and out of her league. But he was in *her* league? He hurt Samantha's feelings, too! How could Cara go behind her back? Lie to her? Be with him knowing how she felt?

Samantha had done everything Cara suggested, but she had yet to take one piece of advice from Samantha. She tried to help her. Tried to be there for her. Cara hid secrets from her, and in turn, Samantha didn't tell her about singing at the Open Mic nights. This was a friendship?

This. Was. It.

The elevator doors opened and Samantha jumped in. Her mind floated back to what she just saw. To think she actually liked someone like Dr. Chambers, initially. A conceited, drug addict, who had no problem taking advantage of a woman with clouded judgment. Were there no good men out there? Were they all nymphomaniacs that made you give them sex behind smelly dumpsters, blowjobs in stairwells, have sex with their gross friends and then pay for it all! Were there no decent guys left?

The elevator door opened on the second floor, and Cooper stepped in. "What a pleasant surprise." He smiled and re-pushed the basement button.

Chapter 30

Cooper was able to leave work on time for the first time since hired. With the kitchen finally running in an organized fashion, the menus handed over to Roselyn this evening, Angie taking control of the cafeteria to some degree, and the diet office fully staffed, he tossed his lab coat over his chair and strolled toward the loading dock.

As he pushed the doors open, the familiar clip-clop amplified behind him. He held the door open and waited for Ms. Bad Mood to exit.

"Still grumbling and pissed?" He extended his arm, welcoming her into the great outdoors.

"Don't ask. This day went from bad to worse."

"My day was great. I think Roselyn will finally get off my case."

Samantha looked at him, puzzled. "Why?"

"Not sure. I just feel the winds of change coming. Like peace is finally within my grasp."

"Ha! Yeah, okay. Let me know when you find it. Send some my way."

Cooper hesitated by the curb. "Want to grab some coffee?"

Samantha jarred to a halt and studied him. Was it a look of disgust? Outrage? She wanted to get coffee with him on Saturday, but now she looked like she had amnesia.

"You know what?" she said.

Fantastic. Here it comes. Another outburst. So much for peace.

"As a matter of fact. Yes. I'd love some coffee. But, you're paying."

They walked into the small, family owned coffee shop three blocks up the road. Fresh brewed coffee, the sweet scent of caramel, and the tingle of cinnamon, pricked Cooper's nose. A Stack of damp mugs, hot from the dishwasher, and a glass case holding scones and assorted pastries, caught his eye.

Samantha struggled out of her jacket and then tossed it into the red, leather booth. Perfectly spaced bistro tables with trendy chairs and padded seats enhanced the sunlit room. Coffee beans whirled in the grinder, while the airy slurp of an empty whipping cream canister topped a young girl's hot chocolate.

"This place is so quaint." Samantha beamed. "It reminds me of the coffee shop my grandfather took me to in Brooklyn when I was little. I always ordered a chocolate egg cream."

"Brooklyn, eh?" Cooper flicked his eyebrows. Alone with Samantha at last. He left his cell phone in the car this time, wanting no interruptions.

"Yup. My grandparents grew up there. We used to visit them every Sunday."

"Brooklyn's a fun place." He eyed her tight blue suit again. Something she hadn't worn in a while, but it looked different on her now. When they first met, she seemed brazen, tough, and well, slutty. He couldn't believe Roselyn allowed the dietitians to dress like that. Cara was worse because of the way she drew attention to herself. Heather, the other dietitian, wore frumpier mommy clothes. These two had stood out like sore thumbs.

Over the last few months, Samantha had toned it down. He finally saw her, and not the clothes. The clothes that blinded anyone from getting to know the real person underneath. Would she ever let him in?

The waitress brought their coffees, and the scalding liquid burned the tip of Cooper's tongue. When his body infused with warmth, he leaned in. "What happened today that made you so angry?"

She emptied four packets of sugar and five creamers into her coffee and stirred. Was she avoiding the question? Why was she so afraid to speak to him? He remembered what she had said about him being mean to her. But, now alone and away from the craziness, he felt at ease. Did she?

"First of all..." she took a sip of the coffee and dumped another creamer in, "Roselyn gave me a two percent raise!"

"What? That's impossible."

"Is it?" Her sarcasm coated her tone. "Please. Spare me." She took a large slug from her now sugary beverage. "I don't care anymore."

"Yes, you do."

"I don't. Seriously. I'm numb. That's the word. Numb. Frozen. Anesthetized. Just utterly blank."

"Did you say anything to her? Please tell me you did."

She held the steaming mug near her mouth, avoiding his question, and pretended to drink. She shook her head once, sighed and then gripped the mug tighter. "And then there's Cara. I don't know what to do with her. I can't stand being around her anymore. I want to help her, but she won't let me, then she's ungrateful and doesn't even appreciate our friendship. She screws me over repeatedly and somehow blames the whole thing on me!"

Cooper's coffee mug shot down so fast that some of the contents sloshed out and painted the table. Okay, maybe he didn't want to know what was in her head. "What're you talking about? I thought you guys were best friends?"

After a deep breath that looked like she was trying not to crush her coffee cup in her hands, she continued. "Last year, me, Cara and Eryn, a former co-worker, started hanging out at this club. I never fit in with the two of them. They're tall and gorgeous. Sexy. Knew how to dance and attract guys, you know?"

Cooper nodded, but he remembered the day he caught Samantha dancing by herself in the hallway. She looked like she could heat up the dance floor the way she gyrated her hips. He pretended he hadn't seen, but had watched her for a good thirty seconds.

"I had decided a few weeks earlier I needed a change. A total transformation."

"Change? But why?"

"I hated who I was. No one liked me."

"Samantha. I don't think it's about changing yourself so that others like you. I think it's about being yourself and finding people that like you as you are."

"No." She shook her head. "I liked the new me. At first, at least. Cara and I got closer. It became her and me, not her and Eryn. We went out every Friday night, some Saturdays, too."

"That person I met nine months ago was a product of Cara's doing?"

She nodded. "We laughed, danced our asses off, flirted. I felt like the life of the party for the first time in my life."

Cooper listened intently. The coffee shop hadn't filled up yet and aside from the understanding waitress, no one noticed Samantha's voice rise with anger, then crash to barely audible whispers.

Samantha hesitated. She took another sip from the green mug and wiped her mouth as if contemplating whether she wanted to tell him anymore. Or, maybe she realized she made a mistake telling him in the first place. "So…um, then it got weird. Cara and I started to argue. A lot. I think it was my fault, but maybe it wasn't. I don't know."

"What happened?"

She gazed out the window, then in a flash, stared directly in his eyes. She was definitely holding back. What was she hiding from him?

"Does it have to do with what I overheard in the kitchen?" He touched her blue shirtsleeve gently.

Samantha's eyes bulged, but then she immediately pretended to blink as if something caught in her eye. She wiped it, stalling further.

"The stories of binge drinking, cocaine, driving home drunk? That was you, wasn't it—"

"No!" Her assertion caused a couple that recently entered to turn around. She lowered her voice and leaned in. "No. I swear."

"It's fine. I don't believe what those guys say anyway. They talk through their asses. If you say the stories were lies, I believe you."

Her chin appeared to tremble, but she squeezed her fist tight, then smiled. "It was Cara they were talking about."

"Everything?"

She nodded again. "Yes."

A family of four sat in the booth behind them and the boy, around five-years-old, stood in his seat and stared at Samantha.

Cooper finished his coffee and changed the subject. "What pissed you off this morning?"

Samantha leaned back in her chair. "Honestly? I was mad that you blew me off Saturday. You know, that fake phone call about the flood in your sister's basement?"

That's why she avoided him all week? "I swear. It was real. She really had a ton of water in her basement. I told her to get to the bottom of the problem months ago, but she ignored me."

"Why didn't you ignore her?"

"That's the problem. I can't. They call, I run."

"How's that fair? Don't you deserve a life also?" Samantha's posture slumped.

"I feel bad."

"Who feels bad for you? Who helps you?"

"You." The words sputtered out before he had time to contain them. *Did he just say that out loud?*

Samantha brought the coffee mug to her lips, but her cheeks turned red before the steam hit. Had he embarrassed her?

"I like helping you," she whispered into the mug, barely audible.

"I thought I was bothering you."

"You do. A lot. But...I like it." She kept her eyes down.

"You do?" He chuckled. "I thought you hated it."

Samantha peeked up from the mug and sucked her lips inside.

"Lately, the only part of work I look forward to, is when I'm around you."

Cooper's jaw dropped. He tried to conceal it by faking a cough. *Wait, what just happened?* Then, without putting too much thought into it, tapped her hand. "Hey. What're you doing Saturday?"

Her face contorted and that annoyed expression returned. "What project do you want me to do now, Cooper?"

"No. No. No project. Nothing to do with work. Just you and me. Getting together."

She hesitated, a little too long if you asked him. But, then, as he raised his palm to tell her to forget it, she spoke.

"Like a date?"

Now *he* hesitated. Did she want to go on a date with him? He wanted to. That's for sure. But, would a date scare her off? Probably. Better act cool.

"Well, like two friends hanging out and doing something fun together that doesn't involve Roselyn, inventory, and annoying co-workers."

Her eyes remained vacant. Would she date someone like him? Dating Samantha would erase this entire crappy year.

"What did you have in mind?" She pushed her hair away from her face.

"I have an idea. It'll be a surprise though. I'll pick you up at your place at 9 a.m."

"My place? No!" Her eyes widened, then she softened her voice. "I mean, why don't I just meet you there?"

"Afraid of me again?" He pointed to his chest.

"Of course not." Samantha waved a hand at him.

"Then meet me at my place."

"Yours? Your apartment? No. Can't we just meet there?"

"It's too far. Plus, getting there's half the fun. How about this? Meet me at the Huntington Woods train station at 9:15 a.m. Okay?"

She squinted. "The train station? Where're we going?"

"Not telling you." He clamped his hands together.

"Well, what should I wear?"

"It's supposed to be an unseasonable seventy-degrees this Saturday. How 'bout jeans, sneakers, a T-shirt and a light jacket? Sound good?" He smirked knowing he was driving her crazy. She deserved it for holding back from him. He'd get inside that head of hers if it killed him. "Oh, and wear those pigtails again."

Chapter 31

Samantha pulled into the Huntington Woods train station at 8:58 a.m. Early, but she had to get away from her mother. After sleep eluded her all night, and the tossing and turning worsened any attempts at a good night sleep, she finally jumped in the shower at 7:15. She exited the bathroom still sleepy, but the alarm of her mother standing in the bathroom doorway with her hands on her hips and mascara dripping down her eyes, erased any last traces of sleep.

A melodramatic whisper ensued as her mother confronted her quietly, without waking her brother who had returned for the long Columbus Day weekend. God forbid her star child was disturbed. After gathering her hairdryer, brushes and a bag of makeup, Samantha hustled down the stairs to get ready in the basement bathroom. Her mother followed, yelling now, that Samantha had woken her up, and what was she doing up so early, where was she going, with who, and why wasn't she invited?

Luckily, the hum of the hair dryer drowned her out. She took the hint and finally left.

During a quick meal of oatmeal and raspberries, Samantha had to listen to her mother drone on about how her boss caught multiple errors in her report - clearly due to Samantha arguing with her the night before. Then, informed Samantha she was lazy like her father and that's why she'd never marry. She went on to tell her, "I have to love you because you're my daughter, but it doesn't mean I have to like you."

Samantha washed, dried and put away the cereal bowl and spoon, grabbed her hooded sweatshirt, and headed out the door. Her mother opened the kitchen window, questioning her ridiculous pigtails.

She had pulled into the train station parking lot and parked behind a huge, black truck. Perfect place to hide so she could compose herself. She stopped a few inches from the trucks back bumper and cut the ignition.

Birds flapped overhead as a family of four hurried to catch the train. Taxis idled alongside the awning-covered concrete landing.

Samantha rolled her window down a few inches and caught the scents from the Station Café kiosk. Sugary bakery items reached her nose. The train doors sealed and the chain of cars soon rumbled and clacked away.

Samantha's thoughts returned to her conversation in the coffee shop with Cooper. She had lied to him. Right to his face. He seemed interested in her problem, and genuinely concerned, but there's no way she could ever tell him about Lou and Bruce. He'd never speak to her again. She couldn't believe what she had reduced herself to. It all felt surreal. Why did she ever think it was okay?

Cara.

Cara had made her feel so guilty about everything she did. Or hadn't done. Was she really doing all this to improve herself, or was it to get Cara to like her more? She remembered what Cooper said about changing to get people to like you.

Slam! The black truck's door disrupted her meditation and she flinched. A guy reached into his back seat looking for something, then emerged, looked at her, smiled, and approached her window.

"How long were you going to sit in your car before saying hello?" Cooper slipped his arms through his jacket sleeves.

"I…I didn't know it was you. I never saw what you drove before." A slight faintness rolled over her as she hopped out next to him. Warmth shimmied up her neck and heated her face. "What are you doing here so early?"

"What are *you* doing here so early?" He nudged her shoulder.

His touch, although teasing, reminded her that she was spending the day alone with Cooper far away from any interruptions. A shiver flowed through her. "Getting away from my mother."

"You still live at home?"

Fantastic. Keep opening your mouth Samantha. She took a deep breath to collect herself, but his adorable smile instantly calmed her. Cooper had a way of unearthing all her deepest feelings and secrets, but any embarrassment seemed to vanish as soon as it appeared.

"Yup. And I live with a narcissistic mother who enjoys letting me know how much of an utter disappointment I am and how I'm so much like my worthless, lazy father who, by the way, had enough sense to leave her, move far away, remarry and work his way up to the president of his company."

"You are lazy! Only working fifteen jobs at once. What a piece of crap you are. Why am I even associating with you?" Cooper strutted off in this overconfident swagger like he was some male, runway model wearing the latest in spandex, furry boots, and see-through mesh.

Samantha snorted, then quickly covered her nose and mouth. She caught up to him with a playful skip and slapped him on his broad shoulders.

And, that's how the rest of the day went.

The forty-five minute ride into Penn Station had Samantha forgetting about work, Cara, her mother, and instead, focusing on Cooper and his never before seen sense of humor. They ate the hot creamery bagels, and the rich chocolate milk he bought, and laughed non-stop while others looked on.

They exited the Long Island Railroad, zigzagged through the bustle of travelers, and then pushed through the turnstiles leading to the subway platform. After being blasted by the wind of a passing train, they hopped on the Number 4 subway. The distant and muffled voice on the loud speaker hummed.

"Where we going?" The fluttering in her belly returned.

"Still not telling." He leaned over and swiped a glob of butter out of several strands of her hair. She could feel his breath on her face.

The subway came to a stop at Brooklyn Bridge/City Hall and Samantha gasped. "Brooklyn? You're taking me to Brooklyn?"

"No. City Hall. We're getting married."

Cooper ran off before she could answer. Before she could move. Her feet finally snapped out of it and she took off after him, snaking through the weekend crowds. She met him on the top of the stairs and then chased him outside. The warmth of the sun hit her as she made her way onto the street with City Hall's gorgeous two-hundred-year-old architecture in the background. The building struck her with such beauty, she didn't notice Cooper had planted himself in front of her, staring at her wonder and admiration of the structure.

"Did you know it's the oldest City Hall in the United States?" He woke her from yet another spell.

"Looks like it. It's amazing such an historic building like this can exist in a modern city like New York. It's stunning"

"Ever seen the City Hall Fountain in the surrounding park?"

"Never. Is it beautiful too?"

"If we have time later, we'll walk by it. Most of the trees haven't changed color yet, but we may catch some fall foliage." He nudged her forward. "Come."

After grabbing two bottles of water from a street vender, they crossed over what looked like a normal street, onto another normal street, but as the congestion of pedestrians swelled, it was anything but normal. The entrance to the Brooklyn Bridge walkway sprayed out in front of her as they shuffled along the right hand side of the sidewalk with hundreds of others.

An occasional bicyclist sped past them in the bike lane, and Cooper continued to gaze at Samantha as she looked around like a little kid seeing the Rockefeller Christmas tree light up for the first time.

"Have you ever walked across the bridge before?"

"No. I went to Coney Island a lot. But never over this bridge. Or, any bridge. How long is it?"

"It'll take at least forty-five minutes, to walk over, shoot a few pictures, look at the Manhattan sky-line—"

"I didn't bring a camera."

"I did." Cooper grasped her hand to pull her around a slow family of six.

Their feet strolled along the wooden planks that stretched a good five-feet across for pedestrians. The bike lane, to the left of them, extended the same five-feet. Although mainly empty, an occasional cyclist whizzed by them narrowly missing those that stopped to take a photo in the open path. Joggers and multiple baby strollers, all shared the congested lane they were in, as the morning sun warmed and Samantha removed her sweatshirt. She tied it around her waist and Cooper chuckled.

"Where do you get these things?" He pointed to her T-shirt.

Her yellow T-shirt with the little stick-figure girl on it, stood out in the bright sun light. The girl held a lemon in her hand. Samantha pointed to it with both index fingers. "When Life Hands You Lemons…Squirt Someone in the Eye."

"Nice. Real nice attitude, Samantha. No wonder your mother likes your brother better." He stuck his tongue out, then ran from her.

She chased after him and veered into the bike lane. An obvious pro-cyclist zoomed down the hill way too fast, showing off his talents to onlookers, and came intimately close to her. Cooper pulled her away just in time.

"Slow down," he shouted. "No wonder she blames you for everything. You almost killed that poor, harmless biker!"

"Me?" she laughed. "Yes, I'm the cause of all her problems. She never does anything wrong. Nothing is her fault. Actually, she is so self-absorbed, she'd purposely throw herself in front of the cyclist just to get attention."

"Cool." He joked. "Let's bring her next time."

Samantha smacked him in the arm. "No way. She destroys all my relationships. She'd probably throw you off the bridge, then pretend to cry so everyone would take pity on her and give her the attention she craves, blame the whole thing on me, then tell me how I made her so upset that she can't eat now."

"Then, you can tell her it was you that helped her lose all that weight."

"But, she'll say she's too thin and then use her sickly appearance to get more sympathy from complete strangers."

Cooper stopped as a couple in front of them took a picture of themselves with the Manhattan skyline behind them. His face turned serious. "Are you kidding, or is this for real?"

"She'll melt like a candle into utter helplessness. Wah. Wah."

He stepped closer and placed his hands on her upper arms. "Let me guess. Then she'll say you're cold and heartless for not being there for your poor mother when she feels so horrible."

"Oh. So, you know her? Gem Lillianna Starr?"

He lifted a single eyebrow. "That's her name?"

"Yup. She had her name changed after the divorce."

Cooper burst into hysterics. "You're making this all up, aren't you?"

"Nope."

"How are you so calm?"

Samantha ran back across the bike lane and leaned over the metal beam on the pedestrian side. Cooper followed. Why *was* she so calm? It really wasn't funny and she cried herself to sleep at times. The only thing that saved her lately was Tuesday's at the open mic night.

"I just make myself numb when I go home. I tried to move out a few times this year, but she cries and says my brother's away at school and how can I leave her all alone? What if something happens to her? What if she falls, or gets robbed, or…" Samantha leaned in close to Cooper's ear to whisper. That heavenly cologne made her forget what she was about to say for a minute. "…or dies."

"Dies? Samantha, you need out. You should be surrounding yourself with people that support you, make you happy, bring out the best in you. From what you told me on the train, she does none of that. I hate to say it, I know she's your mother, but maybe some distance is a good thing."

"I joke about it, but it eats at me every day." Her heart wrenched.

Cooper stepped closer. His fingers touched her chin and angled it up. "Sometimes you have to give up on people, not because you don't care about them, but because they don't care about you." His fingers lingered, and he let his eyes leave hers for a second to look down at her lips. Would he kiss her? She wanted him to.

The wind picked up and the warm breeze tickled the back of her neck.

"Come on, let's get going or else we'll never make to the other side." He prodded her forward.

They reached the second of the two arches and Cooper removed his camera from his back pocket. "Turn around so I can get the skyline behind you."

She looked behind her and then back at him. "Me?"

"No, the ninety-year-old man behind you. I want to hang his photo in my office. He looks hot in those suspenders that're pulling up his pants so high, I can see his olive green socks."

"I bet you do. You'll probably crop me out to get his full outline." Samantha stood awkwardly while Cooper snapped a picture of her. The thought of him having a photo of her caused a lightness in her chest. She became breathless leaning over the railing and feeling the rush of cars pass beneath her.

"Great shot," Cooper said as he approached. He leaned in and let her look at the picture. It was a close range head-shot of the ninety-year-old man smiling and waving at Cooper.

Samantha's uneasiness left her as it always did when around him, and she laughed so hard, it drowned out the chatter of the French tourists behind him.

"Do you want a picture of the two of you?" A woman in her late fifties asked.

Cooper and Samantha both glanced at each other uncomfortably and then looked away, babbling incoherently.

"Come on. You look nice. Get near each other." She waved her arms demonstrating.

They both took a step closer. The woman tilted her head to the side and tossed them a blank look. Cooper took one final step closer and when the woman shook her head in annoyance, Cooper placed his arm around her waist.

Samantha felt the heat of his hands around her stomach and thought about the health fair when Cooper lifted her out of that puddle. His strong hands cradling her and that look of determination in his eyes. Had she imagined it?

Samantha wrapped her arm around his waist, too, and he hugged a little tighter. Despite the woman taking three photos, they remained in place, not wanting to let go of something safe and comforting. They were in Brooklyn, on top of a beautiful bridge, on a gorgeous, warm day, alone.

The woman grabbed Cooper's hand, slapped the camera in his palm, and took off with an exasperated look in her eyes.

Fifteen minutes later, Cooper and Samantha reached the end of the bridge, turned right and headed to DUMBO. Cooper pointed toward the Fulton Ferry Pier. A quaint two-story building that looked like a fireboat house welcomed them. Samantha saw the long line forming in front of it. "The Brooklyn Ice Cream Factory?"

"Yup, homemade ice cream. It's—" Before he could continue, Samantha grabbed his shirtsleeve and dragged him to the end of the line. "We didn't have lunch yet."

"This is lunch." She beamed. Once inside, Samantha chose two scoops of chocolate, chocolate chunk in a waffle cone. Cooper settled on a small dish of vanilla. "How boring."

"I'm boring? Where are you right now? What would you've done if we didn't come here today?"

Samantha took a bite and a large chunk of chocolate wedged in her back tooth. "Probably raking leaves."

"Do you ever hang out with the crowd from that open mic night?" He scooped up a huge spoonful of the thick, velvety ice cream and grimaced. Brain freeze at its best.

She chuckled and licked her lips. "They invite me all the time. Sometimes they go out for a bite to eat before performing, or other times they just hit the beach. One time a Met's game."

"You go?"

"No." She took one of the napkins out of her jeans pocket and wiped away the ice cream that dripped onto her hand.

"Why not?"

She'd told him so much about herself already, and yet he still stuck around to hear more senseless tales. He saw her at her worst. Saw her acting like an idiot. Saw her being teased in the kitchen. Somehow, Cooper stuck around. Was he that blind? Desperate?

"I have a hard time making friends."

"You just said they invite you out all the time."

"Yes, but that's because they only see me sing, maybe talk a little before and after my set, but I never stuck around long enough for them to really get to know me."

"And, if you did?"

"Please. They'd probably find something wrong with me, stop sitting near me, avoid me..."

Cooper placed his ice cream down beside him. "I don't understand."

She tilted her head down, but then let her eyes glide to their corners to look at him. "I'm afraid I'd say something stupid or do something dumb."

He grabbed her chin again and lifted her head up. "I've been with you all day and have yet to hear or see you do one stupid thing. I've worked at St. Elizabeth's for six months now, and I've only seen someone that rises to the occasion and helps her boss, her co-workers, and patients, despite no recognition whatsoever. You do it selflessly, with no incentives, no rewards, and even despite taunts from kitchen workers, lack of support from Cara, and Roselyn giving you a shitty raise."

At once, her face and ears became impossibly hot. "Thank you," she whispered. Her ice cream now dripping furiously down her hand.

"Eat, before I eat it."

Samantha took a large bite, not because of the melting power of the sun, but because she could not believe Cooper's kind words. Had he noticed all that? How long had he been keeping an eye on her? All this time she thought he was mean. Was he only teasing her last year? Trying to help her? Protecting her from her own self?

"Then why were you so mean to me in the beginning?"

"I was never mean, Samantha. Half the time I was probably just joking around. Plus, I told you, I was trying to prove myself to Roselyn, I had Cara sneaking in there on countless occasions, Bruce and Lou talked shit all the time. Then that night you came in while I was naked—"

"I didn't see anything, I swear!"

"You totally saw everything," he teased.

Samantha took another large bite, but between the big fat bagel, the walk in the sun, and now double scoops of ice cream, her stomach was ready to give up on her.

"I tossed my pants on the desk and sensed someone sneak past my window. I had no shoes on so I quickly ran around the bend. I actually saw you tiptoeing, like they do in cartoons, tiptoeing, out of the kitchen."

"See. Embarrassing."

"Not embarrassing. Cute." His eyes twinkled. "I knew then you weren't what I first thought."

"What do you mean?"

"Every time I caught Cara in the kitchen, she yelled at me. Had a total attitude like she was showing off to everyone how tough she was. Poked her finger in my face. Lied and said she was getting patient's food. Never left with anything in her hand, though." He scooped up the last of the melted slop, then sucked it in his mouth as if it were the remains of milk at the bottom of a cereal bowl.

"I didn't realize that. Sorry."

"Why are *you* sorry?" He set the cup on the ground. "You were different, though. That tiptoeing had me laughing hysterically. I shook my head and had to compose myself before I called out to you. I watched you the entire way out. After begging you to come back in, you actually made me laugh a few times. I realized you weren't bad to the bone. Trying to be, maybe, but I saw you were pretending."

"Yeah, you saw, all right. My whole dress flung open for you to see everything."

"It was only fair. You saw me naked, too."

She smirked, knowing it was true.

"Then you thought my sisters were some hookers in Vegas, and you—"

"Oh, man, I forgot about that. See. If you stick around long enough, I do asinine things." She forged on and took a giant bite out of the cone. The whole thing crumbled in her hand. "Shit!"

Cooper leaned over to help, but she took the whole, messy, crumbled glob and shoved it right in his face. Ice cream and melted chocolate pieces trickled down his cheek. Instead of freaking out, he charged at her, smashed his cheek into hers, and let the slimy mess smear all over her face and nose.

A group of three young girls watched as they made fools of themselves. Samantha reached back into her jeans pocket and removed the wad of napkins. She shared half with him, and they wiped the sticky ice cream off their faces.

"Is that pay back for seeing you do something stupid, again?" Cooper tossed the napkins in the trash.

"Consider us even now."

"I still don't know what you're talking about."

She sighed, not wanting to mention it again. He either was being polite, or truly didn't think she was a dork. "Where to now?"

"Give me your hand." He clasped it in a friendly, helpful way, as if not wanting to lose her in the crowd. The way he held onto her, anyone would think they were some happily married couple skipping off together. The feel of his strong, warm hand wrapped around hers, made her feel as if Peter Pan had taken her under his control as they flew over Netherland.

They made their way around the floating river barge and proceeded to the end of the dock. Once there, Cooper and Samantha leaned on the thin, transparent enclosure that separated them from the rest of the glorious world, and they cleared their minds. The blue water lapped and flowed as speedboats soared past them. They studied the grand architecture of the Brooklyn Bridge above them. Not to be outdone, the Manhattan Bridge peeked out from behind with its more modern construction.

The breeze blew in their faces and cooled them from the surprisingly hot October day. "Gotta love Indian Summers." Cooper smiled. "I had to make the most of today, knowing this would probably be it until the spring."

"Can't believe the holidays will be here soon."

"And then my sister's wedding."

"When's that?"

"Thursday, January 23rd."

Samantha swept the strand of hair out of her mouth and entwined it with the pigtail on the right. "A Thursday wedding?"

"Yes, remember she's having one of those destination weddings in Jamaica? We fly out the Saturday before just in case any blizzards cancel the flights, and then the early part of the week we have the rehearsal dinner, bachelor parties, and she's gifting the bridal party spa services before the big day."

"Sounds nice."

"It's actually aggravating."

"For you?"

"Somehow I'm involved with the madness. I think because my dad's not around she's having me walk her down the aisle, which somehow turned into me making a speech, and making sure all the boys are doing what they're supposed to. I got roped into the bachelor party, too."

A speedboat flew by bucking the waves as its passengers held on for dear life. Pedestrians on the pier gave them all a giant wave. Samantha joined in also. "Isn't that the best man's job?"

"Yes, but apparently my sister Hannah thinks he's a spaz and he'll either do nothing, or screw everything up."

"So, you're basically going as the wedding planner?"

"Seems that way. I'm hoping to just sit by the ocean and get tan. Drink a bunch of Bob Marley's and cool off in the ocean."

"Doesn't look like that's happening."

"It never does." He turned away from the bridges. "Come on."

He grabbed her hand again, but this time there were no crowds. She gave his fingers a little squeeze to see what he would do and he squeezed back harder. A grin spread across her face.

Cooper swung their arms back and forth like a bunch of silly kids, then found an empty bench overlooking the wondrous Manhattan skyline. "This was my favorite view." He smiled big and wide.

"Was?"

"When I was little my father used to walk the bridge and push me in a stroller. When I was old enough to walk it myself, he'd take me every year. It was our thing. I loved all my time with him, but times like that, when it was just us, and we'd talk and talk for hours, it just meant the world to me."

He still hadn't let go of her hand and gripped it tighter as if to ward off tears. She squeezed again.

"When he died, the bridge was one of the first things I thought about. We'd never walk across it together again. About a year later, my grandfather, who lived around here, took me one summer for a walk over it. I didn't want to go at first. Too many memories. But, he forced me and I remember being angry and bitter. My grandfather was a very athletic man, though, and he convinced me by saying it was good exercise. I wouldn't be surprised if he used to hang with Jack La Lane in his youth." Cooper ran his fingers through his hair and laughed. "We went over and back, grabbed some Grimaldi's pizza, and he started telling me all these stories about my dad that I never heard before. All the talks *they* had when they used to walk over the bridge together. My anger disappeared, and these walks with my grandfather gave me a way to be near my dad again."

"You've been coming every year since then?"

"We did. Initially. He'd take me for the weekend while my mom did some girlie things with my sisters. Then, the summer before I started high school, we walked across and sat by the City Hall Fountain. I remember him being very quiet that day. Before heading back over the bridge, he told me this would be the last time. My grandmother and he decided to move to Florida after New Years. I was devastated. First my dad, now him."

"I'm so sorry. I wish I knew what to say." Samantha clutched his hand again wanting to do more. Hugging or leaning on his shoulder seemed strange under the circumstances. Holding his hand for so long was already odd, but anything more would cross the line. Why was he holding her hand? Was he that upset?

"My grandfather used to say a bridge was like two arms extending out to keep things near and dear to your heart. Whether it be people, communities, or traditions. My dad though, looked at bridges as arteries where the people were the blood, surging back and forth and nourishing everyone that lived on either side."

"Wow. I never looked at it that way. What do you see it as?"

"Never really thought about it. I guess I was too young to come

THE BRIDGES BEFORE US

up with anything as clever as them."

"Do you come here often with your friends?"

Cooper's eyes lit up and the sun heightened his sudden enthusiasm. "It didn't feel right coming here with anyone else. Today's actually the first time I've been back since that summer with my grandfather."

Samantha flinched. What was he saying? "With me? Why me?"

"You make me feel comfortable. Calm. It's like stress disappears when I'm around you. You make me laugh. A lot. You're the first person that helped me, instead of me always having to lend a hand. I'm not used to that. It feels good." He closed his eyes, sighed and then reopened them. "You're compassionate, caring, and down to earth. Objects mean nothing to you. You're fun, and silly, and quirky. You make things look effortless. Nothing seems to bother you."

"Everything bothers me. I just hold it all in." She released his hand and avoided his compliments. She was blown away by his words, unprepared for them, and didn't know how to react. "That's why I like singing. I express myself through music. I pick the songs because of the lyrics—"

Cooper stood abruptly and started to walk back where they'd come from. Was he mad that she ignored his compliment? There was no way he could like someone like her. His grief over the loss of his father and grandfather muddled his emotions.

She caught up and made small talk, complimented a young girl on her pink, flowery dress, and petted a Doberman puppy. They walked the rest of the way in silence until they exited the Fulton Ferry Pier.

"Want to head back? We can grab some lunch on the other side." He continued to look straight ahead.

"Sure." Still full from all the fat she ingested today, she hoped her appetite would return once they crossed over.

They entered the walkway for the bridge and the noon sun beat down hard on her head. The crowd swelled now that more people realized the weather forecast was for real. The pedestrian lane tipped over into the bicycle lane as cyclists weaved in and out, barely missing anyone that dared to step into their area. Samantha moved in closer to Cooper to avoid them flattening her.

He glanced at her, but kept quiet. What was he thinking?

"So, you think I should hang out with the Open Mic people more?"

He smiled finally. Was it forced? "Yes. Definitely. They seem like a great bunch of guys."

"There's girls, too."

He chuckled. "I wasn't questioning you. I meant guys like in the gang, the group, you know."

"They are great. Funny. Supportive. They push me to try things out of my comfort zone."

"That's what everyone you're close with should be doing. You should surround yourself with people that make you the best person you can be. They should be your mirror. Showing you what you need to work on, what your potential is, and to push you to do things you're scared of, until you love yourself for who you are."

"There's times when I really don't like myself."

"I think you're hanging out with the wrong people, Samantha. I really do. They bring you down. Insult you. Make fun of you. How can you possibly like yourself when that surrounds you?"

She bit the inside of her cheek, her mind raced with thoughts. "I used to walk into a party and wonder if the guests would like me."

"You should walk into a party and wonder if you'll like any of them."

Samantha smiled at his perspective. Regardless of them towering high above the ocean, a feeling of breathlessness took over and heat radiated through her chest. How she once thought a man with this much insight, with this much compassion, was once mean, was mind-boggling.

They neared the first arch of the bridge and stopped to shade themselves from the sun. "Whew." Cooper flapped his red T-shirt up and down to air himself. "I should've grabbed us more waters." He walked to the far end, overlooking the ocean.

Samantha leaned against the cool granite and stared deeply at Cooper while he looked out at the beautiful water. Why'd he invite her out today? Didn't he have other friends he wanted to be with? Why hadn't he brought Tiara here before? She stared at him long and hard. Her hands touched the chilly stone behind her and she tilted her head up and against it. Her breaths increased as she let the ocean breeze revive her.

Cooper's T-shirt clung to his sweaty body and enhanced his broad chest and huge biceps. He had his hair cut last night and the tiny, blonde spikes sprang up as he shook off the perspiration beading on top of his head. He reached up high, grabbing his hands together and stretched forward. His shirt lifted just enough to see how tight his ass looked in his jeans.

Samantha clenched her fist behind her back and attempted to control her breathing. Why was she having these crazy thoughts about him? God, she wanted him so bad. It wasn't the alcohol. It wasn't mixed emotions. They worked well together. They did laugh a lot. They bounced some great ideas off each other. Supported each other with every conflict. He was a wonderful guy and a great friend.

Somehow, despite her goofy, embarrassing moments, Cooper wanted to be around her all the time. He asked her to help him with important projects. Chose her to spend this beautiful day with. Only wanted to venture across this bridge with her, a bridge that meant so much to him.

Had she read him wrong all this time? Was she that blind and stupid? Why'd she brush aside his compliments before? Did she love herself enough to know this could happen? That someone like Cooper could actually fall in love with someone like her?

Cooper finally looked over. Her heart sped up. He paused, took a step closer and watched as her mouth opened in lust for him. Her chest rose and fell. Her breathing intensified. She could hear the gasps escape from her mouth. Her eyes let him know that she wanted him. Now.

He moved in tight. Searched her eyes for the words she couldn't speak. He clearly could not mistake the yearning in her face. She released her arms from behind her and before he had a chance to ask her if she was okay, Samantha tugged his T-shirt towards her. She grabbed the back of his head with her other hand and pulled him in for a kiss.

At that moment, the hum of the traffic below muted. She placed her lips firmly onto his and tasted his delicious mouth. As if in heaven itself, all her fears and regrets, her worries and doubts, disappeared when Cooper pushed her back against the wall and kissed her feverishly. His fingers swept under her pigtails and seized her cheeks. He leaned into her palpitating chest. Cooper's mouth opened as if he needed air, but then covered her mouth again while his tongue linked with hers.

He pulled away finally, but his thumb lingered and circled her lower lip. As his breaths heaved in and out, an overweight man ducked into the shade next to them, breathing just as heavy.

"Hot day," the man huffed while wiping his head with a handkerchief. "Catching your breath underneath here, too?"

Cooper and Samantha laughed, the gasps pouring out of the three of them at the same tempo.

"Yup." Cooper grinned. "Catching our breath."

The man nodded and then strolled over to the edge to look at the ocean.

Cooper stared at Samantha and grabbed both her pigtails.

"These things have been driving me crazy all day." He kissed her once again. His lips more gentle this time, but still passionate and yearning. "What made you kiss me?"

"It just finally hit me. Everything you said today."

His eyebrows squished together.

"Don't change to impress someone. Be yourself and the right person will come. And you did. You were right here all along. I just didn't want to believe it."

"Why not?" Cooper tapped her on the nose.

"I…I just don't get it. I'm nothing special."

"Nothing special? Wow." His brow collapsed into his nose. "Sometimes we envision things in our heads for so long, we believe them to be true. We actually see them."

"How come, then, no matter how many stupid things I do in front of you, you still stick around?"

"You keep saying that. When have I ever seen you do anything stupid?"

"You saw me dancing in the hallway by myself doing some ridiculous undulating move. You saw me singing that song in the diet office when I was banging the pencils against the shelf and thrusting my butt out like some maniac. You overheard Bruce and Lou insult me on the tray line multiple times. Watched me pretend to look for something in my car when there was nothing back there. You said you hid in a patient's room and listened to my whole conversation. I practically tripped onto you in the cafeteria. You watched me—"

"*These* are the embarrassing moments?" His eyebrows shot up. He chuckled, shook his head and looked away.

Samantha took her eyes off him for the first time since they hid behind the bridge's arch. "Yes. And I'm sure there's many more, but I felt dumb even mentioning these."

Cooper eased into her hips again, and clutched her upper arms as if he was massaging them. "Samantha. Before I ever had the pleasure of meeting you, I thought you were just like all the other women out there. I also thought you were a carbon copy of Cara and I wanted nothing to do with you. But…" He hesitated, lifting her chin up. "Every time you didn't think someone was watching you…Didn't know I was watching you…That's when I started to like you. That's when I was able to see the real you. That's the Samantha I fell in love with."

Samantha drew back, but the granite wall pushed harder. Speechless, she continued to stare. This was a dream.

"You also take care of me, defend me, and keep me going when

I feel like quitting. You showed me that when you feel like giving up, try a new approach. You give me a new perspective. One I never thought of."

"I do?"

"Yes. You do." Cooper weaved his fingers with hers, lifted her hands high above, and leaned their arms against the arch. He nibbled teasingly on her bottom lip a few times, and then, when she could stand it no longer, bent in and kissed him hard again.

"Get a room!" A father biking with a young child, shouted.

They both shook their heads and laughed. Samantha and Cooper resumed their walk, but their hands stayed linked together like the bridge, until they reached Manhattan, stopping several times to taste each other.

They never made it to the City Hall Fountain.

Chapter 32

Cooper never drove to his apartment so fast in his life. Why he suggested going all the way to Brooklyn on their first date was beyond him. Then again, he didn't expect Samantha to grab him like that. After months of compliments, flirting and asking her to help him with various projects, he thought she'd respond. Something, anything. Not completely ignore his hints. After that heartfelt moment on the bench, when he revealed his private feelings to her, he had given up. Obviously, she wasn't interested.

When he saw that strange look in her eye under the arch, one that either resembled someone having an orgasm or suffering from heat exhaustion, he became more confused. He was about to ask her if she was feeling okay, when she pulled him into her so aggressively, he had no time to think. From the moment he touched her lips, he didn't care to think anymore. His fantasy came true. Something finally clicked.

He knew it was against Roselyn's rules to date an employee. That's why he tried so hard to maintain a professional relationship with Samantha. But, he didn't care anymore. She was worth this stupid job.

It took them over two hours to get home. All right, the multiple times they stopped to kiss was part of the problem, but he couldn't contain himself. How many months had he daydreamed about being with Samantha?

They blew off the fountain, blew off lunch, and spent the crowded, stifling subway ride back to Penn Station kissing and rubbing their bodies against one another. The subway riders, accustomed to countless indecencies, ignored them. After grabbing a couple of Nathan's hot dogs, they boarded the forty-five minute train ride home to their cars. He was tempted to drag her into the train's bathroom, but contained himself until they arrived at the Huntington Woods parking lot.

Once there, he hoped she wouldn't chicken out and say she had to help her mother change the sheets in the house or something equally ridiculous. Would her mother want her home? Would his sisters call and interrupt them again? He clicked off his phone before they did.

Samantha lingered by his truck, though, and her desire seemed as fierce as his. "Wanna check out my new kitchen mug I bought last week?" He winked. Samantha laughed, and then he leaned her against the driver side's door, nuzzling her neck.

They both jumped into his truck.

He fumbled with his apartment key as she waited behind him, circling her soft fingers up his back. Once inside, he chucked his keys on the table and watched them careen off the edge and onto the floor. Would he remember where they were later?

He scooped up this petite, little girl in his arms and cradled her ass in his hands. God, he lifted dumbbells heavier than her. Would he hurt her? He shuffled down the hallway, entered his bedroom, held her ass with one hand and removed his comforter with the other, gently placing her on the bed. They both fell back and he landed on top - her beautiful blue eyes, only two-inches from his.

Samantha began ripping her clothes off, but Cooper stopped her. "I fantasized about this one too many times. Let me do it."

He slid his hands under her cute yellow T-shirt until they rested just under her breasts. His lips kissed her stomach and his tongue lingered over the hollow of her belly button. Samantha's skin tasted sweet and salty from the day filled with cold ice cream and hot temps. It reminded him of the incredible hours they had just spent together. Wanting to taste more of her smooth skin, he eased her shirt up with his thumbs and pulled it over her head. Although he had seen them jiggle for him under that leather dress, the pale-pink bra teased him now, hiding the unforgettable mounds of flesh that he wanted so badly in his mouth.

He ran his finger over the lace that hung below the bra, knowing what came next would drive his fingers mad. His hands reached up, deliberately, sliding along and rubbing the fabric against her nipples. He surrounded each one and then inched the material down. Her nipples sprung up, rigid and extending toward him. Her leftover summer tan highlighted the soft flesh in his hands, and he wasted no time securing one in his mouth. His tongue lingered over the very tip of her nipple, then sucked on it hard, capturing most of her breast in his mouth.

Her body heaved, her chest arched for him. She let out a soft moan that drove him crazy, then he unhooked her bra, tossing the barrier on the floor. Samantha ran her fingers through his hair and pushed his head down harder. His hand trembled, fighting back the urge to rip off both their pants. He never thought he could want someone this urgently.

When she thrust her groin into him and started grinding his impossibly hard dick, he couldn't wait any longer. Cooper released her breasts and glided his hands back down her stomach. After unlatching her jeans, he wiggled them down to find her matching undies. Heat built up under his already drenched shirt. He whipped it off and chucked it across the room hitting his Ab bench.

Had he imagined it? Did her body heat just rise up like air in a sauna? Or, was it the intense sun hitting the south facing window? He yanked her pants down not wanting to remove her undies yet. Instead, he stood and removed his pants.

Samantha scooted up and leaned back on her elbows. She watched him while he undressed, focusing on his navy-blue briefs. He never saw a girl blatantly stare at his crotch before. Didn't only guys do that? Not wanting to disappoint her, Cooper stared right back, and in one swooping motion jerked his briefs down to his ankles, kicked them aside, and stood in front of her.

That cute, quirky, mind-boggling, little thing, sat there like she was looking at a picture on a wall, like it was no big deal. She eyed every angle of his body, focusing mostly on what was between his legs. No shame whatsoever. What happened to all her embarrassing moments?

Not knowing what else to do, Cooper squeezed the muscles on both his arms. "Like what you see?" Now *he* felt embarrassed.

Samantha laid there motionless, gasps spilling from her mouth. "Yes," she stammered.

"Good." He took one flying leap and pounced on top of her, walloping the bed beneath them. She sprang up, then dangled off the edge of the bed, her arms thrashing in the air to stop herself from falling. Cooper intentionally grabbed hold of her tiny underwear in an obvious lame attempt at keeping her from falling. His dive was too powerful though, and her body gradually… glided…off…the bed. The pink lace in his hands slid down her thighs, her knees, and then her ankles.

Plunk! She landed on her naked ass and let out a stream of laughter. He crawled over to the edge of the bed and rested on his stomach, allowing only his chin to hang off the side. "Whatcha doing down there?" he asked, totally deadpan.

All of these apparent periods of humiliation flew out the window as Samantha jumped back on the bed and laid on top of him. Feeling her naked breasts on his back, while she wiggled her hips into his ass, reminded him what they were in the middle of doing. He rolled over, catching her on top.

She sat up and smiled. "I can't believe I'm sitting on top of you naked, in your bedroom."

"Why?" He rubbed his hands up and down her thighs while staring at her breasts now, on purpose.

She snapped her fingers in front of his face. "Eyes here." She pointed to her eyes.

"I don't recall your eyes being there a minute ago." He pointed between his legs.

She smirked. "First of all, I was blown away by what was in your briefs. Secondly, it reminded me of that day in your office. The only thing you had on was your briefs. I always wondered what was under that one piece of clothing."

"And now you know. And now you're sitting in my room, naked."

She rubbed the base of her neck. "Cooper. I'm sorry I didn't pick up on your cues sooner. I had a lot going on this year and the thought of someone like you liking me, seemed improbable."

"What do you mean 'like you'? Are you an alien or something?"

"I feel like one."

"Hmm. What planet are you from? I like alien chicks."

She slapped him in the stomach. "Stop. I'm serious."

"So am I. I'm sick of the norm. That's why I broke up with Tiara. I wanted you."

Samantha leaned forward and laid her elbows on Cooper's chest. She tilted her head to the side, letting her loose hair drape over his shoulder. She wiggled her nose over his and then kissed him. "I want you, too. I have for a while, but refused to believe you liked me back. I guess I thought if I blocked it out, the ache would go away."

He sighed. "You have no idea how happy that makes me. I can't believe how much time we wasted. And…I know just the thing to get rid of that ache." Cooper weaved his fingers through her hair and pulled her down onto his mouth. After several minutes of fervent kissing, she opened her eyes.

"Why are your eyes always open?" Samantha asked.

"Always. I want to see every inch of you. Experience all that you are, and never miss another moment." He lifted her off him, spun on the bed, and sat on the edge.

Samantha kneeled on his lap facing him, and then rose up on her knees allowing him to guide himself inside. He teased her, only letting his tip penetrate, getting the outside of her nice and wet. She rotated around his cock, knowing she was teasing him more.

Once she dripped on him, he slowly pushed in, an inch at a time. Samantha grabbed hold of his shoulders, stood up straight, and rocked with him.

With his hands on her ass, Cooper drove hard, pulling her into him. When their rhythm matched, he captured her left breast in his mouth, and took turns between his tongue enjoying her hardened nipple, and his lips sucking the mound into his mouth.

Samantha took over and thrust with her hips. When her moans filled the room, he let go of her ass and leaned back on his hands, watching her take control. He gave her the biggest grin he could.

Cooper never thought she'd be this aggressive. Yeah, she strutted around in those slutty clothes, which, now, he wanted to see her in. All of them. Only for his eyes, though. But, all those times he caught her acting silly, he never imagined she'd be a spit-fire in the bedroom. Where was this wild side coming from? Had those stories he overheard from Lou and Bruce been true? Samantha would never lie to him, would she? Suddenly, the thought of her hooking up with them sickened him.

No. Stop. Samantha was obviously one of those quiet ones you'd never suspect until you brought them into your bedroom.

Cooper continued to watch her and she glided her hands up her stomach and onto her breasts. He sucked in a quick breath of air through his teeth. *Damn her.* She twirled her fingers around her nipples hardening them for him. After seizing both breasts in her hands and squeezing them, she put one in her mouth and sucked vigorously.

That was it. He lost it. Cooper leaned back in, secured his hands around her ass once more, and covered her mouth with his. Samantha threw her hands around his neck and rocked with him in perfect pace. His driving force took over and he hammered her as if they were some untamed beasts in the jungle. The two gasped and moaned so loudly, the neighbor in the apartment next door pounded on the wall as furiously as he had pounded her.

Cooper fell back on the bed, Samantha on top of him, and they both chuckled in between gasps of breath. He kissed her one more time, and then she rolled over onto her back. The two co-workers, lying beside each other naked, connected on a higher level than either of them ever imagined. He slipped his hand into hers while they tried to catch their breath.

After another minute, Cooper jumped off the bed and opened the window. He let the air course over his body. No traces of shyness present, Samantha followed and stood beside him, letting the cool breeze harden her nipples again.

Before he got hard again, Cooper bent over. "Hop on. I'm thirsty."

Samantha shook her head like he was the craziest guy in the world, then hopped onto his back.

"I'm dying of thirst. Are you?" He galloped into the kitchen, their laughter echoing in the hallway.

Chapter 33

Samantha knocked on Cooper's door for their weekly Sunday football game at his apartment. Chants and shouts reverberated off the walls, as Harry, Steve, and Vance, his friends since high school, jumped up and down and cheered at the Giant's touchdown she just missed. Wearing their team jerseys and blue headbands, Steve outdid them all by painting his face blue and white.

She strode into the kitchen and placed her tray of curried nachos with mango salsa on his counter. Cooper lifted the tinfoil and sniffed. "Cilantro, eh? Smells great."

"Did she bring healthy food again?" Steve called out.

"You loved my beef and beer chili last Sunday." Samantha screamed back. "I recall someone having two bowls of it."

"I think it was three." Steve's voice low, but still audible.

"Trust me, it was three." Vance grumbled. "I had to drive him all the way home in a small, unventilated car. All four window were down the last ten minutes of our drive."

Samantha held her head high and stuck out her tongue as she and Cooper returned to the living room with the nachos. Vance's spicy, hot wings filled the room and singed her nose. "*Whew!* Vance, did you dump the whole bottle of Frank's Hot Sauce on your wings?"

"You know you love 'em. Don't pretend you're not going to scarf down fifteen of them again! I had to buy an additional package this week just to feed you." He rolled his eyes. "I'll go broke at this rate."

"Yeah, where do you put it?" Harry nodded to her tiny frame. "You practically ate me under the couch last Sunday."

Samantha bounced on her toes and grinned large and wide. "I think Vance makes them hot so I'll drink more beers and end up under the couch passed out like you."

"You were close to it last weekend." Steve threw a potato skin in his mouth and seemed to swallow it whole. "All that hopping on the couch, doing cartwheels, screaming on the top of your lungs. How much did you drink?" Steve glanced at Cooper. "I think she's keeping up with us in the beer department, also."

"She loves her beers, that for sure." Cooper wrapped his huge bicep around her neck, pulled her over to him, and kissed her on her hair. "Mmm. Coconut shampoo?" He bent over until his mouth covered her ear. "You always smell so damn good." Cooper captured her hands in his and led her to his bedroom.

"Hey!" Vance shouted. "Can't you two wait until we leave?"

Cooper ignored him and entered his room. "I bought something for you." He reached under one of four pillows on his bed and pulled out a Giants jersey. In her size.

"For me? How cool! I feel like one of the guys now."

"You are one of the guys."

Samantha clutched the jersey by the shoulders and held it up. A pink envelope careened to the floor. "What's this?"

"Just a card." Cooper glanced at the ceiling and whistled.

"Nothing is ever 'just' with you." After placing the jersey on the bed, she ripped open the envelope and opened the card. The front page swelled her heart.

> *"Love comes to those who still hope after disappointment,*
> *who still believe after betrayal,*
> *and who still love after they've been hurt."*
> *Anonymous*

"I...don't know what to say. It's beautiful. And, so true." As happy as she should be, a wave of uncertainty passed over her. Still feeling as if this was a dream, she swallowed it back down and grinned.

"The past month has been nothing short of amazing, Samantha." He slid his hands over her cheeks and under her hair.

"Well, you're lucky you're a Giants fan, otherwise it'd be over." Her tongue inched out in a mischievous mood.

A beer cap snapped off a bottle in the living room, and a round of high-fives followed.

The corners of Cooper's mouth rose. "It's hard to be romantic when your friends are in the next room eating bacon-wrapped, stuffed jalapeños."

"True. I guess we'll just have to wait until later." She placed her index finger on his chest and playfully pushed him away.

"The game doesn't end until after seven."

"I can wait." She yawned, teasingly.

Cooper pulled her in tight, their hips locked. "Or, you could sleep over again." He slipped his fingers into her rear jeans pockets.

Samantha wiggled her eyebrows. Waking up in Cooper's arms last week was the most intoxicating feeling she ever experienced.

She spent the morning in one of his extra-large T-shirts, while he baked popovers for breakfast. They lounged on his couch all afternoon under a plush blanket and watched '80s movies. "Aren't you getting sick of me yet?" she joshed.

"I told you. I'm just getting started."

Chapter 34

Samantha reclined in her office chair still daydreaming about her evening with Cooper yesterday. The past seven weeks had been some of the most emotionally charged days of her life. Was it possible to be this happy? Did she need to muddle through months of hell before reaching her heaven? It was worth it. She would only move forward now. Any memories with Lou, Bruce, even Cara, started to fade as if they never happened. How strange.

The only downside involved Roselyn. She had a strict no-dating policy with her managers. Although she understood the reasoning behind possible favoritism and bias with evaluations and scheduling, she failed to see what it had to do with her. Cooper wasn't her manager and had no part in her appraisals or disciplines. They weren't chancing it, though. No one could know.

The most annoying part was that Roselyn had no problem breaking her own rule with Kenneth. Maybe that was the reason. Maybe she was afraid Kenneth would wander off and find another woman. Dump her for someone else. The little puppy dog was destined to be with Roselyn forever. She wondered if her husband suspected. Would she leave him for Kenneth one day?

Maybe Roselyn's husband was horrible. Maybe she found happiness when she was with Kenneth. Samantha knew all too well how that felt. She wouldn't judge. If Kenneth and Roselyn were happy together, then that was their business. What she wouldn't give to be a fly on the wall though, on the afternoons they spent locked in her office.

Samantha finished her French toast and chucked her plate in the trash. She glanced over at Heather's desk. She was off today having worked the weekend. Three beautiful silver frames adorned her desk. One was a picture of Laurel, her seven-year-old daughter. The other frame caught this scrumptious picture of Gia, her four-year-old. The last was a picture of the three of them in the park. She hadn't seen a picture of her husband in years. Was everyone that miserable?

Cara had refused to sit with Heather at lunch after a few months. She thought Heather's humdrum conversations of babies and daycare were repetitive and annoying. Heather didn't seem to mind them blowing her off, and she shared lunch every day with Rebecca, a social worker on her floor. Looking at her photographs now, made her wonder what her life was like - to be married with kids and a house. She regretted never developing a close relationship with Heather. They had snubbed her for no reason. Once again, Cara's doing. Maybe Cara was jealous that Heather was married. Why did Samantha go along with everything she said? This was someone she looked up to at one point?

The clock read nine o'clock. Cara had officially changed her hours to 10 - 6 p.m. She wasn't sure if it was to avoid Samantha or to avoid getting in trouble for being late every morning. Maybe she had no choice and Roselyn changed her hours for her. Lord knows what Cara did every night. She stopped asking.

Samantha left the diet office and peeked down the hallway. It was such a tease not being able to see much of Cooper during the day. They snuck out for lunch two to three times a week, always meeting at the chosen restaurant. They spent every weekend together - movies, romantic dinners, and of course, Sunday football with his friends. She had slept over a few more times and wanted it to be more.

Once Samantha reached her floor, she dumped her binder on the counter and chose a chart from the rack. Before she had time to read through it, her beeper buzzed. Cooper's morning hello. It started her day on the right path, and helped them cope with whatever life threw at them.

She snuck a quick peek at the number, and her body tensed. Whose number was this? An outside line?

She jabbed the numbers on the keypad. The hello familiar, yet removed. "Yes, this is Samantha. Did someone page me?"

"Samantha, you goof. It's me, Eryn!"

Samantha hesitated. Why was she calling after so many months? "Sorry. It's been so long. I wasn't expecting you," her sarcasm unmistakable.

"I tried to call Cara, actually, but she didn't answer."

Gee. Thanks. "She doesn't come in until ten now."

"Oh, that sucks. How was your Thanksgiving?"

"Um...Good. And...yours?" Samantha held the phone away from her ear and stared at it. *Odd.*

"Fantastic! Which brings me to why I'm calling. I was wondering if you guys were free Friday night. Can we meet up?"

Terrific. Eryn had no clue what had been going on the past few months. Completely oblivious. Cara had given up trying to call her. "Why, what's up?"

"It's a surprise. I can't tell you. Can we meet at our old stomping grounds? The Liquid Ambassador Bar?"

Ugh. That's where Lou and she had sex behind the dumpster. "Can't we meet somewhere else? Like a restaurant. Maybe talk over a delicious meal?"

"Fuck that. I haven't been out in months. I want to get my drink on and dance my ass off!"

And Samantha didn't. The last thing she wanted was go back to that shithole club and watch Cara and Eryn screw people on the dance floor just so she could drive their drunken asses home later. Her palms grew clammy. She felt the old Samantha returning. An obedient follower. Their plaything.

"Eryn, a lot has been going on the past few months. Things aren't the same."

"Well, nothing has changed with me. You guys are still my closest friends."

Really? Then where was she for the past eight months? Why hadn't she called? She snags a boyfriend and blows the two of them off? Her big news – can we take a guess? Engaged. And now, throw it in their faces. Like Samantha cared. Too much time had passed. Too many bad feelings had come out. If she were a real friend, she'd know what was going on with Cara. She would've helped.

"Eryn. Cara has changed. She's been acting…weird." Okay, that was putting it lightly. She didn't feel comfortable telling her Cara's business, but she needed to know. "She drinks a lot now."

"Ha! That's news? Are you kidding? We always drank a lot. When did you become Mother Theresa?"

"No. I mean all the time. Even during work." A family member approached the desk and Samantha casually turned her head away.

"Who hasn't gone out for a liquid lunch once in a while?"

"Eryn. She drinks *during* work. She has bottles of liquor in her desk. She gets so drunk at clubs she throws up, blacks out, and I end up driving her home. One time I drove her home, there was coke and drug paraphernalia on the coffee table. She picks up strange guys all the time. She comes into work hung over or still drunk from the night before. Tells me crazy stories about not knowing how she drove home or who she was with. Has sex with multiple men every week. She forgets to use condoms. I caught her giving some resident a blowjob in the top landing of the stairwell a few months ago. She lost a ton of weight and she looks like shit. Like a regular crack head!"

One of the nurses Samantha had a close relationship with, gave her a knowing look. Did everyone in the hospital suspect?

"Are you serious?" Eryn whispered, finally catching on. "It sounds like you're just jealous. We've always been big partiers. Suddenly you have a problem with it? Are you jealous that Cara and I are getting action and you're not?"

Samantha rubbed her head. The nurse rubbed her back. "I am far from jealous. I'm concerned. And you should be, too. If you're truly her friend, you'd get involved."

"Fine. The Liquid Ambassador Bar, Friday, seven o'clock. I'll see for myself if it's her or just you being envious."

"I don't want to go to a bar, Eryn."

"It's not about you. It's about me. I was hoping to share some news with you, but now you're ruining it."

"Fine. Fine! I'll meet you there at seven. But, you can drive her home. I'm not dealing with it."

"Yeah. We'll see."

****

Samantha snuggled in Cooper's arms and recounted her phone call with Eryn. She'd never told Cooper about Cara's past, but tonight everything came out. Cara's upbringing, her mother and brothers, the fiancé that dumped her, and her out of control partying this past year, including the blowjob she gave Dr. Chambers. Always comfortable in Cooper's arms, she didn't hold anything back.

"Don't show up then." Cooper stroked her arm.

"I can't. That's rude."

"Who cares? They haven't exactly been nice to you, have they?"

"No, but at times, I still feel bad for Cara. She has no one really. Sometimes, I picture her sitting all alone in her apartment crying. Depressed. Nowhere to turn. Desperate."

"You tried to help her. Multiple times. But, dragging you into her whacked-out life, isn't being a friend."

"She tried to help me change."

"There was nothing to change. You only change when it makes you a better person and leads you to a better future. Not down the path to hell. You just needed to believe In yourself, and the people you were hanging around with didn't let you."

"I think I saw the two of them laughing and having the time of their lives and I wanted that. I wanted—"

"That wasn't real. You think they're happy? They're searching for happiness like every other twenty-year-old. When people make you feel insecure, it's because of something happening to them, and not about you."

"Part of me wanted to be just like Cara. Or, so I thought. And, I was jealous of her relationship with Eryn. I was willing to do anything Cara said." Samantha wanted to tell him everything. Even about Lou and Bruce, but her fear tore through her. She hated hiding things from the man she loved, but there were some things better left untold. It wouldn't solve anything, would it?

"You can't fill your loneliness that way. No one will ever be there enough to fill that ache. Everyone's struggling with their own demons. Singing at Open Mic was the best thing you did for yourself."

She sat up and pushed her hair away from her face. "Cooper, I have to tell you one more thing."

"Is everything, okay?" A look of deep concern dusted his face.

"Yes. Just want to add to the crazy Cara story. As if I haven't said enough already."

"I told you. You can't scare me off." He placed his hands on her cheeks and kissed her on the forehead.

She swallowed hard, then stiffened. "Um…" *This was bad. She couldn't do it.* "Remember when Apollo attacked me?"

"No." He widened his eyes, mocking her.

She forced a laugh. He was so silly. "Well, it wasn't entirely Apollo's fault. It happened because Cara thought I'd be into it. She slept with him herself, and thought she'd throw me a bone - as she put it - and asked him to have sex with me. Out of the goodness of both their hearts," her melodramatic, singsong voice carried in his apartment.

From between his frowning eyebrows came a hardened glare, fury pouring from his eyes. "Wait. What? You planned on having sex with Apollo?"

"No! I had no idea. It was their plan. She failed to tell me, and Apollo thought I knew." Her eyes searched the room, unable to focus on anything. She suddenly regretted her admission. "He did attack me, but thought I wanted it, that I knew. But, I had no clue. I freaked out, he got fired, and Cara was pissed at me."

Cooper lurched up from the couch. "I don't understand. She put him up to this and she was pissed at you?"

"She said due to my 'stupidity and big mouth', he got fired and then stopped speaking to her. She lost a *good thing*."

"First of all, that's a manipulative personality. She blames you for everything. Second…" Cooper's posture slumped. "I never told you about this, but I was so upset about what Apollo had done to you. I couldn't show my feelings for you in front of Roselyn, but I was sick to my stomach that he could've raped you. I didn't sleep all night. I came in early and practically camped out by Roselyn's door waiting for her to come in. I was freakin' thrilled he got fired. Cara or no Cara, he's a pig, and the thought of him hurting you, killed me."

He kneeled down in front of her and put his head in her lap. Samantha stroked his hair. Had Cooper cared for her way back then? "Sorry, I didn't tell you this sooner. It was a bad year. I wish I could erase it all. I don't know what I was thinking. I thought I wanted to be like the two of them, but looking back, it was a nightmare."

"We all do stupid things. Fortunately, we learn from them. Well, some of us do. And, I'm sorry if I added to your stress last year."

"No. Actually, the night I saw you strip in your office..." she nudged him, "...that was the night everything changed for me. You woke me up."

"Seeing my naked body woke you up?" He sat back on his butt and Samantha joined him on the rug.

"Yup." Samantha leaned her head on his shoulder. "I was sick of it. Tired of the whole scene. I didn't want to meet Cara at the bar that night. I forgot my pocketbook at work, which now I wonder if it was some subconscious decision. I came back to the hospital to get it, promised Cara I'd be back, then saw the light on in your office. I never returned to the bar."

"I thought I pissed you off that night, though?"

"You did. But, looking back, I needed a good kick in the ass. You woke me up to what I was becoming. You were my mirror."

"And you're mine." Cooper kissed her tenderly. He rode the waves of her crazy life, never letting it bother him, seeing past all the ugliness. "I have some news, too."

"What?"

"I looked into it, and I'm going back to college next semester. I picked up the paperwork I need. It starts two days after I return from Hannah's wedding. Perfect. I took two classes, back to back on Tuesday and Thursday nights. I'll be a zombie the following mornings, but I figured I can graduate by this time next year."

"That's great! I'm so happy for you. I'll help you anyway I can."

"Then maybe Roselyn will get off my back. If I get my degree, I'm going to shove it so far up that woman's ass—"

"Woah, cowboy. She's not worth it. Do it for yourself. The moment you have to prove yourself to someone, is the moment you utterly have to walk away."

Cooper narrowed his eyes. "Where'd you hear that?"

"I saw it on a plaque at the Open Mic night. Near the ladies room. I read it every night before I go on stage."

"I Love it. By the way, when're you going to perform on Thursday nights so you can win us some money?"

Samantha let out a hoot, then rolled onto her back. "We'll see. I do have some news that you'll like."

"Oh, yeah? What?" He nibbled on her neck and climbed on top of her.

"Tomorrow night, before Open Mic night, I'm going to Houlihans to grab a bite with the gang."

"Really? I'm impressed. But what if you say something dumb? What if you order the wrong food? What if they don't like your goofy T-shirts?"

Cooper's nails dug into her ribs, tickling her. She rolled onto her stomach, then tried to crawl across the floor away from him. She grabbed hold of the carpet and dragged herself over it, but he lunged, and threw his arms around her knees. Before she could wiggle away, Cooper clutched onto the elastic band of her sweats and tugged. With both of them aggressively pulling away, Samantha went one direction, while her sweatpants went the other. Cooper scooted up and rested his head on her thighs, tightening his grip on her knees.

"What are you wearing?" He edged up another few inches.

She turned her head enough to see his eyes on her butt. Her underwear had a yellow smiley face with headphones on its head, and musical notes trailing from one side. "You have a problem with them?"

"Not at all. I like them better than the thongs, actually. They suit you better. But…"

"Yes?"

"I think I like them better when they're off." He scooped her into his arms. Their lips melted into one, and with his free hand, he quickly ripped the cotton material off.

Chapter 35

Samantha cut through the crowd in The Liquid Ambassador Bar at seven o'clock, dreading the night ahead. How long would she have to stay so it didn't looked obvious that she wanted no part of this? She threw on a pair of dark jeans, a fitted, white, long-sleeve shirt, and boots with a tiny heel. Except for a long, dangly necklace, she couldn't look any plainer.

She glanced toward the bar and Cara had already planted herself on a stool with a peach-colored cocktail in her hand. The usual trashy attire barely covered her body despite the chilly December weather.

Relax. You can do this.

"Hello, Cara." She hopped on the stool beside her.

"Samantha." Cara took a long sip, avoiding further conversation.

Samantha removed her jacket and swung it over the back of the barstool. "Why do you think Eryn wanted us here?"

"It's pretty obvious, don't you think?"

"I wasn't sure if she told you or not."

"She called you first, not me." Cara swiveled slightly to the right.

Samantha ignored her and watched as a girl climbed up on one of the large speakers and attempted to dance, but was swiftly removed by one of the employees.

"Why are you even here?" Cara sucked down her drink and banged it on the counter.

"Woo hoo! My friends! Let the celebration begin!" Eryn burst through the crowd and flung her arms up, hugging them both. Cara and Samantha's heads came within inches of one another. The smell of cigarettes choked her. "It's been so long. I missed you guys so much. How's everyone?"

"Great. What's your news? I'm dying to know." Cara sounded fake and sarcastic.

"Ready?" Eryn grinned so big, her teeth looked like they were dentures. "Ta da." Even in the dim light, her giant rock blinded them. "I'm getting married!"

Samantha couldn't help sensing the change in atmosphere from a year ago. Eryn was like a stranger to them. That feeling you get when a family member hasn't contacted you in years, but then sends you their son's graduation announcement expecting money.

Cara looked completely jealous. Samantha knew what she was thinking: *How could she be engaged in less than a year? There should be a ring on her finger.* Cara placed her hand under Eryn's and smiled. No words came out though, as if she was fighting back tears.

"It's beautiful." Samantha finally said. "When's the wedding?" At that moment, she realized how little she cared. Hopefully, Eryn wouldn't invite her.

"We haven't set a date yet. He surprised me on Thanksgiving in front of my family. I just had to tell you two. Can you believe it?"

Still having said nothing, Cara swiveled toward the bar. "Let's get some drinks to celebrate."

Surprise on that one.

"Ladies, how 'bout three Mojitos?" Cara finally looked happy.

"Sounds great." Eryn wiggled herself out of her ski jacket and threw it behind Samantha's barstool. Her tiny, body-hugging red dress said, "single and looking", not "soon to be married".

The bartender approached and Cara gave him their order.

"Actually..." Samantha interrupted. "Do you happen to have any pumpkin ales left?"

The bartender smiled. "You know what? I think we do."

"It's a shame they're only around for a short time." Samantha leaned over the bar as he searched.

He plucked one from the small fridge and cracked open the cap. "True, but then we get to try all the winter ales."

"I love the pumpkin ales, though. They're just like Mallomars. You can only get them in the cooler months. I want to pick up a six-pack of pumpkin ale and a box of Mallomars and scoff them down together."

"Totally! Let's add it to our bucket list. Mandatory." He winked, then placed the bottle in front of her. "Enjoy."

Cara kicked Samantha in the shin and tossed her a dirty look.

The bartender returned his attention to the other two. "Sorry. What'd you want again?"

While waiting for their Mojitos, Cara leaned in close to Samantha. "What're you trying to do? Embarrass us?"

"He seemed pretty into it."

"Look. You come dressed like your taking your kids bowling, then you order a beer and start talking about cookies?"

"Is this what you were talking about, Cara?" Eryn leaned over and grabbed her leafy beverage. "I think she needs to get laid. I hope you're not jealous that I'm engaged and Cara's hooking up. Are you?"

"I tried to help her. She hasn't changed one bit." Cara laughed and a mint leaf stuck to her tooth for all to see. Too bad Eryn couldn't from her angle, because Samantha definitely wasn't going to tell her. Let's see who's embarrassed now.

The next hour dragged on, Samantha desperately thinking of an excuse to leave. With two drinks behind them, and a round of shots ordered, Cara and Eryn had no plans of slowing down or going home. Cara had excused herself to the bathroom at one point, and soon after, started sniffling and licking her teeth. The once moody woman now talked incessantly, throwing her hands all over the place and laughing at the dumbest stories. She spoke so rapidly, Samantha couldn't get a word in.

"My car loan's paid off, my credit card bills, and after this month, my college loan will be paid off, too. Come this spring, I'm looking for a new apartment. A nice, big place." Cara held up her glass for them to clink.

When Cara ordered a fourth drink, Eryn declined. Samantha had stopped after the first, and now Cara egged Eryn to have just one more. Eryn agreed, not noticing Cara's intoxicated state due to her own euphoria. Part of Samantha wanted to leave now. Part of her held on to that motherly instinct to take care of Cara. Would Eryn be able to? She glanced at her watch. She'd stay another half hour.

Samantha headed to the long line already forming at the bathroom. The last time she stood here was with Lou, right before they headed to the green dumpster. She wanted to be with Cooper in his apartment, safely in his arms. This whole atmosphere seemed childish and foreign. As she neared the entrance to the bathroom door, the familiar sign hanging to the left finally made sense. "It's easier to forgive an enemy, than a friend."

Thirty minutes later, Samantha found herself on the dance floor. Eryn, heavily buzzed, was having the time of her life as if this was a rehearsal for her future bachelorette party. Somehow, she snatched a newspaper-boy cap off some guy's head and spun around with one hand on the cap, and the other on her spicy hips. Despite the obvious diamond ring, a group of men surrounded Eryn and cheered her on. That fiery, red hair and matching dress lit up the dance floor.

Cara, on the other hand, presented a much different image. The painfully thin girl held a glass in her hand, the contents of which spilled down her arm. Her black eye shadow, which matched her peeling, black nail polish, dripped down her face as if she had splashed herself, attempted to wipe it, but smudged it down her cheek instead. Her red nose and droopy eyelids made her look like she had a bad head cold and needed medical attention.

Unable to keep her eyes open any longer, or perhaps closed to prevent herself from seeing double, Cara swayed back and forth by herself as if in a trance. Her head bobbed up and down, her arms stayed close to her lower body which barely moved. She bumped into dancers around her, unaware. Occasionally, she shook her hair around in violent bursts, but then raised her hand as if to keep from falling, or to grab hold of someone near her.

Eryn released a stream of powerful snorts and cackles when the guys began clapping and cheering her on. One of their neckties hung around her neck and she hopped around in her four-inch heels like a performer on stage. A man at least six-foot-five, flung his arm around her waist, clutched onto her ass, and grinded her. She laughed as if not a care in the world – and no fiancé waiting at home - tossed her arms around him, and then their tongues intertwined like two snakes.

Sickened, Samantha looked back at Cara, who had made her way off the dance floor, unsuccessfully. She attempted to put her glass on a bar stool, missed and it crashed to the floor. With her hand grasping anything beside her to hold onto, she stumbled to the entrance. Samantha caught up.

Had Cara thrown up a little on her chin? Cara breathed in, bit down on her bottom lip, and tried to keep her head from bobbing. With her eyes barely open, and her legs surprisingly remembering how to move, she crashed through the swinging doors that lead to the parking lot.

Samantha seized Cara's wrist and flung her against the brick wall outside. "Cara!"

Cara only smiled and swayed. "Samantha, baby. You always try to take care of me, but I got this. I got it all under control, toots."

"What're you on? What did you take?"

Cara bobbed her head, then her body joined in until she looked like she was performing a rain dance.

"Your friend all right?" The bouncer pointed to Cara who was obviously high on something other than liquor and coke.

"Yup. Just had a little too much to drink."

"Want me to call her a cab?"

"Nah. I'll take her home." *Again.*

Samantha drove the exasperating route to Cara's apartment, never having said good-bye to Eryn who seemed more than content with her fan club of men. Having already told the two of them her big news, Eryn had no use for them anymore. She'd go back to ignoring them now that she had a wedding to plan. Until, of course, her bachelorette party. Would she hook up with one of those guys tonight? All of them? Had she cheated on him throughout their relationship or was this a cry for help? How would she drive home?

She dragged Cara up the stairs, dropped her in bed and tossed a blanket on top. After filling a tall glass with water and placing it by Cara's nightstand, Cara moaned and held her hand out for Samantha.

"She's married. I'm married. I tried." Cara dug her face into the pillow.

"What? Cara, she's not married yet. And neither are you. Are you okay to leave alone?"

"Alone is where the ships are. Alone on the water. I'm always alone."

"You need help. You have serious drug and alcohol problems."

"No problem, mon."

"Yes, problem, mon. You're a mess and I'm concerned. Really concerned."

"You hate me. I smell like ceiling fans with the wind blowing."

Samantha pulled the covers closer to her ear. "Get some rest. We'll talk next week."

"Talk. Walk. Chalk. So comfortable. Pillows are frothy."

Why was she always sucked back into Cara's bullshit? How was this destructive relationship adding any value to her life? It was dragging her down, like a strong riptide threatening to drown her if she stuck around.

Before she walked out the door, she glanced back. There was something different. The apartment didn't look the same. Not only was the apartment immaculate, but the set up was different. Had she moved furniture around? No. She had brand new furniture. Everything. Where was Cara getting all this money?

Then it hit her. Was she selling drugs? But who was supplying her? Any number of her hook-ups could've roped her in. How much was she selling to make this much money? *Damn her!* No matter how hard she tried to stay away from this girl, she always managed to suck her back in

Chapter 36

Monday morning, Samantha walked into the diet office and Karen let her know there'd be a meeting in the kitchen at ten o'clock. She tried to call Cooper, but his office phone rang multiple times before finally going to voicemail. After doing her sheets, and eating a quick breakfast, she headed into the kitchen for one of Roselyn's draining, tiresome announcements. What would it be now? How no one was working up to potential? How she was going to give us all more work to do? How two percent raises were too much and in the future they'd only get one?

She hurried down the hall and a roomful of employees stared at her in silence. More unnerving was Kenneth standing in the center of the ring, and Roselyn, nowhere to be found. Samantha scanned the room for Cooper, but he had parked himself right outside his office. Bruce blocked most of him.

"Thank you guys for coming. I know you're waiting to take your break, so I'll make this fast."

Where was Roselyn? Why wasn't she speaking? Was she in some fatal car crash?

"As most of you know, I've worked as the Assistant Director of Nutrition for the past three years. I've gained a tremendous amount of knowledge during my time here and am thankful for the opportunity. However, it's time I moved on and explored other career opportunities. Ones I've had my eye on for quite some time. It's with both sadness and excitement, I report my departure from St. Elizabeth's Hospital. My last day will be on January 3rd."

Several loud gasps and immediate chatter broke out in the normally bustling kitchen. Why wasn't Roselyn making this announcement? Why was he leaving? Had their affair been discovered by administration? Were they planning on marrying and one of them had to leave?

"I'm sure my replacement will be just as affective in keeping this department up to the high standards it has always followed. Mainly because you're the backbone of this department and without you, everything would fall apart. You guys should be proud of the hard work you do on a daily basis and I encourage you to continue doing your best. It has not gone unnoticed. Thank you for three wonderful years. You'll be missed."

Applause broke out and Cooper finally caught Samantha's eye. She attempted to ask what was going on, but Bruce saw the exchange and gave them both a look. She shifted her expression toward Ryan and threw her hands up, trying to show general confusion.

Cooper casually held his hand up to his ear, pretending it was a phone.

She tore down the hall, grabbed her books and took the elevator up to her floor. Once there, she dialed Cooper's office phone.

"Good Morning. Cooper Tim—"

"Cooper. It's me. What's going on?"

"I've no idea. I'm just as surprised as you."

"Where was Roselyn during all this?"

"I saw her early this morning when I came in, but she disappeared. You'd think she'd be here for an important announcement like this. Or, make the announcement herself. They never leave each other's side and now she's MIA."

"Maybe she's in her office plotting their wedding. Why else would he leave?"

"Not sure. They're the mother and father of this department. I can't imagine them broken up. But I'll tell you one thing. I'm putting in for his job first thing in the morning."

****

On January 3rd, Kenneth made his departure from St. Elizabeth's Hospital and Cooper anxiously awaited Roselyn's decision. Although he always gave one hundred percent, Samantha noticed he came in even earlier, stayed later, and assisted Angie even more with the many problems she continued to have running the cafeteria. Cooper gladly helped without expecting anything in return, all with the hope that his good deeds would finally pay off. If Roselyn or human resources needed testimonials of his hard work, there was a long list of employees he had helped over the past year.

Cara initially returned to work humbled, and thanked Samantha for driving her home. Samantha was unsure if she was sincere, embarrassed, or sarcastic, but she attempted to give their friendship one final chance. Cooper told her it was time to move on, that her passive-aggressiveness was wearing her down, but Samantha's heart pulled her back in.

The Monday after Kenneth left, Roselyn immediately had Cooper assist with many projects that Kenneth had been responsible for. The long lists of his assignments made Cooper wonder what Roselyn did all day. He juggled his work, Kenneth's, and continued to help Angie.

Cara came in Tuesday morning back to her old self. Samantha wolfed down her breakfast to get away, as Cara rambled on about some hot guy she met at a bar, how he worked in radiology, how much vodka she drank, how she wasn't sure if she used a condom, and couldn't understand why he never called all weekend.

Heather was on the phone behind them, trying to get a word in edgewise to the caller. When Heather finally hung up, Coletta, a tray passer from the kitchen, delivered the devastating news. Rebecca, the social worker Heather ate lunch with every day, had been killed in a car accident on her way to work this morning. Heather bolted from the diet office and charged upstairs.

Samantha's heart broke in two. The room seemed to spin. She regretted never having formed a relationship with her. She wanted to throw her arms around Heather and console her, but it would've looked fake and forced. She pushed her food away, nausea rolling in her stomach. Rebecca seemed to be Heather's only close friend in this place. How would she cope with such painful news?

Samantha dumped her plate of food in the garbage and heard Cara huff. Then a *humph*. "What?" Samantha was in no mood.

"Great. What does this mean now? She's gonna want to eat lunch with us every day again?"

Samantha recoiled. "Are you serious? You did *not* just say that. Her best friend is dead and you only care how it'll affect you?" Samantha slammed her chair back under the desk, shoved her lab coat on, and hurried up the stairs to find Heather.

Chapter 37

Samantha typed quietly on her computer making sure it didn't rouse her mother to question what she was doing. The slow and deliberate tapping of the keys was taking too long though, and she snuck over to her bedroom door and closed it all the way. She glanced at the picture of Cooper and her from Christmas Eve at his mother's house. The large tree in the background lit up her red dress and his matching red dress shirt.

The pictures of her mother somehow returned. She had hid all four of them in a drawer. They were back on the dresser now.

After she finished typing, Samantha headed back to the door to reopen it, but then decided against it. Sure, it would cause yet another fight, but she didn't care anymore. The large boxes she brought home from work yesterday sat in the middle of her room, empty, but not for long. Samantha took all the slutty going-out clothes she used to wear with Cara and dumped them in the box. Then snatched up all the four-inch stilettos and piled them on top. Her painfully inappropriate suits went into another box, along with clingy, two-sizes too small shirts, that made her boobs look photo-shopped in pictures.

When the boxes overflowed, Samantha threw her pocketbook over her shoulder and headed to the mall to buy new, professional suits. She realized the distinct difference between slutty and sexy, and wanted no part of the former. Done with Cara and her never-ending drama, Samantha needed to move on.

****

On Thursday, January 16th, two days before Cooper left for his sister's wedding in Jamaica, Samantha snuck into the kitchen during the busy lunch service. Roselyn had yet to make a decision on Kenneth's job. An obvious ploy for the hospital to save money. Why hire Cooper right away when you can have him do both jobs and save a few bucks along the way? Hopefully she'd make the announcement tomorrow before he left so he'd have something to enjoy during this wedding from hell.

Between Roselyn working him like a dog, and Hannah forcing

him to come over every night with last minute preparations, Samantha hadn't shared a moment alone with Cooper since Saturday morning. Five days without having more than a five-minute conversation with him - never mind holding him in her arms - wore on her patience. Not to mention she had so much to tell him. Coming in the kitchen like this risked someone discovering their secret, but he hadn't answered his phone all day.

Samantha entered his office, closed the door, and kept her foot against it like a wedge. Cooper dropped his pen on the desk and his grin grew steadily, not stopping until his cheekbones collided with his eyes.

"And to what do I owe this pleasure?" He rubbed his eyes. *Was he getting any sleep?*

"I miss you. I miss our lunch dates. I miss our lunch kisses. I miss seeing you during the eight long hours I'm forced to work in this depressing place. And I'm going to miss you so much while you're away."

"Me too." His smile weakened, as his eyelids drooped. He could barely keep them open. "You going to Pablo's retirement party tomorrow night? Forty years that man worked in this damn kitchen. I give him credit. I don't know if I could stay in one place that long."

"Not sure. Got a lot going on in the next twenty-four hours."

Cooper glanced at the blinds, which were all drawn. "I heard Heather gave notice. Only two weeks. She must have another job already."

"Do you blame her? I wouldn't want to work here anymore either." Samantha unfastened a button on her blouse and wiggled her eyebrows.

"You nut." He rose from his chair. "You're in an extra good mood today. I wish I wasn't so exhausted."

She unfastened another one and winked. "It's a new year. I feel good things happening with us this year."

He inched closer to her. "Do you know something I don't?"

"Yes. Actually, I do. Lots of good news."

"And I want to hear all about it." He placed his hands on her shoulders, but then glanced at the door.

"My foot's wedged against it. They have to get through me before it opens."

"Now you're reading my mind." Before she could speak, Cooper swept his mouth over hers and let his top lip roll and brush over her lower lip, dragging it down and opening her mouth. Her breaths surged out and she wrapped her arms around his neck. After weeks of grueling hours, he let himself go and kissed her with such fervency, his hunger oozed from every pore in his body.

Cooper placed his fingers under her blouse, pushing the bra back so he could sneak a peek. "Shit. You're killing me, Samantha." He rolled his fingers around her nipple and then, as if he couldn't control himself any longer, placed his mouth over the hardened tip.

Samantha rocked with his sucking, and ran her left hand through his hair. She reached as far as she could with her right hand and relocated the framed photo of his sisters that threatened to fall from his circling hips. He let go of her nipple and his smirk revealed a man that desperately needed a release. Now. Sin and mischievous thoughts flashed across his face and he pulled her in close locking onto her lips again. With one hand under the back of her head, and one on her ass, Cooper hoisted her into his crotch and gyrated as if he'd have an orgasm just from this alone.

Samantha leaned in, rubbing him with her pelvic bone and felt how hard he was under his pants. She drew her hips in tight and grinded him back wanting so much for him to be inside her. Fantasies surfaced of them coming back later after the kitchen closed and screwing him on his desk.

"Boss, what do you want me to do with all those tubs of Axelrod yogurt—" The door opened and smashed Samantha's heel. The heel that had come undone from the door. It swung open enough for Lou to pop his head in the space and see Samantha's ass in Cooper's hand. The skin around Cooper's mouth - deep red - as hers probably was, too.

None of them spoke. Samantha hid her face, but still coming off his high, Cooper's breaths rushed out. He desperately tried to control them.

"Sorry." Lou nodded to Cooper. "Didn't realized you were...preoccupied." He closed the door and left.

"Oh God." Samantha's hands flew to her mouth.

Cooper pounded his hand on his desk. "Dammit. Right before she makes her announcement! She won't give me the job now. That's department rules. All this hard work for nothing!" He turned back to her. "Go. Just, go. Let me talk to him before he tells the entire building."

Samantha fled, her head down the entire way out of the kitchen. How could she be so stupid? She ruined everything she touched.

Chapter 38

Cooper took one final breath and hurried toward the back fridge. Lou unloaded the Promise margarine onto the shelf and sneered when Cooper entered. Before he could say a word, Lou leaned his arm on the tallest box of Land O'Lakes butter and smiled.

"Sorry there, boss. Guess I should've knocked. My bad."

Cooper wasn't sure what to say. Would Lou be cool with this? Could he trust him not to say anything? "Listen, Lou, You know there's a—"

"No. No." He ripped off his gloves. "No need to explain. Samantha's obviously making her way around the department and you're next on her list."

"What?"

"Don't get me wrong. She's a smart girl moving up the ladder. I mean, why get it on with a lowly storeroom boy when she can have the next Assistant Food Service Director?"

"What are you talking about?"

Lou sat back on a case of milk. "You don't think she's with you 'cause of your good looks and charm do you? She's got her sights on bigger things. I noticed when she started working in the kitchen over the summer she had her eye on you. Kissing Roselyn's ass, always volunteering, working close with you. And, with you as the new Assistant Director, she'll have endless possibilities. Maybe you'll even bring back the Chief Clinical position we used to have and give her the job. Has she asked you about that yet?"

Besides Lou talking in circles, his release of information was coming at Cooper faster than he could process. "Wait. Back up. What do you mean making her way around the department?"

"Isn't it obvious? She's desperate. First, she gets it on with me, then shoots for Apollo, but screwed that one up bad." Lou snickered. "Now she's moved on to you. Maybe she tried to get it on with Kenneth and that's why Roselyn made him leave."

"Lou, you're making no sense. None of that happened. Are you high again?"

"Look, I don't know what she told you, but that girl sleeps

around."

"You slept with her?" His heart felt like it was shrinking. He looked around in confusion and shock.

"Not sure why you'd want my sloppy seconds, but some guys don't care about that shit. Like Bruce. He just wants a piece of the action. If you don't mind, I don't mind. It's all cool."

"Samantha slept with Bruce, too?" His heart fell into his stomach. A minute ago, he was kissing the girl of his dreams, and now a storeroom clerk was telling him his biggest fear.

"Don't forget Apollo. When he got a little too aggressive, she chickened out. She plays a good act. If I were you, I wouldn't trust her. She plays games. Hides things from people. Tells you one thing, then does another. Pretends she's one person, then you start finding out all these puzzling things about her that don't make any sense."

Cooper couldn't speak. So much he wanted to ask. So much he wanted to say. He rubbed the back of his neck.

"I'd make it my business to find out what else she's got up her sleeve. What other surprises. Now that you've got the leftovers, that is."

Cooper's arms felt impossibly heavy. His entire body weighed him down as if it would collapse at any second.

"Boss, be careful. She doesn't care where she does it or what she does. I did her behind a fucking dumpster, for Christ's sake, and she didn't give a shit. And then, she ended up meeting both me and Bruce in a motel, bought the beers, and paid for the room. If you ask me, she's one desperate lady. But if that's what you want…"

Burnt chicken cutlet returned to Cooper's mouth. A distant phone rang behind him. His head spun. He didn't' know what to say. *She had lied*.

That's why she acted so mysterious. How many different lives had she led? Kind-hearted dietitian that sings to innocent children at a library. But then, dresses like a hooker and sleeps with everyone in the kitchen. An alternative rocker chick at night who doesn't even let her best friend know she sings. And, no matter how many things Cara does to her, she stays by her side. Why had Samantha insisted on meeting Cara and Eryn at the bar that night? There had to be more to Samantha's stories. Was he part of her game, too?

"Thanks for the heads up, Lou." He pressed his fist into his stomach.

"No problem."

"You won't say anything, will you? I mean, I'll lose my job. This one. Forget about me getting Kenneth's."

"Nah. Course not. You always say I'm your right hand man, right?" He yanked his thick gloves back on.

"Yeah. Thanks. I appreciate that."

Lou held up his fist and butted Cooper's with his.

Coletta entered the refrigerator. "Cooper. Your phone's been ringing off the hook. Roselyn wants you in her office, now."

Chapter 39

Samantha stepped into the deserted elevator at the end of the day. Why hadn't Cooper paged her? Had Lou told on him? Had Roselyn fired Cooper? Fear ripped through her. As the day progressed, her other fear won out. That Lou told Cooper about them.

What would she say in response? Reveal everything to Cooper? All the details? Wait to follow his lead and see what he said first? Her life had been going so well, with a promising future ahead. Ever since that damn Eryn called, her past started catching up with her. Why did Samantha go that night? She should have refused. She should have told Eryn off. Left Cara at the bar.

She was a good person, with a good heart. Tried to help everyone and still, nothing went right. She should've listened to Cooper and escaped from this juvenile, soul-sucking environment. She hated confrontation, not wanting to make things worse, but that's exactly what happened. Why'd she care what everyone thought of her? She needed to stick up for herself. Tell people off. Tell them how she really felt.

Tired of people taking advantage of her. Blaming her for everything. Blaming herself.

Samantha exited the elevator and paused. Her fear dissipated. Anger rose. *Blaming herself.* She thought back over the past year. The library. The Pediatrics Unit. Lou. Cara and Eryn. Roselyn. Her shitty raise. She had done nothing wrong. But, apologized repeatedly. Tried to change herself so others would like her. Let Lou treat her like a piece of crap. Let Cara manipulate her for her own needs. Never defending herself.

God, of all days, why today?

Before she came up with a plan, Cooper flew out of Roselyn's office. He looked pissed. Was it too late? Did she just fire him? Her stomach knotted. Her heart felt as if it was crushing.

Samantha took off down the hall, but Cooper ran over to her just as fast, yanked her arm and pulled her in the opposite direction towards the linen room. Once in the far back of the basement corridor, Cooper spun her, and the first thing she saw was his blazing eyes.

Fury rolled across his face. "Just answer one question. The same question I asked you several times before. Yes or no. Did you sleep with Lou?"

The hairs lifted on the back of her neck firing off a stream of guilt. The only person that liked her for who she was, believed in her, and looked past all her quirks. The person who supported her and stuck by her, she had lied to. "I...I'm sorry."

"That's not what I asked. Answer me," his voice echoed in the abandoned hallway.

She couldn't even look him the eye.

"I really don't know what to say to you, Samantha. I can't believe you put me in this position."

Put him in this position? How many times had he put her in difficult positions? How many times had she bailed him out, stood by him, and backed him up with Roselyn?

He clenched his fists and an image of her mother's incensed temperament flashed in front of her. The stairwell door behind her opened and slammed shut. The noise reverberated and shook Samantha to the core.

She. Had. Enough.

"How dare you! You blow me off all week, can't return any of my phone calls, don't make time for me, and then you have the nerve to question me? Me? I've had it. What I did in my past is none of your business. I've been there for you every step of the way despite all the criticism from you initially. I helped you through every work crisis. Even when you blow me off for your constant family drama, I'm still there for you. Now, I'm done. Done trying to please everyone and make everyone happy. Somehow, despite all my efforts, I'm the one that ends up miserable!"

Clicking of high-heels approached, until finally Samantha saw who it was. Cara. What the hell was she doing in that stairwell? Cara eyed them both up and down and snickered at Samantha. She reached the diet office and entered, tossing one more pathetic look her way.

"Cooper!" Roselyn, clear on the opposite end of the corridor, spotted them. "You've got to be kidding me. I asked you not two minutes ago to get that report for me and you're hiding out?"

"I'm coming," his angered tone continued.

"Did you think I wouldn't see you if you went to the end of the hall?"

Cooper looked at Samantha, still reeling. "I need to speak to you about this before I get on that plane. If I ever get the hell out of here tonight, I'll call you."

"Don't do me any favors. I won't be home tonight anyway. I tried to tell you multiple times—"

"Then find time tomorrow at work."

"Don't tell me what to do." Her muscles tensed, then quivered from rage.

"Cooper!" Roselyn's hands planted themselves on her hips, her feet refused to budge from their spot.

"We can't talk here anyway. It's impossible." Samantha nudged past him.

"Tomorrow night. Pablo's party," Cooper shouted, as she darted down the hall away from him.

Chapter 40

Samantha missed the first turn for Déjà Vu and continued to the next light, making a left into the parking lot. Her pounding chest worsened the claustrophobia that gripped her, and she pulled her car over to the side, parking along a crumbling fence, under a tree, a few feet from the entrance to Vixens & Vamps. The multi-color pennant banner no longer hung over Dunkin Donuts, and the once lively summer parking lot felt deserted and cold tonight. She cut the ignition and leaned her head back on the headrest. Five more minutes wouldn't matter. She already put her name down on the list when she went Tuesday night, and she needed time to calm down.

No bad vibes tonight. No drama.

She shut the radio and practiced singing the lyrics to the songs she'd sing tonight for the competition. She had hoped Cooper would come with her for support, but after what happened this afternoon, she didn't want him here. She tried to tell Cooper all week, but his busy schedule didn't allow for a measly five-minute conversation.

No bad vibes tonight. No drama.

Why was she here? Her mood was off.

No. She couldn't keep putting it off. Her whole life she put things off. Singing in public. Dating. Hanging with the gang from Open Mic. Her relationship with Cooper. Sure, she had regrets, but at least she had something to regret instead of sitting home every weekend by herself. This year was a blur. A nightmare. A dream come true. A disappointment. A new beginning.

She had to do this for herself. Cooper was right. She couldn't rely on others to make her happy.

Maybe it was better that Cooper wasn't here. She seemed to do better when alone and pushed to the edge. When she didn't analyze every detail and question every thought.

Her thoughts returned to Cooper and his angry tone – once again taking out his stress on other people. Her to be exact. His interrogation - who'd he think he was? Yes, she had a life before him. Did she question things he'd done in the past? How dare he grill her. It was none of his business. She had made mistakes, but she never once questioned him about Tiara or any past sexual conquests.

Samantha sat up and reached for the ignition when a familiar guy exited Vamps & Vixens. Where had she seen him before? He lit a cigarette, took a long drag and exhaled into the sky. Then appeared to look straight at her. It was him.

Could he see her in the car? No. Impossible. Nowhere near a street light, car turned off, she looked like any other car parked here. But, it was him for sure. That steroid-infused beast that spoke to Cara at the club on two occasions. What an ass. A pig! She wasn't surprised he hung out at trashy places like this. He probably couldn't pick any women up at the clubs and came here to watch a bunch of low-life, naked women touch themselves while he jerked off in his car. *Asshole!*

No wonder Cara shrugged him off every time he came near. He probably got too drunk, hit on all the women in the clubs, and asked them to come back to his place. What a dirt bag. She wouldn't be surprised if he was some mad-rapist, serial killer you hear about on the news. They'd catch him and women would come out to tell their story of how he always hit on them and wouldn't leave them alone. He creeped Samantha out. Luckily, Cara had enough sense to stay away from him.

Like clockwork, as if it couldn't be more perfectly timed, Cara came flying out of Vamps & Vixens with a short black raincoat that she clung to with her left hand.

What? Why was she with him? Was he her new boyfriend? Was he one of those guys that liked bringing their girlfriends to strip clubs so they could watch him get off on the dancers?

He handed Cara a cigarette and she popped it in her mouth while he attempted to light it. The January wind swirled and blew out the flame several times. He motioned to her. Cara released the raincoat and held her other hand up and around the cigarette to block the wind. With three of their hands sheltering the cigarette from the wind, it picked up again whipping against the side of Samantha's car window, and flinging Cara's coat opened.

No. Please, no.

Her black, leather thigh-high boots, reached above her knees and a few pieces of black string wound their way around her thighs and stomach in some form of underwear. Two black star tassels hung from her nipples. The silver sequins glimmered from the street lamp.

All the blood drained from Samantha's face and her stomach immediately tightened into a knot. A stripper? This wasn't real. Cara was stripping in this sleezeball place? Was this why Cooper and

Samantha saw her in this parking lot that night?

Samantha wanted to drag her into the car and take her home. Shocked, pissed off, betrayed, heartbroken. What was she doing? Is this how she paid off all her loans? Is this what she did after work and why she was late every morning? How could she? Did that steroid beast force her to do this? Who was he? Her pimp? How did any of this work?

Samantha looked at the clock on her dashboard. She had to go. No one was ruining her evening. Not Cara. Not Cooper. They could all go to hell.

The beast walked back into the strip club while Cara finished her cigarette. Samantha started her car and floored it until it rested parallel to the curb in front of Cara. Before Cara had a chance to see who was driving, Samantha jumped out and stormed over. Rage and disbelief competed for words, but as her hands shook and formed into fists, rage won.

"I have no words for what you've become. You've become a stranger to me, Cara. A stranger I no longer want to know. I can't even look at you anymore. All I see is this fucked up person that once meant everything to me. I can't believe I wanted to be just like you."

"Fuck...you."

Did she expect any more from her? "Great response. You know, the whole time I was trying to save you, you were killing me. Dragging me down further. I no longer have the energy. I can't protect you anymore, nor do I want to."

"Ha! I can handle myself. I've never been happier. Away from your nagging, making hard cash, paying off bills, and starting my life over."

"This is starting your life over?"

"This is only the beginning. I've done many incredible things this past year."

"I'm sure. Like what? Cocaine? Stripping? Giving Dr. Chambers a blow job in the stairwell?"

Her face contorted. "He told you? You little shit. You couldn't leave him alone when he didn't want your sad ass. You had to keep trying, didn't you? What'd you do? Fuck him and he revealed everything to you?"

Why was she arguing with this deranged person? Why was she wasting her time and her breath? "The mistake was mine for trusting you. I did everything you asked. I'm still recovering from all the lies." Samantha pulled Cara's coat back to reveal the shiny, star tassel.

"Lies? I never lied." Cara yanked the coat closed again.

"You withheld information."

"Interesting." Cara took the last drag from her cigarette and flicked it across the parking lot. "It appears you've been withholding information from me. How long have you and Cooper been fucking around?"

She should've known Lou would tell her. "Lou told you?"

"Lou? No. Not Lou, darling. You gave me an earful in the hallway today. Still blaming everyone else for your mistakes?" She turned to leave. "I have to go. You can stop stalking me now."

"I wasn't stalking you."

"Oh, yeah. What're you doing here then? Looking for a stripper job?" Evil laughter echoed off the building.

"No. I'm meeting some *friends* at Déjà Vu. Real friends. Have a nice life." With that, she jumped back in her car and careened to the far end of the parking lot.

****

"Samantha's in the house!" Chuck, one of Samantha's Open Mic friends, handed her a beer and gave her a huge hug. "Tonight's the night. Are ya excited or what?"

"Actually, I'm scared to death." Samantha flung her coat around a chair at the rectangular table the seven of them occupied. Her heartbeat thrashed in her ears.

"What the hell for? You're talented. Your friends are here to cheer ya on. My brother's gonna hook up the music for you."

"Thank you so much. I don't even know what to say."

"Say you're gonna kick ass and buy us all beers at the end when you win."

"Win? Oh, God, you're crazy. It's my first time doing this and I'm surprised if I don't throw up."

"Samantha!" Roger's wife ran up to her and squeezed tight. "How you doing, girl?"

"I'm going to faint. I can't do this."

"Nonsense. I didn't get a babysitter so I could watch you lose."

Samantha wished they'd all stop saying that. She didn't want to see the look of disappointment on their faces when she didn't win. They'd all toss her one of those awkward faces where you don't know what to say and suddenly have to come up with some great encouragement. Some would look away. Some would pat her on the back, but it'll all be the same. Then she'd drive home knowing this was a stupid idea from the get-go.

Damn Cooper forced her to come here and where was he now?

This is why she hated getting close to people. She bared her soul to Cara and she took the information and used it for her own amusement. Like she was some Barbie doll to dress up and play with. Cooper said he would love her no matter what, but as soon as he heard about Lou, he's off and running. Or actually, off and screaming. Screw him. Screw Cara. Screw everyone.

Tonight was about her. No one else. She wouldn't let anyone ruin it. This was the beginning of her new life. Starting over as Cara had said. New year. New her.

A hand clasped over her eyes and she clawed at the fingers to remove them. They were man-hands for sure. Had Cooper figured out what her big news was and shown up? Did he realize how wrong he was and came to apologize? Samantha ducked down and spun, removing the fingers from her eyes. Roger.

Now her heart felt like it was shriveling.

"Hey, hey, hey. You ready to blast this place into a new dimension, Sammy?"

"What number am I?" She didn't want to be first. Although, maybe first would be great. She could get this over with and then just relax, drink a few beers, and listen to the other performers.

"Dead last, I'm afraid."

"Great. Here. Take my beer. At this rate I'll be passed out by the time I go on."

"More time to check out the competition! Don't sweat it. You're going to rock it."

Two hours later, Samantha's eyes drooped. She woke at 7 a.m. for work and had to be up early tomorrow. Her initial energy and enthusiasm abandoned her. Watching one great performer after another killed her high spirits as she sipped on her warm beer. With one singer left, she guzzled the rest of the beer and shoved a mint in her mouth.

"Up next, a regular from our Tuesday night mini-mic, and her first appearance tonight. Please give a warm welcome to Samantha Hart!"

Applause rang out and her own table stood, clapped, and whistled. She took to the stage and positioned herself in front of the standing microphone. Even though she had performed on this stage many times, the vibe in the room felt different.

Chuck's brother helped set up the music and she tightened her fingers around the microphone. Her hands shook and she squeezed harder. Sharp nails dug into her palms. Samantha closed her eyes and tried to suck in deep breaths. The darkness shut out the audience, but Cara's ferocious look, Cooper's accusations, and her mother questioning the outfit she wore tonight, surrounded her instead.

The music to Avril Lavigne's "I'm With You" began, and hushed the crowd. The calming violin rhythm and the slow strumming of the guitar comforted her. She released her tight grip and gently swayed to the tune. Although only twenty seconds long, the opening melody seemed to drag on forever as the silent crowd waited.

Samantha opened her eyes and let herself escape into the only thing she did right in her life. Rich, powerful words escaped her lips in a hypnotic whisper. The tender melody and poignant lyrics took over and Samantha reached out to the crowd as if speaking to each one of them directly. Her eyes squinted with desperation. Her hand extended and grasped for understanding and acceptance.

Music to the chorus burst from the speakers and she ripped the microphone from its stand. Her strong, captivating voice ignited across the packed bar and the lyrics surged out, as did her anger and heartache.

The words paralleled everything she buried inside her for years. Confusion. Anger. Betrayal. Fear. Loneliness. Her tight fist punched the sky, then her finger pointed to the crowd. A girl in the back of the room stood and mouthed the words with her. Two guys at the bar whistled, and her own table bobbed their heads while waving their arms in the air.

Samantha edged toward the end of the stage, closer to the audience, closer to the warm feeling that surrounded her. She squatted until her butt touched her calves, then sang to three guys occupying the first table, looking deep into their eyes.

Were they getting it? Did anyone understand the pain? Would anyone help her?

She leaned back until she landed on her ass with a thud. She dangled her legs over the edge of the stage, banging her biker boots against the front panel. She wanted to be close to everyone here tonight. Those cheering her on, and those singing along with her. They got it. Only they understood her.

A group in the far back corner swayed to the right and left, their shoulders hugging each other as if glued. The bartender lit his lighter and gave her a thumbs-up.

The last chorus approached and she stood, strolled back the stand, drove the mic into the holder and grasped it with both hands, releasing her final fears and uncertainties.

Her eyes closed again. Not from anxiety this time. From relief.

Like a tremendous weight had lifted from her. Loud applause and cheering rang out, and she nodded her head a few times as if locked inside a dream. She opened her eyes to find not only her friends standing to cheer her on, but the entire bar. An unyielding chill coursed through her body, causing her to shiver.

A smile raced across her face and she held her hand up again, thanking everyone for their support. She'd done it. She could do anything she put her mind to. She didn't need anyone. Only herself.

That was it. She made up her mind. She would do it. She made her decision even before showing up tomorrow morning. It would be "yes". A big, fat, yes.

Chuck's brother hopped back on stage to change the song, when Samantha saw her watching near the entrance. Cara. Her arms clamped around her chest as if in a strait jacket. How long had she stood there, watching, listening?

Cara scowled. Samantha, in a moment of enlightenment, grinned. Then sneered. In here, her happy place, all the evils of her world seemed imaginary, like some bad nightmare. They weren't real. Cara wasn't real.

As the clapping died down, and requests for her second song began, Samantha turned to Chuck's brother. "Wait. I changed my mind. I want this song instead." She pointed to the one she sought out.

"You sure? It's a tough one."

"Yup. Never more sure of something."

"You got it, Samantha."

Tonight's host leaned over their shoulders, looked at the song, and his eyes widened. "Looks like we saved the best for last, huh?" He winked at her. "Go for it."

With Cara still watching, a martini glass now in her hand, Samantha took her place at the mic once more. The intense drumbeat began, the audience already bopping their heads to the pounding, then the bass rhythm pulsed, and a few banged on the tables in front of them, including the hot guy with the black wavy hair.

"Oh yeah!" Some big guy screamed to the right of her, standing and pumping his fist.

Samantha removed the mic and strutted across the stage, mimicking the strumming of the bass. Her thick-heeled biker boots pounded the stage. Her red, plaid mini-skirt flared out as No Doubt's "Hella Good" pulsated from the speakers.

The last time she sang it with such fervor was in the diet office, before Cooper overheard her, Apollo tried to rape her, and Cara later admitted to setting up the whole thing. The night she sang it, she thought she'd finally taken control of her life.

How wrong she was.

Today started another phase. One of many, she was sure. But this time, Samantha was in control. Things would go differently this time.

Samantha took her army jacket off and tossed it into the crowd. It landed on that hot guy's head. Her black tank top with the white skeleton reflected the flashing stage lights. She swayed her hips, and panted like Gwen Stephani did. When the chorus rang out, she hopped up and down as if on a pogo stick and waved her free hand in the air.

Cara chucked her drink on a small, square table and dashed out the door.

Chapter 41

Samantha couldn't wipe the smile off her face as she sauntered into work Monday morning at nine o'clock. Her first order of business: Roselyn's office. She hung her winter coat on the hook behind the diet office door and grabbed the crisp, white sheet of paper between the blue folder. After everything that went on this past year, this felt right.

Before she could leave the office, Karen stopped her. "Roselyn's having a meeting in the kitchen at nine-thirty. Everyone's to attend."

"Thanks." Not caring about her stupid meetings anymore, Samantha tore down the hall with confidence. Half way there, Cooper popped into her head. Did Roselyn announce his promotion on Friday? She forgot to ask Karen. She had called in sick Friday and thought it would look obvious if she called to ask. Cooper never gave her a call, so why'd she care? She'd find out later. With Cooper in Jamaica, she needed a clear head for this.

Samantha's knuckles rapped upon Roselyn's door and an annoyed, "come in" resounded. Roselyn darted around her office searching through mounds of papers strewn all over her desk. Never had she seen her desk like this before. Not even a stray paperclip took up space on the pristine desktop.

"What is it, Samantha? Can't this wait?"

A stack of papers toppled off her desk and sprayed across the floor. Samantha took a step forward to help, then changed her mind.

"Don't touch them! Don't touch anything, you hear? Goddammit."

Samantha stiffened like a soldier while Roselyn reorganized the papers and stacked them on her chair. She looked absolutely frazzled. Hair in a ponytail. Dress slacks instead of the usual skirt. Was she wearing flats? Had Kenneth's departure caused this much disarray? Hadn't Roselyn run a tight ship?

"What do you want, Samantha? Can't you see I'm busy? God, its Monday morning for Christ sake." She tucked a stray clump of hair behind her ear.

"It'll only take a minute. I promise." She bit down on her lip to suppress the giggle.

"When they clock changes to 9:07 you better be out of here."

Samantha leaned forward not knowing where to place her needle in the 'haystack of doom'. She finally decided to put it on the corner of the desk where Roselyn stood.

"What? What is that? Don't you see I have enough papers to go through?"

"It's my resignation. I'm giving you three weeks' notice. Which is more than Heather gave."

A manila folder fell from Roselyn's hand and landed on her shoe. "Notice? What? You can't leave."

"I am. February seventh's my last day. Says it right there on the first paragraph." Samantha pointed to the top of the document.

Roselyn's index finger pointed squarely in Heather's face. "I can read. But, you cannot leave."

"I can and I am. Since I'm assuming you already put an ad in the paper for Heather's job, you're ahead of the game and can interview and pick two candidates instead of one." Her sneer, obvious.

"Put an ad in the paper? Do you think I had time to do that?" As if her appearance couldn't get any worse, her face flushed and looked like it was molting. "Do you see this mess Kenneth left me? Cooper's vacation even took precedence over the needs of the department."

"Considering he told you six months in advance about his sister getting married, I'm sure you made arrangements. Correct?"

"He shouldn't have gone!" Spit flew from her mouth, narrowly missing Samantha.

"To his sister's wedding?"

Roselyn slammed her desk drawer shut. "Where? Where are you going?"

Samantha stood erect, shoulders back and grinned. "Someplace I know I'll get the respect I deserve. Someplace that recognizes my worth."

A vein seemed to throb in Roselyn's neck as she stepped forward, nostrils flaring. "What is that supposed to mean?"

A small knock tapped on the door. "Come in!" Her guttural roar, undeniable.

Angie entered with her eyes ablaze at the chaos. "Um, you wanted to see me, Roselyn?"

"Yes, yes. Come in." Roselyn glared at Samantha, then gritted her teeth. Her voice took on an exasperated tone. "Done?"

"Completely." Samantha grinned as if she just won the lottery, then turned to leave, but not before Angie slipped on a large stack of papers. She flew up like a cartoon character, and landed on her ass.

"What is wrong with you, Angie? Can't I count on anyone in this department?" Roselyn collapsed into her wide, black leather chair and huffed. Angie bent down and sorted the papers she had just scattered across the rug.

Samantha laughed to herself as she closed the door behind her. Before she made it back to the diet office, Lou stepped in front of her.

"Good morning, sexy." He winked and attempted to put his hand on her hip.

"Seriously, Lou?" She twisted to the left, knocking his hand off.

"I just thought since you and Coop broke up, maybe we could have another go at it."

"Broke up?" Did Cooper tell Lou they broke up? *Good.* One less thing on her to-do list. "Another go at what? There was never any thing going on. Re...mem...ber?" She widened her eyes until they almost popped out of their sockets.

"Baby. How could you say that? Everything was fine until Cooper came along. We had a real good thing, didn't we?"

Samantha snorted at his delusion. "Lou. I went through a lot last year and unfortunately, you didn't date the real me. You dated some fake version."

"Huh?" Lou squinted and shook his head.

"The me you met was not real. And that's the me you like. That's fine, but it's not the real me. Whenever I showed you who I really was, you ran."

"Girl, you on drugs?" His tone, uncertain.

"I can't explain it. I was going through this thing last year and you met me at a time I was trying to change who I was. But, I didn't like that person. I never felt comfortable being her. When I was her, you couldn't get enough of me. When you saw the real Samantha, you avoided me like roadkill."

"That's not true, baby. I like all of you." He tried to place his hand on her hip again.

She slapped his hand away this time. "Lou, you're not getting it. I don't want someone that likes the fake me. I want someone that sees behind the mask and likes me for who I really am." As the words left her mouth, she thought of Cooper. *Oh no. What had she done?*

"And Cooper likes this real you? I can like the real you. Give me a chance, baby." He wiggled his eyebrows. "The Sam I saw in Coop's office was pretty damn hot."

"Stop! Are you even listening? I'm not interested in you! You used me and treated me like a piece of shit. You had your chance and blew it. You could've had a great thing, but you were too busy showing off your *babes* to your *boys*."

Lou stepped back and frowned. As if a switch went off, he reverted to the dirt bag he was. "Yeah, well, now you have no one."

"What?" Thank God in three weeks she wouldn't have to see Lou's face anymore.

"Friday night. At Pablo's retirement party." He hesitated on purpose, wanting that perfect delivery. "Cara and Cooper were all hot and heavy making out near the bathrooms."

Her body tensed and a flood of adrenaline pulsed through her. Why was it, whenever her life looked up, there was always someone to bring it back down? "What are you talking about? You're lying. He would never. She would nev—"

"You talkin' about Cara and The Coop, and their lip locking session?" Bruce popped his head around the corner and leered at her. He rested his hand on the wall above her head, pursed his lips and nodded as if acknowledging how hot she was today.

"Yeah. She don't believe me, but we saw it. With our own eyes."

As if they saw it with someone else's eyes. Why was she entertaining these two buffoons? "You're both lying to get a rise out of me. Nothing's going to put me in a bad mood today. Especially your BS stories."

"You think we're lying? Go ask Cara yourself." Bruce snickered.

"We went through the door leading to the bathrooms and there they were. Sucking face like two fish. Guess they figured they could hide in there and not be seen."

"Cara had her hands all over his face. He didn't seem to mind." Bruce demonstrated by rubbing his hands over and around his head while puckering his lips.

"Yeah, he wasn't pulling away or nothing. Guess you couldn't give him what Cara has. She sure is more daring between the sheets then you ever were." Lou nodded.

"How would you know?" Samantha narrowed her eyes.

Bruce and Lou both looked at each other now. "You don't know 'bout that either?" Bruce bent over and grabbed his stomach. "Damn girl. What kind of crazy friendship did you and Cara have? Doesn't she tell you anything?"

Samantha glared at Lou, the saner of the two, which wasn't saying much. Her fist clasped onto the front of his shirt, tugging him down. "What are you talking about?"

"Yo. If she didn't tell you. I'm not spilling anything."

She yanked harder. "Tell me. Now!"

Bruce stepped in. "We had a bunch of threesomes. You know,

ménage à trois?" He attempted to look sophisticated. *Nice try.* "She brought the beers and even a little snif snif."

She let go of Lou. He patted down his cheap-ass, filthy work shirt as if it was a five-hundred dollar dress shirt. They both stared at her with total straight faces.

"When? When did this happen?"

"The first time?" Lou surveyed the ceiling. "That night you took off and left her in the bar. Forgot your pocketbook or something."

"No. You're lying. She hooked up with these two GQ, model looking guys. She had her eye on them and she told me she left with them."

"The guys with the pink and purple shirts?" Lou pressed his lips together.

"Yes. See. You know who I mean. She left with them."

"Girl." Bruce broke out in hysterics. "You are so lost. Those two were as gay as they come. She flashed some titties and they politely told her they were gay. She left with *us*."

Lou turned away. "I'm out of here. This is all too embarrassing. Samantha, wake up. Cara slept with us multiple times and now she stole Cooper from you. Maybe you shouldn't have called out sick Friday. Maybe you should've showed up to Pablo's party." With that, he strolled back to the kitchen, leaving Bruce to continue to leer at her.

Samantha's heart wilted. Was she always destined to feel like a loser? No matter how hard she tried, she would always be that loser from middle school. Bruce leaned in as if none of this just happened. Without missing a beat, he came close to her ear. "I still want you, babe. Now that no one wants you, I'll take you. What do ya say?"

Her eyes fixed on the white linoleum in front of her feet, then slowly rose to meet Bruce's tongue licking his crusty, chapped lips. As if in a daze, she turned away and strolled back to her office. There were no words left.

Before she stepped in, Karen exited. "Aren't you coming, Samantha? Roselyn's meeting's now. Remember?"

Samantha followed Karen like a zombie, as she jabbered on about her weekend. She let her talk, for her words were absent. She wouldn't put it past Cara to hit on Cooper. But, Cooper kissing her back? Was he that angry with her? Was this his payback for her lying to him about Lou? Did he kiss her on purpose to get back at Samantha? Did he know others would see and tell her?

Obviously, Lou hadn't told Roselyn he caught them kissing. Roselyn hadn't fired him, and he got the promotion. Maybe getting the promotion swelled Cooper's head? Did he go out Friday night to celebrate and got too drunk? Or, was he pissed Samantha called in sick Friday? That she didn't show up at Pablo's party? Didn't call him before he left for the wedding? Too bad. He didn't call either.

Maybe they should have spoken before he left, but for the first time in her life, she put herself first. She needed to do what was best for her, and he only seemed to care about her past sexual experiences. But, he did love her for who she was. He loved every ounce of her, no matter how quirky or dorky. Even when she felt like the biggest loser, he had loved her.

Why did he scream at her then? Why did he kiss Cara? Why hadn't he tried to call her? A frenzied ringing took over in her ears.

Karen and Samantha stepped into the kitchen surrounded by at least thirty dietary employees. The crowd glanced at their watches, whispered in each other's ears, and a bunch of guys in the back showed off their less then muscular calf muscles. Ryan and Angie sat on the supervisor's desk. The pot washer turned off the sink and ambled in with his long, black rubber gloves still in place.

Samantha looked around for Cara. Had she even made it into work yet? She'd question her as soon as she came in. Maybe Lou and Bruce lied. *Shit*. The last time she spoke to Cara was in front of Vamps & Vixens. That seemed so long ago. *Wait*. Is that why Cara kissed Cooper? Because of their fight? Because she saw her perform on stage? Was she jealous of her?

That. Was. It. Her mood was destroyed. She clenched her fist and shook with rage. Her eyes closed and she tried desperately to calm her anger. That bitch. That skank. They could all go to hell. She had it with all these assholes. It wasn't her. She'd surrounded herself with a bunch of bullies. She gave one-hundred percent of her heart to these people and got used. Repeatedly. And she let them! What the hell was wrong with her?

As if a wave washed over the entire department, it instantly silenced. Her eyes opened and Roselyn took center stage. Her hair was now down, but looked unwashed. A pair of high heels graced her feet.

"I'll make this quick, as I have a lot of work to do it seems. I've been abandoned. Deserted with no help. And, I have a selfish management team to thank for it."

The room immediately swelled with employees glancing at each other, and whispering voices elevated until the kitchen grew loud once more. Samantha caught Bruce staring at her, pursing his lips, and throwing kisses her way.

"Shh." Roselyn held her hands up. "I've been so busy, and buried with work I haven't had time to post for Heather's job, which some of you may not know, her last day was Friday and she only gave two weeks' notice. I've now been informed that Samantha is deserting us as well."

Gasps circled the room, and all eyes focused on her. *Now* is when she decided to announce this? Now? Samantha hadn't had time to tell anyone yet. In the corner of her eye, she saw Lou stroll over to Bruce, lean in, and whisper.

"I guess when the director is down and out, that's what everyone does. Kenneth leaves, my dietitians leave, Cooper goes on vacation during a critical time. What's next?"

How dare she! What had Roselyn done for any of them? She didn't even give her a decent raise after all she'd done. Cooper worked long hours, every day, for months. Heather gave over eight years of service to this dump. For what? Why were they all breaking their asses and working so hard? For this *great* leader? No recognition? Shitty raises?

"Anyway, none of this has anything to do with my meeting. I just needed to get that off my chest in case any more of you decide to jump ship." She pushed the loose strands of hair behind her ears. *Had she lost weight?* "The reason I'm here is I never had a chance to hire someone to replace Kenneth's position. And, before I get accused again, for not getting around to doing anything, I'm going to do it now."

She hadn't offered Cooper the position yet? *What the hell?* She didn't get around to doing it? Honestly? Is that why Cooper didn't call her? Was he pissed off and frustrated with everything and everyone in his life? Did that drive him to kiss Cara Friday night? Frustration mixed with some extreme drunkenness?

"During this crisis, I wanted someone to prove that they were a hundred percent loyal to *me* and put our department before their needs. I wanted someone that handled every task thrown at them, with no notice and rose to the occasion. Someone that enjoyed what they did, took it seriously and knew this would be a lifelong career path for them."

Thank God she recognized all his hard work. Why she didn't announce it Friday was a mystery. It would've been great for Cooper to hear these kind words. Finally. But, then again, maybe she had a hard time complimenting people to their faces. At least she was doing it now. Too bad Samantha didn't have a tape recorder.

"With the ever mounting work that needs to be done, I can wait no longer. I have made my decision and would like to share it with all of you." Roselyn raised her arms like a queen waiting for applause from her royal subjects. "I have chosen someone just like that. Angie."

Half the room broke out in applause, while the other half looked completely confused. Even Lou, who got his job because of Angie, hesitated in clapping. He looked up at Bruce, who shook his head.

Samantha slumped. Her entire body felt as if it had caved in, unable to think or move. She did not just say that. She couldn't have. Angie? The woman was clueless. She didn't know how to do anything. Cooper had to help her with every task. *Cooper!*

"Angie took on the job as a cafeteria manager without hesitation, needing very little guidance, and stopped by my office every evening with updates of her day and what she accomplished. Excellent communication."

That little shit! Cooper trained her and she screwed up on a daily basis. She couldn't even work the damn cash register. What lies had she told Roselyn every evening?

"Her biggest accomplishment this year was revamping the entire cafeteria menu and salad bar by herself. Her ideas have shown a significant increase in profits, which was recognized in her raise I authorized. Excellent creativity, innovation and financial gains."

This was not happening. The fluttering in her belly, twisted into a dense knot. Angie was going in there every day and lying? And they believed her? That thief. While Cooper tried to avoid Roselyn, Angie was in there kissing her ass, lying about what she was doing, and not giving Cooper any credit? Cooper let her hand over the menu ideas because he didn't want to see Roselyn's face, and Angie stole the credit? What other things had she told Roselyn she'd done when it was Cooper?

"The deciding factor though, was her discipline and seriousness with her college education. For those of you that don't know, Angie has a bachelor's degree. This shows her dedication to improving herself. I encourage all of you to go to college and better yourselves, too."

What a conceited ass! Better ourselves? Was everyone in here a bunch of losers?

Bruce slowly rocked his crotch back and forth demonstrating what he wanted to do with her later. *Okay, well, Bruce...*

"When Cooper gets back from his relaxing vacation, Angie will start, and until I can find someone suitable enough to replace Angie, Cooper will have to run both the kitchen and the cafeteria. Any problems, please contact him. Oh, and Ryan...I forgot to tell you.

You'll need to do Cooper's job this week, in addition to yours. That'll be all."

Roselyn marched out. Ryan's face plummeted and he tossed his clipboard into the air. Shouldn't Ryan get the cafeteria managers job? What the…? What next? How could Angie lie and steal when she majored in *religious* studies? When a group of Angie's old, kitchen friends surrounded her and provided hugs and pats on the back, Samantha took off in a frenzy.

Before Roselyn's door shut, Samantha kicked it open with her foot, then slammed it shut.

Roselyn had just removed her heels and jerked at the noise. Her lips pulled back, baring her teeth. "What do you think you're doing barging in here like this?"

"How could you? You know Cooper deserved that promotion!"

"Excuse me? Are you questioning me?"

"Yes, I most certainly am!" She raised her voice to new decibels, ones she had never reached even while singing.

"It's not your concern or your decision. That's why I'm the Food Service Director, and not you."

"Cooper worked fifty to sixty hours a week for you, without any extra pay or increase in salary."

"Who do you think you are speaking to me this way?" Roselyn repeatedly raked and tugged on that clump of hair, yanking it behind her ear as if she might rip it from her head.

"He did everything you asked, even putting his own work, his family, his personal needs aside for you. And stop making it out like he's a lazy piece of crap and taking another vacation. This is the first one he's taken in almost a year!"

"He's management. That's what happens."

"And, he tried to finish his final year of college, but you made it impossible for him. Making him work ten and eleven hour workdays. When was he supposed to go?"

"He should've thought about that before he applied. I told him I only wanted managers with degrees, and warned him. If he wanted it that badly, he should have found a way."

Samantha felt her throat start to tighten. "You sabotaged him."

"Don't you stand there and accuse me, I—"

"And, just so the record's straight…" Samantha flashed a cold smile. "Cooper did ninety-percent of the cafeteria menus. I did the other ten. Angie just stood there and nodded. He also redecorated the entire cafeteria himself, some of it with his own money."

"That's it! I will not sit here and have you attack my decision and make a liar out of Angie. Obviously working with Cooper all those months, poisoned your brain."

"You have no idea what's even going on in your department. If you did, you would've noticed that Cooper did the menus. He redesigned the setup of the cafeteria table and chairs. He revamped the grab-and-go structure making it easier to get what you needed. He took his own money and bought new framed art for the walls and gave Angie themes to try out during every season and holiday. He did it! He did it all!"

"Get out! You don't want to work here anymore, fine. But, I will not condone an employee lying about another employee, pretending someone's ideas are their own, and trying to screw the other person in the process of getting ahead."

She backed away, her response toneless. "Why not? You already have." Before Roselyn could answer, Samantha slammed the door behind her.

Samantha's heels punished every floor tile on the way back to her office. This was insane. Why did she put up with it for so long? Roselyn would find out soon enough who really did all the work in the cafeteria. Hopefully, Cooper will have enough sense to just let Angie drown, instead of bailing her out anymore. She'd tell Cooper first thing on Monday. If he was still talking to her.

She marched into her office, squeezed behind the open door and reached into her coat pocket for a piece of gum. Her sore throat needed something to moisten it.

"Hey, hey, hey, Karen. What's up shorty?"

Ugh. Samantha stayed hidden behind the door, avoiding Bruce and his antics.

"Mind if I use the phone?"

"You use it every day, Bruce. Why bother asking anymore?" Karen's heels clip-clopped across the floor, and out the door towards the kitchen, possibly to bring call backs to the line. Or, to avoid Bruce. Samantha knew the feeling all too well.

Fantastic. Now she was alone with him. Could she quietly sneak out from behind the door? She still needed to grab her books and papers. She'd have to wait until he finished.

"Baby. Helloooo. How's my sweet pussy cat?"

Barf. Did she have to sit through one of his disgusting phone calls to some unsuspecting girl? How did his wife not know? That poor woman must be clueless.

"I can't wait to see you tonight either...yes, five-thirty. The Harbor Motor Inn on 8th street. Reserve the room and leave the room number on your car's windshield. Park near the front entrance so I can find your car. ...yeah, of course, I'll reimburse you. I just wish they hadn't asked me to stay a half hour late to set up for a party."

What a liar! And, he used that same pathetic trick Lou used on her. Surprised he didn't ask her to pick up the beers, too.

"Oh, and one more thing. Since I'm getting out of work late, I won't have time to stop and pick up beers. Can you be my honey bear and pick up some beers, pretty please?"

Vomit City. And, to think she fell for the same BS last year. What an idiot she was. How embarrassing.

"Baby. You remind me of my pinky toe. Small, cute and I'm probably going to bang you on a coffee table later tonight."

Wow. Where'd he get this crap?

"Okay, baby, I'll see you later. Kiss Kiss. Can't wait." The phone crashed back in the cradle and Bruce sauntered out.

Samantha, still reeling from Roselyn, rushed to her desk to grab her books before any more drama could happen. She glanced at the phone. Then at the employee phone number box. *Hmm.* She dumped her books, and thumbed through the list of numbers until she found Bruce's home number. And dialed it.

"Hello?"

Samantha took a deep breath and raised the pitch of her voice. "Hi! Is Brucie there?"

"Brucie? Who's this?"

Samantha froze, then figured what difference did the name make? "It's Chiffon. Is he there? We have a date tonight, but I just wanted to confirm it. He hasn't answered his phone."

"Phone? When did he get a phone? What date? Who the hell is this?"

Samantha giggled like a schoolgirl. "I told you Chiffon. His girlfriend."

"Girlfriend?"

"Yes, Who's this. His mama?"

"Mama! I'll give you mama. I'm his wife."

"Wife? What?" Samantha gasped in an exaggerated manner. "My Brucie has a wife?"

"He aint your Brucie, girl. You better start explaining."

"No. He said he loved me. I was supposed to meet him at five-thirty at the Harbor Motor Inn on 8th Street. Park in the front and leave our motel's room number on my windshield, then wait for him in the room. I thought he was going to propose tonight!"

"Propose in a motel? Girl, you're a sucker."

Samantha pretended to cry. "I'm so sorry. I didn't know he had a wife. I hate him. What should I do?"

"I'll tell you what your ass is gonna to do. Nothing. Stay away from the motel. I better not see your ass there. You hear me?"

"Yes. Of course. I hate men! I thought he was the one." Karen reentered and Samantha slammed the receiver down. "See you later Karen. Have a great day." She grabbed her binder, and hightailed it out of the office and down the hall. Right. Into. Cara.

"Well, well. Look who it is. The next American Idol." Cara whipped off her tiny winter coat and scoffed at her.

"We need to talk. Now." Samantha grabbed her wrist and walked a few yards away from the diet office.

"What drama is Samantha starting this week?" Cara leaned against the wall and yawned.

"Don't play dumb with me. Did you or did you not make out with Cooper Friday night?"

"That's what this is about? Ha! You snooze you lose. He seemed more than happy to please me. I guess, once again, Samantha can't please a man."

Of all the anger, of all the words bubbling up in her throat, all the tears, the regrets, wasted time and wasted arguments, the countless things she wanted to say to her, Samantha closed her mouth.

"I didn't think so. You lose again."

Samantha's shoulders relaxed. Her breaths came easier. Her features softened. "You know. I feel really sorry for you Cara," her speech unhurried. "At one time, I wanted to be like you. I really did. You need help, though. You're an alcoholic, a drug addict, and have sex addiction issues. You had a shitty upbringing, and that sucks, but you need to fix your demons before you can move on." Her calm, encouraging voice rolled off her tongue.

"FUCK...YOU!" Cara's scream was so thunderous, Karen ran out to check on the commotion, as did several employees from the kitchen. Cara shook her head. "You fuckin conceited bitch. You think you're' so perfect? *You* need help. You." Cara sniffled. Was she holding back tears or did she just do another load of coke? "You bailed on me! You're not a friend. I did everything for you. How could you desert me! I thought you cared."

Then it hit Samantha. "Wow."

"What?" Cara's tone carried a hard edge, as if she might explode.

"All this time you told me to get away from my controlling, selfish, narcissistic mother, and I just realized something. You are her. You're my mother! That's why I clung to you. You make me feel bad about everything I do. I'm never good enough. You make me feel sorry for you. But, no matter what I do, you insult me, make me feel guilty that I'm not doing enough, or screw me over. You don't care about me. You only care about what I can do for you. When I stopped feeding into your bullshit, you turned on me."

Samantha shook her head and walked down the corridor toward the loading dock. A large crowd formed at the end of the hallway. Despite the shitty day, a sudden giddiness took over. She thought about what Roger told her the other night. "Have the courage to let go of what you can't change. One of the hardest things is letting go. Move on, little Sammy."

Chapter 42

Cooper paused before entering the hospital. Walking through those doors was getting harder and harder. Even a week away from this place didn't help. Then again, the wedding from hell wasn't much of a vacation.

He strolled into his kitchen. At nine o'clock, the breakfast line was finishing up. He managed to stride past without anyone noticing. Not one, "good morning" or "welcome back". *Odd.* Maybe they were too engrossed with their stations. Was the hospital census high?

He placed his mid-morning protein shake in the corner of the juice fridge located directly in front of his office. He turned to leave when Lou's familiar voice materialized. "Welcome back, boss."

"I guess I'm still employed here." Cooper quirked his eyebrow.

Lou waved his hand in dismissal "Nah. I told you I wouldn't say nothing."

"And I thank you for that." He stepped out and entered his office.

"You sure did miss a hell of a lot though."

"What? Paperwork? Reports? Kitchen gossip?" He laughed. "Who's pregnant this month?"

"Nothing like that." Lou followed Cooper to his office and sat down before Cooper could.

"Make yourself at home, Lou."

"Don't mind if I do." Lou leaned back and rested his hands behind his head. He attempted to place his feet on the desk when…

Cooper scowled. "Don't even think about it. Spill it before Darth Vader buzzes me in there."

Lou tweaked his chin. "What do you want to know first? How Angie got Kenneth's job, or how Samantha was fired and escorted out by security for having a knock down brawl with Cara in the hallway over your making out session at Pablo's party?"

"What?" His voice boomed and ricocheted off every wall in the kitchen. Now the line employees turned around. Is this why they all ignored him when he came in? Cooper closed his blinds, but not before the taste of coffee returned in his mouth. He swallowed it down and grabbed his water bottle.

He didn't know what to say. What to ask about first. This was not how he intended on starting his day. He pictured Roselyn congratulating him on his hard work and giving him his promotion. Then finding Samantha and finishing their conversation. *Damn*. Why didn't he call her before he left? Why didn't he leave Pablo's party when he had the chance? *Wait*. Angie?

"Angie got the job? How the hell—"

"Roselyn announced it last Monday. Said she was the most qualified. She worked the hardest."

"Most qualified? Worked the hardest? That woman can't even tie her own shoes!" Cooper paced around his small office. "I did all the work. Angies. Kenneths. Even some of Roselyns. Why the hell was I doing Roselyn's work?" He kicked his empty, metal garbage can.

"Don't know boss. If you must know, we all thought you were getting the job. You deserved it."

He plopped into his chair and sighed. "Thank you. That actually means more to me than getting the stupid job." He wanted to ask about Samantha, but didn't know how without looking obvious. He glanced at Lou, then pretended to read the paper sitting on his desk. Then, looked back at Lou. Lou smirked. Cooper shook his head, then put the paper in his top drawer. Awkward silence followed. Lou continued to stare at him - his huge smile mocked Cooper.

"You love her don't you?" Lou nodded.

"Roselyn? Yeah. Love her as much as my grandmother."

"Not her. Samantha." He looped his thumbs in his front pockets and tilted his head.

"Huh? Lou, what you saw was nothing. I was just—"

"I see it. In your eyes. Hers. You might think I'm just loading boxes of frozen meat into freezers, but I notice things. I knew long before I caught you two."

"I don't know what you're talking—"

"Coop. It's cool." Lou held up his hand. "She always had this look on her face when she was around you. Never had that look with me. She never laughed with me, either. I fucked up. I didn't see what you saw. I only saw what I wanted. My needs. You saw something more. Something I never bothered to find out. And...well...I actually walked in on the two of you on purpose. Jealous. I heard the two of you laughing out loud all the time. Who the hell has fun working on projects for Roselyn?" He stood and turned toward the door. "Don't fuck it up like I did, all right?" With that, he walked into the fridge, never looking back.

With his mouth still open, Ryan flew into his office. "Thank God, you're back! That woman's Satan. Warn me next time you go away. I'm calling in sick!"

Cooper continued to stare in Lou's direction. *What had he done?*

"You okay? How was your sister's wedding? Hello?" Ryan waved his hand in front of Cooper's face. "Oh shit. Did Lou just tell you about Angie? Bad break, bro. Not sure what went on there. Never saw that coming."

Cooper took a step forward, still ignoring him. "I...I don't know what happened either, Ryan. But I'm going to find out."

Without waiting for the royal pain-in-the-ass to call and start barking out orders, he took the liberty of finding her himself. Hopefully, he wouldn't pass Angie on the way. Why Roselyn picked a nitwit like her, was baffling. And, if Angie thought he'd congratulate her, she could kiss his ass.

He stormed out of his office just in time to see Dr. Chambers sneaking out with a handful of juices and two yogurts. Cooper squeezed his fists together until his knuckles cracked and popped. His arms shook so violently he thought he'd have a stroke right there in front of his employees.

Cooper raced from the kitchen and down the hall before Dr. Chambers had a chance to hit the door to the loading dock. With his hip ready to push the door open, Cooper grabbed him by the arm, swung him around and pinned him to the wall. His powerful shoulder lodged in Dr. Chamber's chest, restricting any further movements. Or, his ability to breathe.

Dr. Chambers froze - the size difference unmistakable. Cooper leaned in until only an inch remained between their faces. A container of orange juice pelted the floor dispersing its contents.

"You think you're better than everyone else in the hospital? Think you can repeatedly steal from me without any consequences? Think again, asshole. You messed with the wrong guy. This time *I* caught you, and there's no getting out of it." Cooper snatched the other orange juice out of his trembling hand, held it over the resident's head, and crushed it with his palm. Orange liquid trickled down his face.

"The next time I catch you in here, I won't be so nice. Consider yourself warned." Cooper smashed his shoulder into his chest one last time. Dr. Chambers released a *woosh* of air. Cooper ripped the remaining containers from his hands, and stared him down, finally releasing his anger on the right person.

Dr. Chambers Adam's apple bobbed up and down. He sucked in air as if Cooper smashed his windpipe. He walked backward, afraid to lose sight of Cooper. Once his heel hit the back door, he pushed on the handle and fled like the coward he was.

Cooper exhaled, but with the adrenaline tearing through him, he continued with his mission. He knocked on Roselyn's door and without waiting for a response, charged in. Unfortunately, Angie sat by her side.

"Welcome back!" Angie beamed. "How was it?"

"Leave. Now." His jaw tensed, his posture stiffened.

"Angie, obviously Cooper is a tad upset he didn't get picked. Please, give us a minute."

The second the door closed, Cooper lunged forward. "What happened to Samantha?"

"What? Samantha? What're you talking about?"

"I heard she was fired. What could she have possibly done? She did everything for you. I think she single handedly worked every job in the department. And, for what? A crappy raise? Then you turn around and fire her?"

"If this is your way of expressing anger about not getting Kenneth's job, I'm not falling for it. The bottom line was Angie had the college degree."

His scathing tone intensified. "I couldn't care less. I'm asking you a question."

"I gave you a year to finish your degree and you failed to do it."

"Are you even listening to me, you ignorant, self-centered…" He laughed, for that was all he could do. "You feel so guilty, that you're only hearing what you think I'm angry about. I couldn't care less about the stupid promotion. I care about Samantha. You're a selfish, miserable woman. You deserve what you created here. Good luck with it."

****

After multiple phone calls to Samantha's home with no response, at five-thirty, Cooper took a ride over. He rounded the corner, then slumped in his seat when her car wasn't in front. He knocked on the door, anyway. *Where could she be?* He waited a few seconds, heard a noise, then caught Samantha's mother peeking through the small bathroom window to the right of him.

"Mrs. Hart? I mean, Ms. Starr. It's Cooper. I need to speak to Samantha."

She ducked down and out of view.

"I know you're there. I saw you. Please. Just for a minute?" Had her mother erased all his messages on the answering machine? Did Samantha even know he called? Where was she?

He rang the bell again. Then knocked. He peeked through the window that led into the den and saw her slip behind the wall. "Ms. Starr. Please."

"I don't feel well. I'm sick." Fake coughing ensued.

With one of her eight thousand diseases, he was sure. "I just—" Cooper stopped. He had to think this one through. Samantha wasn't home and she wasn't letting him in. How could he get a woman like this to listen? He grinned. "It must be terrible to feel so sick with no one home to help you. Is there anything I can get you? Some soup? Cough medicine? Eggplant parmesan and garlic knots from Raimo's Pasta?"

He pretended not to look her way, but saw her inching closer to the window. He kept his main vision on the driveway. "Okay. If you have everything you need, I guess I'll be going."

The door opened all of twelve inches, and she poked her head through. One last round of coughs, then she tightened her robe around her neck, but not before Cooper noticed the gold necklace and matching earrings still in place. A ton of makeup coated her face, as well. "Eggplant parmesan sounds good." Her eyes drooped as if she was dying from the Bubonic Plague.

What sick person wants such a heavy meal? "Sure. No problem. I'll be right back."

"Oh, and don't forget the garlic knots!"

He returned, and she immediately answered the door, actually allowing him into the foyer. "Thank you for the dinner. I was way too sick to cook for myself tonight. Lord knows what I would've eaten."

"I'm sure Samantha would have cooked something nice for you." He gestured toward the kitchen.

"Huh! That deserter. She's only visited one since she left." She clutched her robe, then took the brown paper bag from him. The scent of garlic seeped from the container

Cooper tilted his head. Squinted his eyes. "Visited? What do you mean?"

"Don't play dumb with a sick woman. You know well enough she moved out."

"Moved? When? Where? I was out of town. I just got back late last night. How could she have moved out so fast?" His hands flew around wildly.

"Apparently, she'd been plotting this all along. She waited until the last minute to tell me. After all I've done for her." She pried open the brown bag and sniffed. "I really should go. Before I have another attack."

"Where'd she move to? Can you give me her address?"

"I'm not sure where I put the address. *Hmm*. You know, she hasn't even invited me over yet. I'll have to look for the small, crumbled napkin she managed to scribble it on before she took off." She loped toward the kitchen, not realizing he followed close behind.

On the fridge, typed in a huge font, on an 8 x 11 piece of computer paper, was the apartment building's name, the complete mailing address, and her phone number. He glanced it over, knowing exactly where the apartment complex was, then took one giant step back before she noticed. She jotted the address on a fancy note pad, which had her full name embossed on top in elaborate lettering.

"Here you go. You'll let her know how sick I am, right?" she moaned.

"Of course, Ms. Starr." Cooper hurried out the door.

"And make sure you let her know you drove all the way to Raimo's to get me food. Unlike her."

Chapter 43

Samantha attempted to hang the rest of her clothes in the apartment's small closet. Luckily, she had donated all of her slutty outfits to Goodwill. With the last of the clothes hung, she collapsed onto her mattress set upon the hardwood floor. The bedroom set would take at least four weeks to arrive.

She adjusted her clock radio on the makeshift end table she created from one of the empty boxes. *Click*. With no TV or stereo yet, music from here would have to do. Samantha raised the volume as high as it would go, exited her bedroom, blew out the candle in her exceedingly pink, tiled bathroom, and skipped to the tiny kitchen. The lack of counter space allowed for only a small toaster oven to sit on the twenty-by-thirty inch space. *Screech*. She turned the dial, and tossed in a frozen meal before the oven had a chance to heat up.

With the Stouffer's French Bread Pizza heating up, Samantha strolled into her all but deserted living room. Aside from an old director's chair, her beanbag chair, and the large box her kitchen table came in, which she tossed on top of two milk crates for a make shift coffee table, there was no living room furniture. That would take six weeks.

She squatted in front of the beanbag chair, grabbed her book, fell back, and snuggled into the soft material until her meal was ready. Two pages into chapter one, the doorbell rang. She flinched at first, not expecting anyone. Who knew she was here? Her landlord? *Oh, no*. Please don't let it be her mom. She had already left two messages. One saying she almost had a car accident on the way home from work, and the other how she almost got fired from her job because of all the stress from Samantha abandoning her.

Samantha chucked her book onto the floor, then placed her hand around the doorknob. "Who is it?"

"A very tan, but extremely sorry man, bearing dinner."

Her pulse sped up. Her hand instinctively released the door handle. No, no, no. Not tonight. So much had happened today as it was. Even moving out didn't give her a break. When would she get some peace?

"One second." Samantha glanced at the bare apartment, then thought of running to look in the bathroom mirror. She didn't have a spec of makeup on.

"Samantha, I've seen you with a hairnet, apron, and chocolate pudding dripping down your pant leg. I've seen you after we spent six hours cleaning my sister's musty basement. Please, let me in."

Damn him. How'd he always know what she was thinking? How did he even know where she lived? There's no way her mother would tell him. With one last breath, the door opened to reveal an indeed tan hunk, with blonder hair. The jerk *would* look so damn good. She needed to stay strong.

"Yes? Can I help you?" Samantha folded her arms over her chest.

"I believe we have some unfinished business." He shifted back and forth, then slumped onto the door jam.

"Business, eh? That's what you want to call it? I think you already let me know what was important to you."

Looking as if he was unable to fill his lungs completely, his voice hitched. "Samantha, can I please talk to you? I feel terrible how we left things off. And, it happened during mass chaos and confusion."

"My life didn't have any chaos in it." She refused to budge, despite the cold air billowing in from the unheated hallway.

He glanced around the apartment. "Well, it looks like there's some now." He winked.

Instead of being embarrassed, for the first time in her life, she truly didn't care what anyone thought. It was her apartment and she loved it. "Fine. Come in. Pick a chair."

Cooper looked at the two seating choices and laughed. "I don't think I'd be able to get up from the bean bag chair, and the director's chair looks a little snug."

"I can disassemble my expensive coffee table and give you a milk crate. Your choice."

"Hmm. Tough one. Being that I brought dinner, how 'bout we sit at your kitchen table?"

"Fine." Samantha took the seat on the far end and he placed a brown paper bag on the table.

What should've been awkward silence, morphed into an intense staring contest. At first, both their expressions remained deadpan, then the gleam in his eye caught hers. The corner of his lips rose ever so slightly, but she noticed. What were they fighting about? Why were they fighting? What had gone so wrong?

"Samantha, I'm so sorry about the way I spoke to you. I'm not sure what I was really mad about. That you slept with a bunch of boneheads?"

She recoiled. He held up his hand.

"That you lied to me about it? That I had to hear it from Lou? Or, maybe none of that. I think I was so stressed that Lou just caught me off guard. I snapped."

She relaxed and sunk a little deeper into the chair.

"Between Roselyn, the wedding, then Lou mocking me, I took it all out on you. It was wrong and I'm beyond sorry. You were right. I take my anger out on the wrong people." He huffed out a huge breath.

Samantha drove her big toe in between two other toes. "I'm sorry I didn't tell you. I'm not sure what I was doing last year. The whole situation was embarrassing, and—"

Cooper held up his hand again. "You don't have to explain. What you did in your past is really none of my business. I never told you all the crazy things I did in college."

Her eyebrows rose. "What? What did you do?"

"Nothing...I mean, just that—"

Samantha laughed. "I'm kidding. I really don't want to know."

His lips stretched into a grin. "So. We're...good?"

She rubbed her collar bone with her thumb. "The past month was insane and it wasn't how I wanted the new year to start. I thought all these wonderful things were going to happen for the two of us."

Cooper stood and took a few steps toward her. He opened his arms wide. Her heart sprung back to life. She flew into his open arms. Feeling his strong, warm body made everything instantly better. She never wanted to let go.

"Yeah. And look at us now. You got fired, and I—"

"Fired?" She pulled away. "Who told you that?"

"Lou. He said security escorted you out of the building."

"No. No. Not really. I actually handed in my letter of resignation last Monday."

"You did? What! Why?" Cooper unzipped his coat and tossed it behind the chair.

"I found another job. I tried to tell you everything that week, but never had the chance." She closed her eyes and took a deep breath. "There's so much to tell."

"But he said security...?"

"After I handed in my letter, Roselyn announced that Angie got Kenneth's job—"

"Yeah. Another unforeseen thing. Wasn't expecting that." He led her to the beanbag chair, plopped down and pulled her into his lap.

"Neither was I. I'm not sure what happened but...I just stormed in there. I freaked out on her."

"Wait. You yelled at Roselyn? About me not getting the promotion?"

"More than yelled. Angie lied. Everything you did for the cafeteria, including the menus and redecorating, she told Roselyn she did it."

Cooper's head jerked back. "Are you kidding? No wonder. I couldn't figure it out. I was pulling my hair out all day."

"The most ridiculous part was Roselyn believed her."

"That shows how clueless she is."

Samantha rubbed her forehead. "You have no idea."

"What do you mean?" He gave a slight headshake.

"Nothing." Samantha buried her head in his chest, not prepared to tell him everything yet.

"I heard you got fired because of...well, what you...someone told you about Cara and me. That they dragged you out because you two were fighting over me."

Her body tensed at the reminder. "No. After my fight with Roselyn, she called security. By the time they arrived, I had just finished my 'argument' with Cara. Is that what everyone's saying?" Samantha laughed. "I guess it did look that way. We did draw a bit of a crowd."

"Look. About Cara, I—"

"It's okay. I did some stupid things, too. I can't really yell at you for whatever you—"

"No. What did they tell you? I didn't do anything with Cara. I thought...I thought it was you."

"Me?" Her eyebrows squished together.

"You didn't show up for work Friday. I thought you were avoiding me. Roselyn worked me like a dog that day and I almost didn't go Friday night. I headed home, but then I thought you might be there. I got to the bar a half hour after everyone else, and when you didn't show, I stopped in the bathroom before I left. My phone buzzed. I went to answer it and someone grabbed me from behind and put their hands over my eyes. They smelled like coconut body lotion. She spun me without removing her hands and kissed me. The first thing I noticed was the weird movements. They weren't yours. I tried to remove her hands, then pulled back and away." Cooper shook his head. "Did she tell you I kissed her?"

Samantha's forehead sank into her palm. All she could do was laugh. "Unbelievable. Actually, Lou and Bruce walked in on you and saw the two of you kissing. They were more than happy to tell me, and Cara was thrilled to let me know that you were leaving me for her."

"Are you kidding!" His gaze circled the room. "I would never. You know that."

"Cooper, my last day at work was so bizarre, I didn't believe what anyone was telling me. All the stories, the lies, deceit. The cluelessness on everyone's part. I was actually happy Roselyn escorted me out instead of making me work there another three weeks. I figured that was payback enough for Cara. She'd have to do both mine and Heather's work now."

"Actually…no."

Her chest tightened. "What?"

Cooper rubbed her shoulder. "Ryan told me Cara took a leave of absence this morning."

"For what? She's not there half the time anyway."

"He said she took a medical leave of absence for…substance abuse treatment."

Samantha leaped out of his lap. "Are you serious? No way!" She paced the room. Was this much true at least? "I'm actually happy for her. Really happy. I hope what you're saying is true."

"Ryan said Cara lost it when she had to do all the floors. This morning she filed for a leave of absence. Ryan said Roselyn almost needed medical leave." Cooper let out a stream of laugher.

Samantha joined him. "That damn Roselyn got everything she deserved. Good for Cara!"

"I thought you guys weren't friends anymore." Cooper struggled out of the beanbag chair and put his arms around her waist.

"I just wish her well. I hope she gets the help she needs." She placed both her hands on Cooper's chest. "Who's seeing the patients then?"

"Don't know. I left before finding out."

"Ask someone tomorrow." Samantha squeezed him tighter and rested her head in his warm chest.

"No. I left. I quit, Samantha."

Her head shot up. "What? No. You worked so hard." Her voice cracked with emotion.

"And look where it got me."

"You can't. All that time and work. All those hours." Samantha squeezed her temple. "What happened? Did you tell her you deserved the job? That Angie was a fake?"

"I didn't leave because I didn't get the job. I left because I thought she fired you."

"Cooper! That's insane. Why would you quit over me?"

"Why did you?" He let go of her. His arms fell to the sides.

A sudden feeling of breathlessness took over. She pulled away and played with a string on her sweater. "There's so much you don't know."

"Tell me."

Ding! The timer announced the completion of her pizza. Before she walked into the kitchen, the smell of burnt cheese filled the air. The powerful new oven completely burned the cheese covering. After gliding it out with a spatula, she chucked it onto the side. Her appetite had vanished.

"Smells...good. What was it?"

"Burned pizza. I can't eat now anyway. I have to tell you some things first, Cooper." Samantha took a step to her right. "You want some water?"

"Sure."

She filled two glasses with ice and water, and reached for his hand. She led him into the bedroom. His eyes widened at the shabby, motel-looking room. "It's temporary. Don't look so sorry for me. Plus, there's more room for you in here."

After Samantha clicked the clock radio off, they laid across the dark purple sheets and he placed his arm around her waist. "I think this might be my favorite room. With or without furniture." He kissed her on the nose. "I'm all ears. Shoot."

She took a large gulp of water, then released a long, cleansing breath. "About a month ago, when it became obvious that we wouldn't be able to talk or hang out at work without you getting fired, I started looking in the paper for jobs."

"You did not have to do that, Samantha. We could have found a—"

She held up her finger. "I also decided it was time to move."

"Yes. That was a big surprise, too."

"It was time for a change, again. A positive one this time. I looked through the classifieds for jobs. Gathered boxes from work and donated a lot of clothes and things from my room. Then I drove to this apartment complex to look around and ask questions. At first, the entire process freaked me out. I gave up. Went back to trying to make it work with us in the hospital."

"But it didn't." Cooper ran his finger down her cheek. "I'm sorry. I didn't know you were feeling this way."

"When I was at my wits end, they paged me overhead to an outside line." Samantha paused, then smiled. "It was Kenneth."

"Kenneth?" Cooper's mouth fell open. "What?"

"Check this out." Samantha sat up on the bed and tucked her hair behind her ears. "Besides the fact that he called me several times at home and left messages..." Samantha rolled her eyes.

"And your mom 'forgot' to tell you."

"Yup." She threw both hands over her face and let the laughter flow out. "He'd been trying to reach me and was about to give up. He decided to try one more time, and paged me in the hospital."

"Why?"

"Just to make one thing clear, he told me very little on the phone. Today, he told me everything."

"Today?" Cooper sat up on the mattress now, too.

Samanth took another sip of water. "Roselyn had a serious crush on Kenneth. Big time. He didn't like her that way though. In fact, after a while, he didn't like her at all. Roselyn also had no idea what she was doing."

Now Cooper rolled his eyes. "That's no secret."

"She had worked in a hotel as a waitress for years, then promoted to hostess, then some form of management. Her husband, whom she met in the hotel, insisted she go to college to better herself. She refused until he repeatedly humiliated her in front of relatives and friends at parties. She obtained a degree in hotel management and landed this job with the help of his contacts."

"So, he forced her to go to college? Then why was she so hard on me?"

"Who knows. Maybe she took her frustration with her husband out on you. There seems to be a lot of that going around." Samantha winked, and he nudged her in the shoulder. "Anyway. Kenneth started working at the hospital only three months before Roselyn. He learned a lot and was trying to work his way up the ladder. His eye was on a Food Service Director position in the future."

"But, he worked at St. Elizabeths for three years. Why'd he stay so long?"

"Exactly. Roselyn had no idea what she was doing. Kenneth basically did her entire job for her. She made him follow her around everywhere and go to every meeting with her. He did all her reports and financials."

"What did she do?" Cooper's brow frowned.

"Nothing. That was the problem. While she fell in love with him, he tried to find a way out of there. He applied for a Food Service Director position in another hospital, but she refused to give him a reference and then begged him to stay. He thinks she may have even sabotaged his chance at the job."

"What an ass." Cooper punched the mattress.

"He started networking with a lot of the administrative staff in our hospital and other area hospitals. He went to various conferences and met a bunch of important people. Two months ago, a regional manager for Hunter's Grain Food Service Company, let him know they planned to take over the nutrition department in Chelsea Morgan Memorial Hospital and they wanted him as their Food Service Director when the deal went down."

"I know that hospital. Tiara lived near it. How'd he get away from Roselyn, though?"

"He never told her. He sat tight until the position was ready, then gave notice. He said she lost it. Completely fell apart."

"So, there was no wild sex going on in her office in the afternoons?" Cooper ran his finger down her thigh.

"Not at all. That's when he did all her work. Yes, she flirted with him. Even brought in wine and liquor a few times, but he kept it strictly business. She kept the door locked with the hope he'd change his mind, perhaps? Maybe so no one would know he was doing her work? Who knows?"

"Wait. Why'd he call you to tell you this?"

"That's not why he called. He only told me that today." She crossed her legs and leaned in. "His facility needed a Chief Clinical to manage and oversee the dietitians. Once in, he told them he knew the perfect person for it. He called me to come in for an interview. I went that Wednesday after work, and tried to tell you the following day, in your office when all hell broke loose." Samantha pouted.

"Again, I'm sorry. I was so wrapped up in everyone else's crap as usual. You're right. I never put myself or the things that're important to me, first."

Samantha kissed *him* on the nose this time. "Kenneth paged me at work again Thursday morning to say they wanted to bring me in for a second interview to meet the regional manager. Friday morning. That's why I called in sick Friday. Not because I was avoiding you."

"And, I was too busy all week for you to tell me." He rubbed his face and sighed.

"I went for the interview Friday morning, and by the time I reached home, Kenneth already called to say I got the job. I strolled into work Monday, handed in my resignation, and Roselyn gave us the gift of letting me leave immediately. I told Kenneth I could start the next day, but he made me take the week off to get things in order. When I hung up, I immediately jumped back in my car and put money down on this apartment. The landlord said if everything went through, I could move in this weekend. I spent the rest of the week packing, shopping, ordering furniture. I started moving all this beautiful furniture in Saturday."

"*You* make the apartment beautiful. You don't need objects to brighten it up." He kissed her hand gently. The warmth made her lie back down. He followed. "One thing I'm confused about, though. It doesn't make any sense. Why was Kenneth always spying on us and asking questions?"

Samantha chuckled. "He wasn't spying for Roselyn. He noticed all the hard work we did. He saw how I juggled five hundred different jobs, and how you redesigned the entire cafeteria and kitchen yourself. He noticed. And, watched. Then acted on it when he could."

"Why didn't he tell Roselyn?"

"Why? So she'd keep us and never let us go? Kenneth said he knew he had enough of her crap when he found out what she'd given me for a raise. He was so angry at her stupidity and jealousy, he knew he needed out."

Cooper shifted on the bed. "Once he got the job as Food Service director, he hired you on his management team? That's awesome. I'm so happy for you. You truly deserve it."

"Thank you. It feels good. Today was my first day. Today's when Kenneth told me everything. Over lunch. Obviously, he couldn't tell me anything during the interview or until I was out of St. Elizabeths."

"Sure. Loyalty and confidentiality is huge. Congrats, Samantha. This is a big year for you. New job, a promotion and a raise. Your own apartment."

"There's more actually." She smirked.

"Really? What else?"

"The Friday Kenneth offered me the job, he said he heard you applied for his job. He'd been watching you for months and that's why he asked you so many questions at the health fair. He said he wanted you on his team as the Assistant Director of Food Service. I told him you busted your ass for weeks and were waiting for Roselyn's decision. He said he understood."

Cooper's eyes narrowed. "But…I didn't get the job."

"I know." Her eyebrows wiggled.

"And…"

"I told him last Monday after I was *fired* what happened with Angie"

He perked up. "What'd he say?"

"He laughed and said, "that idiot couldn't even order milk and

THE BRIDGES BEFORE US

bread correctly!" And, he told me he had warned Roselyn she was making a huge mistake hiring her as the Cafeteria Manager. Roselyn was out to prove him wrong. Throw in Angie lying about all the tasks she accomplished, and Roselyn thought she won." Samantha leaped up on her mattress and jumped up and down like it was a trampoline.

Cooper latched on to Samantha's hands and joined her. "You nut!" He stared, waiting for her to finish, and she pretended to be bored. After an exaggerated yawn, he leaned in and tickled her. "So..?"

"So what?" she teased.

"Samantha!"

"Okay, okay. So, as of today, I didn't know you quit. I told him to call you and see if you'd be interested."

"Of course I am. Are you kidding!" He stopped jumping. "What about school though? I'm supposed to start tomorrow night."

"He knows. He'll make sure nothing interferes with your night classes if you're interested."

Cooper jumped off the bed and looked at himself in her full-length mirror. He downed half his glass of water, then turned to her. "I was going to take more classes and hold off finding a job for the next four months, but I'd be an idiot not to take this."

Samantha hopped off the bed too, and threw her arms around him. "Can you imagine? The three of us running that department?"

"Yeah. Actually I can. It's going to rock! Kenneth's a decent guy, huh?"

"Amazing. He was as miserable as we were. He has a lot of great ideas, too." Samantha twirled around and then kicked her leg in the air.

Cooper hugged and kissed her with renewed energy. She tried to relax, but the day had been mind-boggling.

"Hey. I almost forgot." Cooper paced the room. "I caught Dr. Chambers stealing food."

Samantha's eyes bulged. "You did? Oh my God? What'd you say?"

"Didn't say much. It's what I did."

"Cooper..." She placed her hands on her hips.

"At least I took my anger out on the right person this time. Right? He won't do it ever again."

"How do you know?" Samantha sauntered over to him and hugged him tight.

"I stopped in the Medical Director's office on the way out and reported him. I wasn't going to, but since I quit, I needed my guarantee. That, and drizzling some fresh squeezed orange juice over his highlighted hair."

"Cooper!" She slapped him on the shoulder. "Poor Ryan's left there all alone, now."

"Well, he'll either take one of the two jobs available, or, if he's smart, he'll just leave."

His compassionate eyes locked onto hers. How she had missed him. He leaned in, placed his soft lips on hers and made her forget every horrible thing that happened this year.

"By the way. You look gorgeous without any makeup on." Then his stomach grumbled like a lion. Wild and loud.

"Thank you." Samantha laughed. "Hungry?"

"Starving. I haven't eaten since eleven o'clock." Cooper latched onto her hand and led her to the brown paper bag he'd brought with him.

"I hope the food didn't get cold while I jabbered on. So sorry."

"Nope. I stopped at the deli." He reached into the bag and lifted out two heroes. "I hope you like tuna fish."

Chapter 44

They finished their sandwiches, then Cooper tossed the remaining trash, and washed their water glasses. He watched as she wiped down the kitchen table with a new, pink sponge.

When he had exited the plane in Jamaica, it hit him how much he missed her. What an ass he was for yelling at her like that. He knew he made the biggest mistake in his life.

"I bought chocolate-chip ice cream. Want some?" She opened the freezer door.

"Sure."

She leaned in and her cute ass poked out as she searched through the surprisingly filled freezer. "How was the wedding? You look nice and tan, as opposed to us pale New Yorkers. Another brutal winter, it seems."

"It was nice to get away, but I missed you, Samantha."

The freezer closed. With the carton in her hand, she bit her bottom lip. "I missed you, also. I thought it was over."

"When you didn't call me Thursday…then called in sick Friday, I thought it was over, too."

"I had a lot going on and I needed to put myself first." Samantha walked back to the kitchen table and placed the carton down.

"I understand. I figured that out when I got off the plane. You and I do things for everyone but ourselves."

"Isn't that weird?"

He searched through the drawers until he found spoons. "Anyway. I checked into the hotel, and as I made my way to the ocean to relax, Hannah handed me a piece of paper with all my tasks on it. That was it. I lost it. I threw a bathing suit on and took off. I walked as far as I could on the beach and hid behind a palm tree for the rest of the day."

"What did Hannah say?"

"She didn't know. She thought I was doing my *tasks.* Until I didn't show up for dinner. I had quite the liquid dinner that night. I passed out in the chair and woke in the middle of the night when a search party found me."

"Who?"

"The groom. The bachelor party. I told Eric my sister was nuts and he should run now while he's still a single man!"

"You did not." Samantha plopped a few dollops of ice cream into each bowl.

"I did. We talked for at least an hour. Then I got hungry."

"Not you." She tossed another scoop into his bowl.

"Eric admitted she was needy, and realized I was doing more than I should. He manned up, said I was relieved of my duties for the rest of my life..." Cooper chuckled. "...and told me to enjoy the rest of the week. He would talk to Hannah for me. So, except for walking her down the aisle, I really didn't do much."

"Nothing?"

"Not unless you include, wind surfing, parasailing, catamaraning, snorkeling..."

"Gee. What a tough week." Samantha sat down and dug into her bowl.

"I spoke to my mom and sisters separately. I told them I loved them dearly, but I needed to focus on my life. Told them about you, our fight, going back to school, Roselyn. Told them they needed to find men, or neighbors, or co-workers. Someone else to help them. And, to delete my phone number."

"Cooper!" Her eyes widened.

"Just kidding. But, they got the point. They thought I liked helping them, and that I was bored and needed something to do."

Samantha choked on her ice cream. "Are you kidding?"

"I guess I was so busy helping them, I never had a chance to tell them much about my own life." He took a mouthful and leaned back in the chair. "It was exhausting, draining, cleansing, and a very beautiful wedding. I'm happy for Hannah and I wish her and Eric the best."

"I'm glad. It's your time now."

"Guess what else I thought about that day?"

Samantha dumped her spoon into the bowl. "What?"

"The bridge. And what it means to me."

Samantha pushed her ice cream bowl aside.

"I was thinking how we passed so many people on the bridge that day. So many lives we interacted with. But, that's kinda what life's like. People come in and out of your lives. Some good, some bad. We learn a lot about ourselves that way. Who we are. Who we want to be. Who we want to be around."

Samantha walked over to him and sat in his lap.

"A bridge gives us an opportunity to not only meet new people, but learn about ourselves on the way. We grow, and change, and learn to love who we are. Thousands of people and we're all different. All one of a kind."

Samantha swept his hair back, a grin grew on her face. "I like that." She stared at him, a gleam grew in her eyes. "Maybe you weren't supposed to know that when you were younger. Maybe it's something you have to learn."

He raked his fingers under her soft hair, and pulled her in for a kiss. He wanted nothing more than to be in Samantha's arms for the rest of his life. "Now. To work on us."

She leaned back and wiggled her eyebrows. "I have one more thing to tell you." She wrapped her legs around him. "The day of our fight…"

"Yes?" He hesitated. *What now?*

"Relax. Only good news today." She inhaled a deep breath. "I tried to tell you that I finally signed up for the Thursday Open Mic competition."

"You did? I'm so glad. You'll be great!"

Samantha smirked. "Well…I went already. That night. And…I won."

Cooper leaped up, with her still in his lap, and she wrapped her legs around him. "Samantha! This is awesome. Wow! I can't believe I missed it." His expression shrunk. "Oh. I missed it. You tried to tell me. I feel terrible. God, I wish I was there."

"At the end of each month, the judges take the winners from each week and choose a monthly winner. That person gets a crap load of free beer and food. Then at the end of the year, they have a grand prize competition, and the winner gets five-hundred dollars cash."

Cooper kissed her on the neck, tasting her salty skin. "And, that winner will be you."

She leaned back, allowing him to devour her flesh. "Mmm. And hopefully you'll be there for it."

He pulled away and shook his head. "I wouldn't miss it for the world. I'm showing up every Thursday no matter what. I only met your friends a couple of times."

"The group's growing. I seem to have a fan club now. They like my singing, I guess."

"I think they like you, Samantha. And what's not to like?"

Epilogue

Three Months Later

At 8:45 p.m., on Easter Sunday, Samantha cleared the dessert dishes from her mother's dining room table following their feast. After the cooking extravaganza in her apartment yesterday, she brought over several appetizers, the side dishes, and a dessert. Her brother, Michael, brought his girlfriend.

"Samantha, did I tell you how Michael and Rose took me out to dinner last Saturday? We had such a nice time. I don't think I've ever been treated so well."

Cooper glanced at Samantha and hid his smirk.

"Yes, mom. You told me when I first got here."

"And I believe you told us during dinner, too," Cooper added. A fake smile planted on his face.

"Well, it was such a lovely evening. I just can't stop talking about it."

"What about the Broadway show Cooper and I took you to last month, mom?" She kicked Cooper under the table.

"That was okay. Anyone want more coffee?"

Samantha shook her head. *Pointless.* "No. We have to get going."

"So soon?" Her head lowered, her gaze focused on the kitchen tile. After her shoulders slumped, her lower lip protruded, and her feet dragged across the floor, she let out the loudest sigh ever spewed from her mouth.

"Yes, mom. It's almost nine o'clock and we both have a big meeting in the morning."

"Rose isn't leaving. Michael's not taking her home yet."

"Michaels's on spring break, and Rose, she…well, I'm not sure what she does during the day. Maybe Rose would like to watch a movie with you? *Gone with the Wind*, perhaps?"

Rose flinched. She looked at Michael who was too busy playing with the crust on his pie.

Cooper finished washing the last of the dishes while Samantha dried. When they neatly arranged everything back in the cabinets, Samantha grabbed their coats and her pocketbook.

"Okay. I guess you have to leave. Not sure when I'll see you again." Her mother stared at her empty hands.

"You see me twice a week, mom. At least." She bent over to put her shoes on. A manila envelope hid behind the foyer end table. Cara's name was on the return address. She plucked it out. The envelope was addressed to her. "Mom, when did you get this?"

She waved her off. "Oh, that. I just got it today."

"It's Easter Sunday. There's no mail delivery."

"Yesterday, then."

The stamp on it's from April 12th. "This was mailed over a week ago. Why didn't you give it to me?"

"I never see you anymore. It's not my fault you moved."

Samantha grinded her teeth. Cooper gently rubbed her back. "You came over Thursday for dinner, and I went food shopping with you yesterday for today's meal."

"I guess I forgot then. You know how busy I am now with that ballroom dancing class I'm taking after work."

The pain in her jaw traveled to her head. "If it wasn't hidden behind a piece of furniture, maybe you'd remember." Samantha shoved it under her arm and headed for the door.

"Aren't you going to say goodbye? After all the hard work I did to serve you and your boyfriend Easter dinner?"

Samantha pulled the front door open. "I paid for the food, cooked everything, and cleaned the dishes. Are you kidding?"

"Rose brought a lovely veggie platter."

"I'm sure Stop & Shop supermarket appreciates her support."

Samantha charged to her car. Cooper tried to keep up. How dare she hide this from her! What was it? Why was Cara mailing her something? Was it an Easter gift? She squeezed the puffy envelope.

"Hey!" Cooper grabbed her arm. "You, okay?"

After a deep breath of the frosty air, she relaxed. He hugged her, then kissed the top of her head. "Sorry. Not sure if I'm even mad at my mom. I'm more anxious about what's inside here."

"Look. It's late. We have to be up early. Go home. See what it is, and if you want to talk, call me."

"Are you sure? I don't want to blow you off." A sinking feeling pooled in her stomach.

"You forget. We work together every day. We're at each other's apartments five nights a week. Go home. See what it is and I'm here for you if you need me." He opened her car door and motioned her to get inside.

The entire drive home, Samantha had to stop herself from pulling over and ripping the large envelope open. Once home, she threw her coat on the floor and jumped on the couch.

Something soft was covered in wrapping paper, and there was a white envelope on top. She put the gift aside and tore open the envelope. Her fingers trembled. Her mouth went dry. She could hardly see the words hand-written on the page. The paper shook in her quivering hands.

Dear Samantha,

Hi. I started writing this so many times, I'm still not sure what I'm trying to say. I decided today to just write it. I hope it all comes out correctly. Forgive me if I ramble on. I'm not drunk though! Completely sober. In fact, I've been clean for three months now. I know. Hard to believe. After you got fired, (sorry our fight got you fired. I never intended for that to happen. I swear!) I checked myself into rehab. I was scared shitless, Samantha. But, I was so ready. I know you don't believe that, but I really was.

No one seemed to mind my drunken, high on God-knows-what, partying. Except you. I hated you for that at first. I mean, who are you to tell me what to do? But, I realized, you were my friend. My only friend. The only one that cared. The only one that tried to help me.

You deserted me. Or, at least I thought you did. I thought I was such a loser. I mean, my only friend dumps me. But hey, everyone in my life abandoned me. My mom, my brothers, my unknown-to-him dad, my fiancé, Eryn. Why not my best friend? I've been high for so long, I forgot what the old Cara was like. I forgot all my dreams and goals in life. Thought there was no point in living. I just floated through my days and nights as best I could. I was lost and scared and didn't give a crap anymore. No one else did, so why should I?

When you told me to get help, I was so angry with you. You, telling me what to do. I couldn't work all day. I went home, popped open some vodka and all I could think about was the look on your face. You were so calm. So determined. So sure of yourself. As if, nothing could bother you. I've never seen that look on you before. Just composed and peaceful. I wanted that. To have no worries and be happy again.

But, you're smart. You always had your head together. Not sure where you are now or what you're doing, but I hope you found what you wanted. Not sure what it was. I liked who you were. A good friend.

Compassionate. Funny. Quirky. Just an all-around good kid.

Three months ago, I walked into a hospital near my apartment and told them I wanted to go to rehab. They were really sweet and helpful, and it made me feel worse. All these wonderful people in the world willing to help me, and what was I doing that was good? I almost snuck out of the ER, but this nice nurse kept checking on me. So, off I went. 8 weeks in rehab. It sucked at first. All the meetings, asking me questions, having to tell strangers my business! After a while though, it felt so good to talk. It's all I wanted to do. It felt like I was purging myself. All the bad shit came out, and left. And after a while, every day, I felt better and better.

I have a long way to go. I've been out for three weeks now, and it's frightening. I couldn't go back to St. Elizabeths. I needed to get away from all the poison there, and, well, you're not there either. I'm in a new apartment, too. One with working heat, and new windows, and a toilet bowl that flushes every time.

Anyway, usually at this point in my letter to you, I wonder what the hell I'm trying to say, or why I'm even writing to you and I give up. I guess I just want to let you know that I'm sorry if I hurt you. We were great friends. I think when you wanted to become me, (someone I hated) I saw who I really was and it made me sick. Then, I wanted to be someone else. Unfortunately, I picked a worse version of myself. Cara x 10. When Eryn stopped calling, and then you moved on, I lost all hope. I just wanted to die.

I realize why you gave up on me. I get it now. But, at the time I was hurt. I see now, how badly I treated you. The terrible things I did to you. I can't even believe it was me doing those things. I deserted you, too. It was just a messed up year.

I hope you're doing better and can forgive me. If not, I understand. I miss the old days. I miss you. If you can forgive me, drop me a line. I bought a cell phone and canceled my old phone number. I need to start clean and move on. My new number's below.

Wow, I just re read this letter and it's so lame. But, I promised I'd send it no matter what. Maybe you can read through the lines and see what I'm trying to say.

Your friend, always, Cara

P.S. Eryn's fiancé broke it off with her. He caught her cheating on him. I didn't give her my new number or address. Need to wipe the slate clean.

Samantha placed the note beside her and fell back into the couch cushion. Part of her wanted to toss the letter in the garbage and forget it all. She had moved on with her life and wasn't sure she wanted to revisit Cara and her drama. Part of her wanted to call her immediately. She tapped her index finger on her lip.

What would the old Samantha do? What would the new one do? What was the right thing to do? A tightness formed in her chest. She weighed the pros and cons, blew her cheeks out, then released the air within.

Samantha glanced at the letter once more. The gift-wrapped item caught her eye. She could open that at least. Her fingers crawled to the package and tore it open, flinging the wrapping paper everywhere. Inside was a Led Zeppelin T-shirt. She smiled. The one with the blimp on it.

The End

Author's Notes

Dear Reader,

Thank you for reading *The Bridges Before Us*. I hope you enjoyed it. If you did, I would love it if you would write a review on your book review site. Reviews are the best way for readers to discover great new books. I look forward to seeing your review on Amazon, Goodreads, or any of your favorite sites.

I would also love to invite you to visit my Website:
Christine-Ardigo-Author.com,
or on Facebook:
Christine Ardigo – Author,
to stay in touch with me.

Thank you for spending a few hours of your day with my story and its characters. I hope you had fun living in their world as much as I did. Curious about Samantha's other co-worker, Heather? Read her story in *Cheating to Survive* and *Every Five Years*, Book One and Two in the series.

Christine

About the Author

I'm a registered dietitian/personal trainer who writes contemporary romance novels in my spare time. When weight lifting, rock climbing, white-water rafting, and jumping out of airplanes wasn't enough, I decided to fulfill a dream I had as a child: to write a book.

I've lived in New York my entire life and can't imagine living anywhere else. I have the beaches, the bay and the city, all a half hour away. I've built memories here with my husband, two quirky daughters and a bunch of crazy friends, all whom I love very much.

The Fix It Or Get Out Series

Book 1 – Cheating to Survive

Hate your boss? Want to Strangle Your Husband? Be Glad Your Co-Workers Can Keep a Secret. Can Cheating on Your Husband Bring Unimaginable Pleasure or Completely Destroy Your World?

To her three daughters, Heather is a fun-loving, silly mom. Her co-workers at Norlyn Plains Hospital think she has it all, including a handsome lawyer husband.

But when a flirtatious new doctor chooses Heather to spend his down time with, he reminds her of the man she regrettably gave up so many years before. Each interaction breathes new life into her and she gives in to the doctor's seductions, threatening her fifteen year marriage.

Her co-workers Victoria and Catherine, are stunned by her actions, but when they see the positive transformation in Heather, and question their own crumbling marriages, they wonder if she has the right idea.

Can cheating on their husbands bring the three of them happiness? Or will they be destroyed by the consequences?

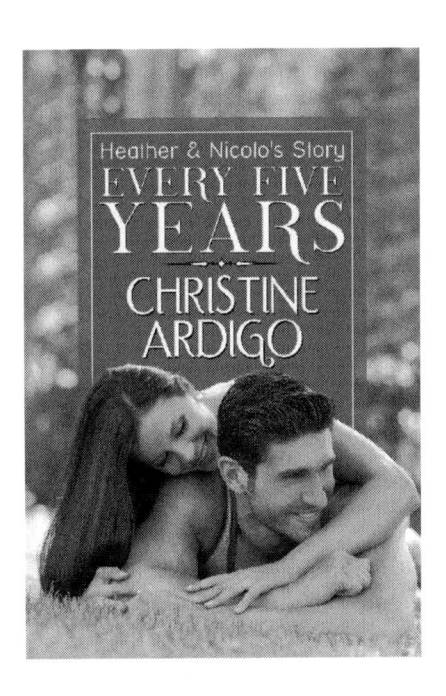

Book 2 – Every Five Years

Do you believe in second chances? Third? Fourth? Destiny's determined to keep offering another shot...if they're brave enough to grab it.

Heather, the quirky non-conformist, is the complete opposite of her conventional, yet highly sought after boyfriend, Lance. She doesn't know it yet, but her perfect boyfriend isn't perfect for her. When Nicolo, a vibrant new employee starts at her job, he ignites a fire inside her, and she finds herself second-guessing her boring future as a lawyer's wife.

Nicolo always questioned his purpose in this world, until Heather's dynamic personality finds a way into his heart. She makes him believe he can conquer the world, while he gives her a glimpse at an adventurous future. Before they reveal their true feelings, a vindictive boss fires Nicolo, leaving Heather with no possibility of contacting him.

Five years later, Lance, deeply engrossed in law school, has yet to propose. During a rare night out, fate reunites Heather with Nicolo and that old spark is still very much alive. Torn between losing him again and the emotions she can no longer suppress, they launch into a powerful love affair. Heather discovers passion and warmth, and knows she must leave Lance.

With love this perfect, what tears them apart a second time?

Fate continues to step in, as Heather and Nicolo cross paths every five years. Will they ever fulfill their destiny, or will insecurities keep them apart?

Every Five Years is a witty, heartfelt story of true love and what happens when life keeps getting in the way.

Printed in Great Britain
by Amazon